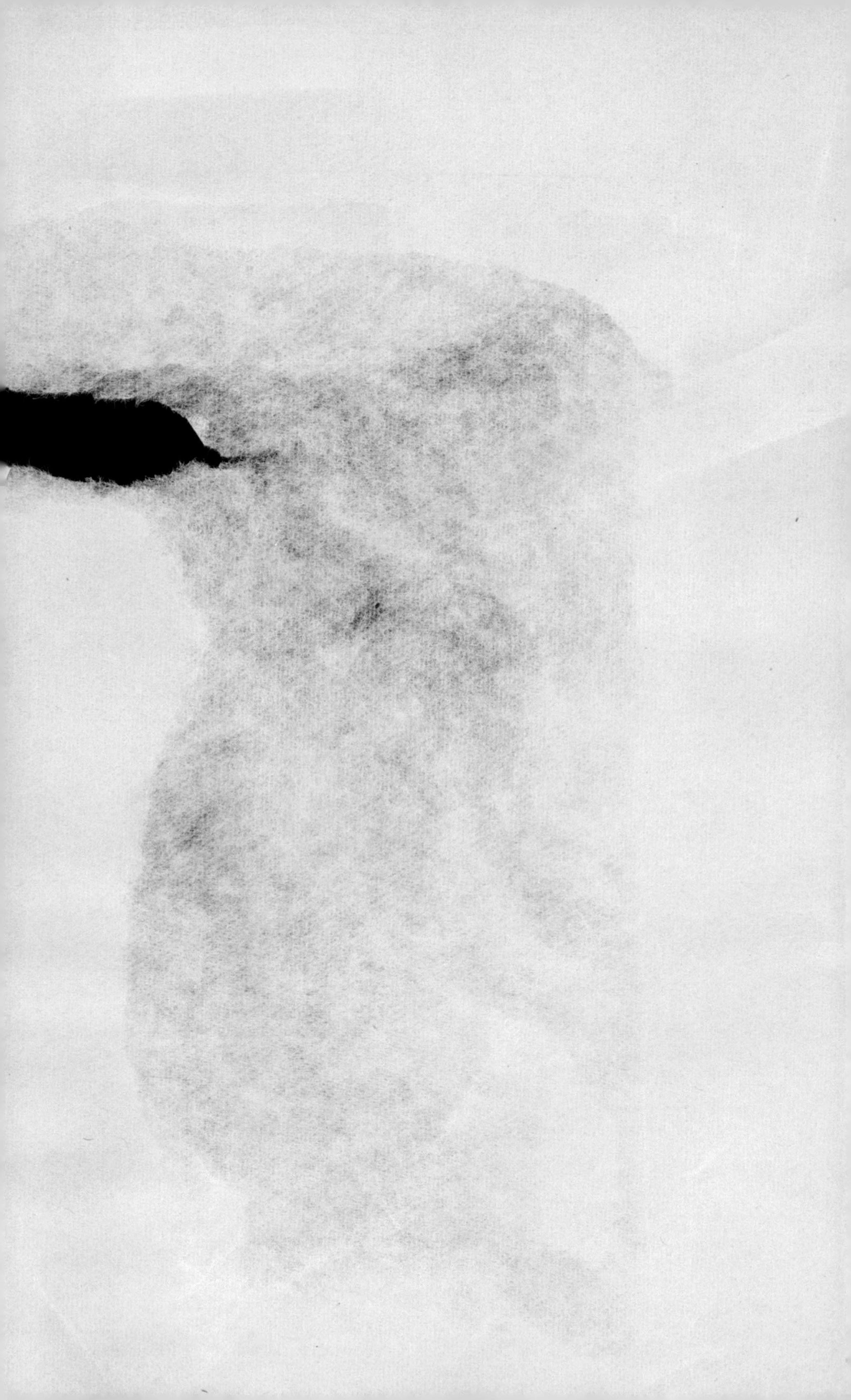

PATTERNS IN LITERARY ART SERIES

The Art of Narration: THE SHORT STORY
A. Grove Day

The Art of Narration: THE NOVELLA
A. Grove Day

Themes in the One-Act Play
R. David and Shirley Cox

The Bible as Literature
Alton C. Capps

The Comic Vision
Peter J. Monahan

Dramatic Tragedy
William C. McAvoy

The Hero and Anti-Hero
Roger B. Rollin

Dramatic Comedy
Harry Schanker

The Classical Heritage
George Kearns

African Images
Harold Scheub

Themes in Science Fiction
Leo P. Kelley

THEMES IN THE ONE-ACT PLAY

Themes in the One-Act Play

Edited by

R. DAVID COX

Head, English Department,
Suffolk County Community College,
Selden, New York

SHIRLEY S. COX

Instructor in Acting,
Suffolk County Community College,
Selden, New York

WEBSTER DIVISION
McGRAW-HILL BOOK COMPANY

New York St. Louis
San Francisco
Dallas Atlanta

ACKNOWLEDGMENTS

For permission to reprint copyright material in this volume, grateful acknowledgment is made to the following:

R. David Cox; For *The Beer Can Tree* by R. David Cox. Copyright 1964 by R. David Cox. Published here for the first time. All rights reserved.

Peter Crouch Plays, Ltd.: For *Monica* by Pauline Macaulay. Copyright © 1966 by Pauline Macaulay. All rights reserved. Reprinted by permission of Peter Crouch Plays, Ltd., London.

Ramon Delgado: For "*Waiting for the Bus*," Copyright © 1968 by Ramon Delgado. ALL RIGHTS RESERVED. This play originally appeared in TEN GREAT ONE ACT PLAYS edited by Morris Sweetkind. Copyright © 1968 by Bantam Books, Inc. Copyright © 1964, 1966 by Ramon Delgado (as an unpublished work). ALL RIGHTS RESERVED. All inquiries for amateur production rights are controlled by Baker's Plays, 100 Summer Street, Boston, Massachusetts 02110. Inquiries on other rights may be addressed to the author's agent, Mr. Warren Bayless, W. B. Agency, Inc., 551 Fifth Ave., New York, New York 10017.

Dramatists Play Service, Inc.: For *Sorry, Wrong Number* by Lucille Fletcher. *Sorry, Wrong Number* Copyright, 1952, 1958 by Lucille Fletcher. All Rights Reserved under the International and Pan-American Conventions.

Sorry, Wrong Number is reprinted by permission of the author and of the Dramatists Play Service, Inc. The use of the play in present form must be confined to study and reference. Attention in particular is called to the fact that this play, being duly copyrighted, may not be publicly read or performed or otherwise used without permission from the author's representative. All inquiries should be addressed to Dramatists Play Service, Inc., 440 Park Avenue South, New York City.

Mario Fratti: For *The Bridge* by Mario Fratti. Published here for the first time by permission of the author and Robert Lantz Literary Agency, New York City.

Harper & Row, Publishers: For *Pullman Car Hiawatha* by Thornton Wilder. "Pullman Car Hiawatha" from *The Long Christmas Dinner & Other Plays in One Act* by Thornton Wilder. Copyright, 1931 by Yale University Press and Coward-McCann, Inc. Copyright, 1959 by Thornton Wilder. Reprinted by permission of Harper & Row, Publishers. Caution: *The Long Christmas Dinner and Other Plays in One Act* is the sole property of the author and is fully protected by copyright. The plays herein may not be acted by professionals or amateurs without formal permission and the payment of a royalty. All rights, including professional, amateur, stock, radio and television, broadcasting, motion picture, recitation, lecturing, public reading, and rights of translation into foreign languages are reserved. All professional inquiries and all requests for amateur rights should be addressed to Samuel French, 25 West 45th Street, New York City.

Robert Lantz—Candida Dondadio Literary Agency, Inc.: For *Crawling Arnold* by Jules Feiffer. Copyright 1961, 1963 by Jules Feiffer. All rights reserved. Reprinted from *Feiffer's Album* by Jules Feiffer by permission of Robert Lantz—Candida Dondadio Literary Agency, Inc., New York City.

Margaret Mayorga: For *The Long Fall* by Carroll V. Howe and *The Golden Axe* by Ralph Scholl.

The Long Fall. Copyright 1949 by Carroll V. Howe. All Rights Reserved. Reprinted by permission of Margaret Mayorga.

The Golden Axe. Copyright © 1958 by Ralph Scholl. All rights reserved.

(Acknowledgments continued on page vii)

ISBN 07-013295-X Library of Congress Catalog Card No. 75-138990

Editorial Development, Jack Dyer; *Editing and Styling*, Bea Rockstroh; *Design*, Ted Smith; *Production*, Richard Shaw

New Directions Publishing Corp.: For *Something Unspoken* by Tennessee Williams. From *27 Wagons Full of Cotton* by Tennessee Williams. Copyright 1953 by Tennessee Williams. Reprinted by permission of New Directions Publishing Corp. Caution: Professionals and amateurs are hereby warned that this play is fully protected under copyright laws of the United States of America, the British Empire, including the Dominion of Canada, and all other countries of the Copyright Union, and is subject to royalty. All rights, including professional, amateur, motion picture, recitation, lecturing, public reading, radio broadcasting, and the rights of translation into foreign languages, are strictly reserved. For permission to produce this play, address all inquiries to New Directions Publishing Corp., 333 Sixth Avenue, New York City.

Margaret Ramsay, Ltd.: For *The Governor's Lady* by David Mercer. Copyright © 1965 by David Mercer. All rights whatsoever in this play are strictly reserved and applications prior to rehearsal for performance of use of the play shall be made to: Margaret Ramsay, Ltd., 14a Goodwin's Court, St. Martin's Lane, London, W.C. 2, England. No performance or use of the play may be made unless a license has been obtained.

Random House, Inc.: For *The Rope* by Eugene O'Neill and *Riders to the Sea* by John M. Synge.

The Rope. Copyright 1919 and renewed 1947 by Eugene O'Neill. Reprinted from *The Long Voyage Home: Seven Plays of the Sea*, by Eugene O'Neill, by permission of Random House, Inc.

Riders to the Sea. Copyright 1935 by the Modern Library, Inc. Reprinted from *The Complete Works of J. M. Synge* by permission of Random House, Inc.

William Saroyan: For *Coming Through the Rye* and *Hello Out There* by William Saroyan. From *Razzle-Dazzle*. Copyright 1942 by William Saroyan. All rights reserved.

University of North Carolina Press: For *Sunday Costs Five Pesos* by Josephina Niggli. Copyright 1937 by Carolina Playmakers, Inc.

Reprinted from *Mexican Folk Plays*, edited by F. H. Koch, by permission of the University of North Carolina Press.

The Viking Press, Inc.: For *Here We Are* by Dorothy Parker. From *The Portable Dorothy Parker*. Copyright 1931, copyright renewed 1959 by Dorothy Parker. Reprinted by the permission of The Viking Press, Inc.

CAUTION NOTE: Professionals and amateurs are hereby warned that the plays reprinted in this book, except for *Pyramus and Thisbe*, are protected by copyright laws, and none may be acted, read in public, or presented as a radio or television broadcast without special permission of the author or his agent.

Contents

About Plays

Plays are for people. In many senses plays deny attempts of scholars to define them, describe them, analyze them, categorize them. You can find some help, however, in knowing some of the basics of the form of plays even though the form is not always consistent.

The general description which follows is a start on form. It is simplified, but it can help you in arriving at the meaning or value of a given play.

Time, Place, and Circumstance

Plays must happen during a specific time—time of day, time of year, time in history. Occasionally, the playwright does not give the time, in which case the reader must assume the time from the other elements in the play. A play which centers around romantic love, for example, would be markedly different depending on whether the time of the play is 9:00 A.M. or 9:00 P.M., January or June, 1900 or 1970.

Plays must happen in specific places. Plays about romantic love will differ, depending upon whether the place is a hotel in Miami in 1970 or a farm in central Kansas in 1970.

The circumstances of the people in plays—whether they are rich or poor, old or young, married or unmarried—are as important as time and place. Thus, a play concerning romantic love, in 1970, in June, at 9:00 P.M., in a Miami hotel room containing two unmarried people will be decidedly different from a play concerning romantic love in 1900, in January, at 9:00 A.M., on a farm in central Kansas owned by two older people. An understanding, then, of time, place, and circumstance is necessary for a clear view of a play.

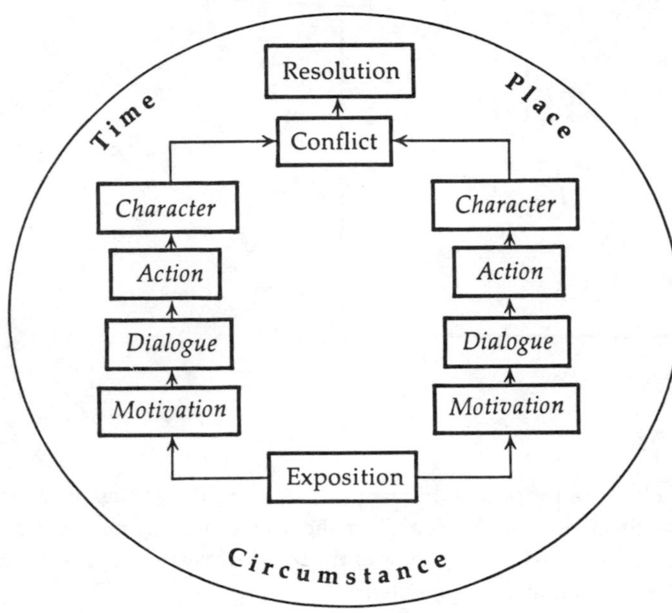

Exposition

Exposition is the explanation of events that have occurred before the play begins (the past action). The reader, or playgoer, should keep these events in mind as they are revealed to him, for the exposition often explains the actions occurring on stage. Exposition is not always revealed at the beginning of the play, however. Sometimes it is revealed a little at a time throughout the play. Suspense is developed in this way.

Motivation

Motivation is something (conditions or character traits) which causes a character to do or say certain things. Because I am poor and hungry, and because my best friend stole the money left to me by my father, and because I live in central Kansas, and because it is the height of the Depression (1932), I am motivated to *do* a number of things. I can get a job (difficult), find my "friend" (difficult), commit suicide (difficult), or steal food (dangerous). There are obviously many other choices, but it is clear that at least I would be sufficiently motivated to complain about my situation.

Dialogue

Dialogue is talk which reveals what a character is as a person. Speaking is an action. The way people speak and what they say indicate something about what they are. For example, a simple greeting says something about a person.

GEORGE: Good morning.
FRED: Morning.

GEORGE: Good morning.
HARRY: Hi.

GEORGE: Good morning.
DAVID: Sure is.

GEORGE: Good morning.
STEVE: Yeah.

GEORGE: Good morning.
BILL: What's so good about it?

You can immediately see that each person is different. Different things cause different reactions to a simple greeting.

Action

Action is what happens in a play. Dialogue may happen, fighting may happen, loving may happen. Action is caused by the interaction of exposition, motivation, character, and conflict.

Character

A character in a play is a human being (although occasionally an animal can be a character). The playwright can tell you what a character says and often what he does. He cannot, like the novelist, tell you what a character thinks or feels; he can only tell you what a character says.

Character is, at once, the easiest and the most difficult element in a play. It is difficult to form a picture of a person only from what he speaks. Yet, when a play is performed on the stage, character is easy to determine; we can then use all our senses to understand the character. The actor helps us. It is through character that the theme and the conflict are conveyed.

Conflict

Conflict is the core of a play. It is easily defined as any two (or more) opposing forces. Thus, two people are brought into conflict as a result of the exposition (past action), the motivation, the dialogue, and the particular makeup of the characters.

Once characters are in conflict, the play has begun in earnest. You should note here that there are different kinds and levels of conflict: man against an inanimate object, man against nature, man against man, man against himself. Generally speaking, different kinds of conflicts produce different kinds of plays. A man in conflict with a banana peel usually produces a comic reaction—farce. A blind, lame man in conflict with a banana peel produces a pathetic reaction—melodrama. Conflict, combined with character, determines the outcome of a play.

Resolution

The resolution of a play occurs when the major conflict has been resolved. The end of the play has arrived or is near. The characters work throughout the play to resolve the conflict. Thus, in a murder mystery, the resolution occurs when the detective finds the criminal. The conflict between good and bad (right and wrong) has been resolved. Good wins. In a romantic play the resolution occurs when the couple gets together or when it finally breaks apart. The elements of exposition, motivation, dialogue, action, character, and conflict must contribute logically to the resolution of the play. When they do not, the play is often unsuccessful.

About One-Act Plays

The one-act play differs from the full-length play primarily in length. It has all the elements of the longer play and often carries as great an impact. Since the one-act play is shorter, however, it is somewhat restricted.

There are usually fewer characters in a one-act play, because there is not time to develop a large number thoroughly. In the one-act, the playwright must characterize quickly—often with one line of dialogue. Also, the one-act usually takes place at *one* time and in *one* place. A longer play can change time and place between acts or scenes.

The conflict in the one-act play is often restricted, as well. Again, the time limit does not allow the playwright to build one conflict upon another; he usually deals with a single major conflict and resolves it (although there are often many minor conflicts). The exposition is minimal; the story is usually simple; the motivations are often uncomplicated. (Briefly, the one-act play is brief.) Brevity, however, does not mean simpleness. A one-act play is often as funny, as sad, as serious, as a full-length play.

In one sense, one-act plays are uniquely modern. Short plays were written before modern times, but often they were part of a longer work—a play within a play (*Pyramus and Thisbe* is part of Shakespeare's *A Midsummer Night's Dream*). August Strindberg, a fine Swedish dramatist, is usually credited with creating the form as we now know it. Eugene O'Neill, one of America's finest playwrights, used the form early in his career and did much to popularize it. His one-act plays are now classics. (One of his plays, *The Rope,* appears in this book.)

One-act plays gained popularity with the emergence of little theater groups and community theater groups across the United States. Such groups found that these plays were particularly suited to the performance conditions under which they worked: low budgets, few actors, limited facilities.

William Saroyan and Thornton Wilder continued to develop and popularize the form in the 1940s. In the 1950s the theater-of-the-absurd caught the public's fancy, and the one-act play seemed particularly suited to this approach to the drama. Eugene Ionesco's plays are perfect examples of how versatile the form can be.

Today the one-act play is very popular. The form lends itself to the off-Broadway movement. Many of our best current playwrights began by writing one-act plays—Tennessee Williams, Edward Albee, Murray Schisgal, and others. The one-act play has found its way to Broadway as well in such plays as *Plaza Suite* and *The Last of the Red Hot Lovers* by Neil Simon and *You Know I Can't Hear You When the Water's Running* by Robert Anderson. Even one of the most controversial of productions, *Oh, Calcutta,* is a series of one-act playlets by a number of anonymous authors.

In short, the one-act play is here to stay. After all, a standard television show is in a sense a one-act play.

About Themes

Lots of people talk about *theme.* Yet, *theme* is a very confusing word and it is often misused. It should not be confused with *plot.* Plot is the order in which the events in a play occur or simply what happens in a play. *Theme* should not be confused with *moral.* A moral is a lesson in right or wrong, and it is usually expressed as a pithy truism like "Look before you leap." More often than not, the plays in this book do not fit into moral truisms.

If you can answer either the question, What is the play about? or the question, What does the play mean? you have, at least on one level, discovered the *theme* of the play. That seems simple enough, but plays—even one-act plays—are usually *about* more than one thing. For the purposes of this book, the plays have been arranged under these *general* themes: Youth, Alienation, Love, Age, and Death. The general theme for each play has been given. The general theme is discussed at the beginning of each section. *Monica* (the first play) is generally about Youth. Yet, you will find as you read it that it could be about Love. In fact, it may be about many things. Thus, there are general themes and specific themes. In *The Beer Can Tree,* for instance, we find that the play is generally concerned with the problems of Age. More specifically, however, we find that it concerns the nature of public parks, conservation, beauty and ugliness, and success. The play has many implications.

The Reading Guides at the beginning of each play and the Questions for Discussion at the end of the book help you to arrive at the specific theme in each play. There is seldom a simple answer to the questions. It is important to try to answer the questions, for it is through thought and discussion of *theme* that values are discovered. We broaden our own understanding of people and circumstances and add to our own experience. We gain understanding and knowledge and from this we, hopefully, grow in maturity and wisdom.

About Reading Plays

Plays are meant to be seen and heard. Thus, when you read a play, you must attempt to create the play production in your imagination. You must attempt to visualize how the characters look and act, how they dress and talk. You must attempt to visualize the place and the atmosphere. You must attempt to visualize what the characters do when they are *not* speaking as well as what they do when they *are* speaking. This is not easy to do, but a number of techniques will help you.

1. If possible, read the play aloud.
2. If you cannot read the play aloud yourself, have the play read to you.
3. If you must read the play silently, always read the name of the character speaking. If you do not do this, you will get confused as to who says what. Remember, it is by what the characters say that we understand the play.
4. Read *all* of the stage directions. This will give you some idea of the action occurring on stage. Also, vital information is often conveyed through the stage directions.
5. Be sure you know who is on stage at any given time, even though the character does not speak. Sometimes the mere presence of a character affects the actions and dialogue of the other characters.
6. Read the *entire* play at one sitting. You would not leave a performance in the middle of an act. When reading longer plays, read at least one act at a sitting.
7. Read carefully and slowly. As literature goes, plays are short, and one-act plays are even shorter. You have time to take time.

THEMES IN THE ONE-ACT PLAY

About Youth

Youth is not an age, it is a condition. The condition often occurs, however, between childhood and adolescence, for youth is characterized by some degree of emotional immaturity. It is also characterized by uninhibited joy, by spontaneity, by enthusiasm. In short, youth does not necessarily mean "young people"; people of all ages have the qualities of youth.

We all strive for maturity. We do not strive to be old; age occurs naturally. Maturity does not. The transition from immaturity to maturity is slow, often uneven, and occasionally very painful. Some people never make the transition.

Maturity involves judgment and control. We find that we must learn to control our emotions or we remain childish. We must develop judgment if we are to function successfully in the world. We learn to live with emotional pain, especially in matters of the heart—we learn to "take it like a man." We learn to respect the rights and needs of human beings and other animals. We hope that we learn these things without losing joy, spontaneity, and enthusiasm.

It is amazing to find that maturity is a matter of developing techniques of control. It is equally amazing to find that immaturity (irrational and overemotional behavior) lurks alarmingly close to the surface. (*Even* Presidents have been known to lose control and lapse, momentarily, into immaturity.)

The three plays in this section are all concerned with one or more aspects of youth and the struggle for maturity. *Monica* concerns a young man and an older man in an affair of the heart. The relative maturity of one of the two decides the outcome. *Coming Through the Rye* takes an unusual look at a number of individuals before they are born. There are interesting comparisons between maturity and immaturity. *The Long Fall* deals with a very important aspect of maturity—guilt.

The struggles of youth are by no means thoroughly explored here, but some of the aspects are strikingly presented.

Monica

PAULINE MACAULAY

Characters

SIMON ELLIOTT
LEONARD
PORTER

Reading Guides

1. *Monica* was originally produced as a television play. Therefore, it is extremely important to read the stage directions carefully so that you can visualize what the camera saw. Because the play is somewhat of a murder mystery, the details are vital.
2. The character Monica never appears in the play, but you should try to get a picture of her in your mind. The actions of Simon and Leonard are explainable if you understand Monica's role in the play.

Monica

SCENE. *Simon Elliott's apartment. Evening.*

The apartment consists of one room, quite attractively furnished in a rather haphazard fashion with things picked up in Portobello market. It is an obviously bachelor apartment, with nothing around except a few books and one or two silver cups won for rowing at a university. There is, however, one beautiful red rose lying on a table. In front of a rather ordinary gas fire is a white polar bear rug. There is a divan couch, rather badly made up, with a few cushions lying squashed at one end and at the other a paper bag. There is an abstract sort of painting on the wall up center. The window, up left center, is closed. Nothing much can be seen from it but some clouds and the tops of a few distant buildings. There is a very narrow balcony outside. The roof slopes toward this window, and toward the narrow alcove balancing it right center in which the divan is placed. The main door is down left. There is also a small door to the bathroom above the fireplace.

When the curtain rises, SIMON ELLIOTT *is discovered seated at the small desk writing a letter. He is an attractive young man, but takes himself a little too seriously and is a shade pompous. He wears a blazer, sports trousers, and an old school tie. He finishes the letter, folds it up, and places it in an envelope on which he writes a name—Monica. He rises, leaving the letter on the desk, and goes to the low bookcase on which are several bottles of spirits, glasses, etc. He takes a swig from a bottle and wipes his mouth with the back of his hand. Then he goes to the divan, picks up the paper bag and takes out a giant roll of Cellotape and a pair of scissors. He blows up the bag, bursts it, and throws it into the wastepaper basket under the desk. He goes to the window, climbs on the chair below it, and starts to seal it up with the Cellotape. For a moment he stops and gazes out into space with a morose expression, then returns to the taping, which he finishes quickly and not very efficiently. He cuts the tape with the scissors, then gets down, moves to a cupboard up left, and throws the tape and scissors to join a pile of sundry articles inside. He then looks at his watch, pauses for a moment, then walks determinedly to the telephone on the desk and dials* TIM, *checking with his watch as he holds the receiver to his ear. He replaces the receiver and goes to a small mirror on the wall above the low bookcase. He takes a comb from his pocket, combs his hair carefully, replaces it, and flicks his shoulders. Then he goes to the desk, takes a fairly large safety pin from a drawer, and pins the envelope on the front of his chest. He goes to the mirror, stepping back a pace or two to make sure the envelope is pinned dead center. He then takes some of the cushions from the divan and places them at the downstage end of the polar bear rug. He picks up the rose from the table and lies down on the rug, head down stage on the cushions. He places the rose on his heart, lifts an arm carefully to look at his watch, reaches out slowly to the gas tap of the fire, and turns it on.*

There is a hissing sound of gas. SIMON'S *eyes stare vacantly toward the window. Suddenly he raises his head slightly, looking annoyed. At the window a large black cat with a misshapen fat face is looking in.* SIMON *turns off the gas tap and sits up, holding the rose. He goes: "Pssssssh!" and the cat vanishes.* SIMON *lies down again, arranging the rose. He reaches out and turns on the tap.*

The hissing noise starts again. SIMON'S *eyes stare vacantly into space. After a second or two his expression begins to look rather pleasurable. His eyes have a sleepy look and almost start to close. Suddenly they open wide. They look startled. His hand reaches out and turns off the tap. With his hand still on the tap he mutters: "Phew!" His other hand brings the watch up to his face. He looks at the time and replaces his arm. He lies still, as if listening for something.*

There is a noise off left of a lift gate clanging. SIMON'S *eyes alter and he again turns on the gas tap. He looks toward the window with an expression of extreme sorrow carefully arranged on his face. The noise of the hissing becomes louder.*

The doorbell rings. A look of annoyance crosses his face and his hand reaches out again to the tap and rests on it. The doorbell rings again. SIMON *turns off the tap and sits up, holding the rose. He looks at the door, puzzled and annoyed. The doorbell rings for the third time, more prolonged.* SIMON *looks very angry. He flings the rose away, gets up and wafts the air hurriedly with his hands. Then he crosses to the door and throws it open, speaking as he does so.*

SIMON: You bitch—you forgot your key!

(*An immaculately dressed man is standing outside, wearing an expensive dark suit, bowler hat, and carrying an umbrella. He is verging on the elderly, his face a little pudgy, his eyes a little sad. He has a very pleasant voice. He looks a well-dressed City business man.*)

THE MAN: I haven't got a key.

SIMON (*in an embarrassed mumble*): I thought you were somebody else.

THE MAN: Sorry to disappoint you. (*He smiles.*) May I come in? (*He crosses past* SIMON, *removing his hat, and turns to look at him.*)

SIMON (*still holding the door*): Well, what is it?

(*The* MAN *says nothing, staring at* SIMON'S *chest.*)

What are you staring at? (*suddenly aware that he has left the envelope pinned to his chest*) Oh. (*He releases the door, which swings to, and begins to wrench at the pin. After what seems an eternity he gets it off, looks at the man and gives a nervous laugh.*) I'm rather forgetful. I pin these little notes on myself to remind me of things. You know what I mean—like putting a rubber band on your finger, only better—because with a rubber band—sometimes—you forget what it was meant to remind you of. . . .

THE MAN: You're very young to have such a bad memory.

(SIMON *folds the envelope over in his hand.*)

Aren't you going to read it?

SIMON: It's—all right. (*He moves up to the wastepaper basket.*) You see, I remember what it said. (*He throws the envelope into the basket.*)

(*The* MAN *moves quietly to the door and closes it with his foot.*)

(SIMON *turns.*) Now, what can I do for you?

(*The* MAN *doesn't seem to hear him. He is looking around and sniffing the air.*)

THE MAN: I can smell gas?

SIMON (*ingenuously*): Gas?

THE MAN: Yes. (*looking at the gas fire*) Perhaps you've knocked the tap on.

SIMON: Oh, I don't think so. I'll have a look. (*He goes toward the fire, and as he does so trips over the cushions. Discomfited, he picks them up and turns to the man.*) For the dog. (*He throws them on the divan and bends over the gas tap.*) No, it's not on.

THE MAN: Well, you may have a leak. (*He puts his hat and umbrella on the table.*) We'd better open a window. (*He goes to the window and tries to open it. It does not budge. He pushes harder. With a sticky, tearing sound the window opens, pulling off some of the tape. He fingers the tape curiously, and looks round at* SIMON.)

SIMON (*moving up to him*): It's for the draft. I tape it for the draft.

THE MAN: Oh, I see.

SIMON: Of course—on the Continent they have double windows. . . .

THE MAN (*gazing out*): You're very high up here, aren't you? Where does that narrow balcony go to?

SIMON: I've never been out there.

THE MAN: Not a very impressive view, is it?

SIMON (*defensively*): Well, you can see the sky—clouds and things.

THE MAN: You can see the sky from a prison cell sometimes.

SIMON (*pompously*): Are you suggesting that my apartment is like a prison cell?

THE MAN (*turning*): We all live in some kind of prison, don't we? (*He looks at the low bookcase.*)

SIMON: Look, I'm sure that's very profound, but I'm rather busy. So if you wouldn't mind telling me exactly what you want . . .

(*The* MAN *moves to the chair below the door.*)

SIMON (*raising his voice slightly*): Look, can I help you at all?

(*The* MAN *studies the chair, picks it up, turns it upside down, examines it closely.*)

THE MAN (*looking at* SIMON): You've got woodworm in that chair. You'd better get rid of it before it spreads to the table.

(SIMON *takes the chair and replaces it.*)

SIMON (*sarcastically*): How very kind of you to tell me—how very kind. You're an antique dealer, of course.

THE MAN: No, no—not a dealer. Nothing like that. I dabble a little. I'm interested in furniture.

SIMON: I see. (*at the door*) Well, may I assure you I have nothing for sale—nothing at all.

THE MAN: You intend to take this furniture with you when you go?

SIMON: Go? Go where?

THE MAN (*pleasantly*): Well, that's entirely up to you, isn't it?

SIMON (*staring at him, then clearing his throat*): Er—I wonder—do you think, by any chance, you're in the wrong apartment?

THE MAN: Number fifty—Mr. Simon Elliott?

SIMON: Yes.

THE MAN (*moving up center*): Call me "Leonard." (*He stares at the painting, goes closer, then steps back and turns to* SIMON.) Slade School?

SIMON (*flushing*): Look, I wonder if you'd mind explaining exactly what you want. You ring my bell—at, I may say, a very inopportune moment—you walk in, a complete stranger—you walk in, criticize my view, condemn my furniture. . . . If you're not looking for antiques, what *are* you looking for?

LEONARD: A *pied-à-terre,* Mr. Elliott. Somewhere intimate—suitable for a quiet weekend—or an afternoon with a friend. (*smiling*) I live outside London, you see. It would be ideal for my purpose. How much is it?

SIMON (*stiffly*): I think you've been misinformed. I don't let rooms.

LEONARD: Very well, I'll buy it. How much do you want for the lease?

SIMON: You're making some kind of a mistake. Mr.—er—Leonard. I'm not selling the lease. I live here.

LEONARD: But you were intending to vacate it, were you not?

SIMON: I certainly wasn't. Whatever gave you that idea?

LEONARD (*after a pause*): Are you sure you weren't intending to vacate it, Mr. Elliott?

SIMON: I . . . (*looking slightly embarrassed*) Well, of course, I don't intend to stay here for ever.

LEONARD (*musing*): How long is for ever? I sometimes ask myself that question.

Perhaps you could give me some idea of when you might be going?

SIMON: No, I'm afraid I couldn't. I couldn't possibly.

LEONARD: What a pity. What a pity, Mr. Elliott.

SIMON: I wonder if you'd mind telling me who gave you my name?

LEONARD: Nobody gave me your name, Mr. Elliott. I came across it—on a piece of paper.

SIMON: What piece of paper? Where?

LEONARD: It was just lying about, Mr. Elliott—just lying about.

SIMON: I don't leave my name lying about on bits of paper, Mr. Leonard. Forgive me if I say that it sounds an odd and doubtful story. (*He looks at his watch.*) Now, I wonder if you'd mind . . . my apartment is not to let, I'm not selling the furniture, and I'm expecting someone. I wonder if you'd mind going? My friend will be here at any moment.

LEONARD: You can't rely on people, Mr. Elliott. You can't rely on people at all. They have a habit of letting you down when you least expect it. Don't you agree?

SIMON: Your friends, possibly. Not mine.

LEONARD: And the fair sex, without a doubt, are even less reliable than ours, wouldn't you say?

SIMON (*angrily*): No, I wouldn't say. (*He looks at his watch again.*) Now (*going to the front door and opening it*) would you mind leaving my apartment! (*He holds the door back.*)

LEONARD (*picking up the rose from the floor*): What a pity! (*He holds it up.*) Such a beautiful rose. Some of its petals have fallen off. It's sad, isn't it, how quickly things die.

(SIMON *crosses quickly and snatches the rose.*)

SIMON (*throwing it in the wastepaper basket*): If you don't go, I shall be compelled to call the porter.

LEONARD: Now, now, Mr. Elliott, that's not very hospitable of you. May we not have a drink and a little chat?

SIMON: Chat? What about? I've never seen you before in my life. I don't know you from Adam. What could we possibly have to say to each other?

LEONARD: We might discover that we have something in common. (*He goes to the drinks.*) You never know. (*He pours himself a drink.*)

SIMON (*furious*): What *do* you think you're doing?

LEONARD: Won't you have one with me?

SIMON: How outrageous! Now you've really gone too far. (*He goes to the telephone, picks up the receiver, and presses a button. Several buzzes are heard. Turning to* LEONARD.) I'm ringing the porter.

(LEONARD *sits above the table with his drink.* SIMON *buzzes again furiously, without success. He looks at his watch. Rather to his surprise, he cannot make out the figures. He blinks, and brings the watch closer. Then he wipes a hand over his forehead and buzzes again.*)

LEONARD (*pleasantly*): Perhaps he's nipped out for a quick one.

SIMON (*muttering*): Unlawful entrance—trespassing—(*He looks at* LEONARD'S *glass.*) stealing!

PORTER (*through the telephone*): 'Allo—yes?

SIMON: Porter? This is Mr. Elliott, flat fifty. I wonder if you'd mind coming up here for a moment. (*He turns his back to* LEONARD.) I'm—(*lowering his voice slightly*) it's rather urgent. . . . (*raising his voice slightly*) I've got a little bit of trouble here. . . . Yes, I appreciate that, but if you could . . . No, I can't discuss it. Come up right away, Porter. (*He puts down the receiver and looks over at* LEONARD *sitting calmly with his drink.*) If I were you, I'd leave now. Rather ignominious to be thrown out, isn't it?

LEONARD (*pleading*): Won't you join me in a drink?

SIMON (*pacing between the fire and the desk*): Don't think I like doing this, you know. But really you leave me no alternative. I mean, you can't just barge into someone's flat, try to intimidate them into letting it to you, and, when they won't—refuse to leave the premises, making yourself a nuisance into the bargain.

LEONARD: I shall be happy to pay for my drink. (*He takes some change from his pocket.*) One tot of whiskey—at saloon bar prices—(*He puts two half crowns on the table.*) That should well cover it.

(SIMON *exits to the bathroom, runs the cold tap, takes a couple of aspirin from a bottle on a shelf, puts them in his mouth, and drinks some water. He can be seen by* LEONARD.)

LEONARD: Headache, Mr. Elliott?

(SIMON *returns and closes the bathroom door.*)

SIMON: You know, it's just occurred to me. You might have just come out of prison.

LEONARD (*looking at his suit somewhat ruefully*): In that case I'd better see my tailor.

SIMON (*resuming his pacing*): Something you were saying when you looked out of that window—and—(*looking at* LEONARD) a certain pallor.

LEONARD: I am not a young man, Mr. Elliott.

SIMON (*pacing*): Prison—(*He mutters.*) or some other place. (*He takes a cigarette from a packet and picks up some matches from the desk.*)

LEONARD: I wouldn't—if I were you.

(SIMON *turns.*)

Gas, you know—in the atmosphere. (*He smiles.*)

(SIMON *throws the cigarette down.*)

Where's your dog?

SIMON (*sharply*): What?

LEONARD: The dog you mentioned earlier.

SIMON (*nastily*): He's out. (*He resumes pacing.*)

LEONARD: By himself? (SIMON *continues to pace. There is a tap at the door.*) Perhaps that's him now—back from his walk.

(SIMON *strides across and opens the door.*)

SIMON: Ah, Porter—come in.

(*The* PORTER *enters. He is short, middle aged, stockily built with powerful shoulders. Cockney or Irish. His face does not inspire trust.*)

PORTER: Good afternoon. (*glancing at* LEONARD) 'Afternoon. (LEONARD *inclines his head politely.*) (*To* SIMON) Now, sir, what's the trouble?

SIMON: Porter, I should like you to escort this gentleman off the premises.

(*The* PORTER *looks at* LEONARD. LEONARD *sits unperturbed.*)

PORTER (*faintly surprised*): Off the premises, sir?

SIMON: Well, out of my flat, anyway. And, I would suggest, out of the building. He's a public menace.

PORTER: May I ask what offense he has committed, sir?

SIMON: Trespassing! Trespassing on my property!

PORTER: A burglar, sir! (*He looks again at* LEONARD.) This gentleman?

SIMON: Well, not exactly a burglar, no. He hasn't actually stolen anything—apart from helping himself to my liquor. I suppose you'd call it "loitering with intent"—although what intent I'm damned if I know.

PORTER (*after a pause*): May I ask how he got *into* your apartment, sir?

(*There is a pause.* SIMON *hesitates.* LEONARD *rises.*)

LEONARD: Tell the porter how I got in, Mr. Elliott.

SIMON: Well . . .

LEONARD (*to the* PORTER): Mr. Elliott let me in.

SIMON (*crossing below* LEONARD *to the* PORTER): Well, he rang the bell; so naturally I opened the door. I mean, it's the usual . . .

LEONARD: And what did you say when you opened the door?

SIMON (*flushing*): What do you mean?

LEONARD (*smiling*): Tell the porter what you said when you opened the door, Mr. Elliott.

SIMON (*discomfited*): "I was expecting somebody else." (*to the* PORTER) The point is—the bell rang and I opened the door. All right. This man, a compiete stranger, walks in, makes himself at home, and tries to intimidate me into letting my apartment. When I refused, he refused to leave. He seems quite impervious to reason. Will you kindly escort him off the premises? And I would suggest that if you see him around the block again, you call the police!

LEONARD (*sniffing*): Strong smell of gas in here, isn't there?

SIMON: Rubbish.

PORTER (*sniffing*): There *is* a smell of gas, sir.

SIMON: The gas fire blew back, that's all. It's all right now.

PORTER: You want to be careful, sir.

SIMON: Yes, I know all about that. What I want now is for you to escort this man off the premises.

(*The* PORTER *looks past* SIMON *at* LEONARD. LEONARD *casually takes out his wallet and glances in it. Then he smiles at the* PORTER *and puts it back. The* PORTER *coughs.*)

PORTER (*to* SIMON): Of course, if you let him in, sir, he hasn't really committed any offense, has he, sir? Technically speaking, that is.

SIMON (*irately*): Of course he has! He refuses to go!

(LEONARD *picks up a book from the table. The* PORTER *shifts his feet and glances across at him again.*)

Well, what are you waiting for? Kindly remove this man from my apartment.

(*The* PORTER *looks past* SIMON *at* LEONARD again. LEONARD *looks up from his book and once more takes out the wallet.*)

PORTER (*to* SIMON, *who has not observed* LEONARD): Well, I'd like to oblige you, sir, but the truth is, I've got a bad back—dislocations, I think I've got. You know—where you can't bend nor lift nothing. I'm afraid I couldn't be using any force at the moment, sir, or I might put myself out altogether.

SIMON: But it's part of your job. Do you mean to say ...

PORTER: I'm very sorry, sir, it wouldn't be worth it—not with my back, you see.

SIMON: Oh, yes—I see!

PORTER: I'm very sorry, sir.

SIMON (*clapping his hands to his head*): Go away, man, go away! (*He moves away upstage.*)

PORTER: Yes, sir. (*He looks at* LEONARD.) I'm sure the gentleman will leave shortly, sir. (SIMON *swings round at him.*) Yes, sir. (*The* PORTER *exits quickly.* SIMON *waits for the door to close, then looks at* LEONARD. LEONARD *closes the book in his hand and puts it back on the table.*)

LEONARD: Interesting.

SIMON: You bribed him, I suppose—that porter—when you came in.

LEONARD: Bribed? Mr. Elliott! If by that you mean inducements offered to procure action or nonaction in favor of the giver, I suppose I cannot demur.

SIMON: How despicable!

LEONARD: Of him, or of me? (*after a slight pause*) Of me, you may think what you will. Of him, I think you must be a little more tolerant. Some people, you must understand, are like machines. They work for those who know how to handle them. That's one thing we older men have learned, you know—how to keep people of a certain mentality happy and efficient. It's not their fault, you know. It's a certain robot quality. ...

SIMON: He'll be reported.

LEONARD: I wouldn't advise that, Mr. Elliott. He's probably been here longer than you have. What is his name?

SIMON: I have no idea.

LEONARD: Find out. (*moving to the fireplace*) Don't call him "porter"—it's pompous. (SIMON *glares.*) And what do you give him? Half a crown at Christmas? In future I would suggest a bottle of whiskey and a small offering every Saturday. I think you'd find an extraordinary difference.

(SIMON *looks daggers at him, then goes to the telephone. He picks up the directory and thumbs through a few pages. He stops, peers hard at the page, then stops again with his finger on a place. He looks up.*)

SIMON: Mr.—er—Leonard, as you call yourself. If you were not an old man, I would throw you through that door myself.

LEONARD: Chivalrous.

SIMON: As it is, not only are you old, but you look sufficiently nasty to distort the story if I happened to break your nose. Therefore, unless you go through that door now, I intend to call the police station and have a policeman come up here and show you the way to go home. Perhaps you might also like to explain to him what you are doing in my apartment.

(*Still looking at* LEONARD, *he picks up the receiver.*)

LEONARD: Well, of course, if it was necessary, I should simply say I was passing and smelt gas, rang the bell, and saved you from suicide—which, I believe, if unsuccessful, is a criminal offense, is it not? (*a slight pause*) You were about to commit suicide, weren't you?

SIMON: Don't be ridiculous.

LEONARD: Fake suicide, no doubt—but then I wouldn't be expected to know that. Nor would the porter. I'm sure the police would agree my motives were purely charitable. A man in a depressed state is better kept an eye on.

SIMON (*putting down the receiver slowly*): You seem to hold all the cards, Mr. Leonard. Although what the game is, only you seem to know. Well (*picking up a book from the desk*), as far as I'm concerned, you can play it by yourself. (*He lies down on the divan. He puts the book up to his face and turns a page or two, but is not really reading.*)

(*There is a pause.* LEONARD *picks up one of the silver cups on the mantelpiece and reads the inscription.*)

LEONARD: Bit of a sportsman, Mr. Elliott? (*He puts it down and picks up another.*) I used to be—in my younger days. Too old for it now. (*He puts the cup down and wanders over to the drinks.*) Too old for most things, I'm afraid. (*There is no response from the divan. Picking up the whisky bottle, looking towards* SIMON) May I? (*Taking some silver from his pocket with the other hand*) The same arrangement?

SIMON (*lowering his book*): The arrangements are all yours, Mr. Leonard. And since it looks as if you're here for the evening, just continue to make yourself at home. Only let me know if you're thinking of staying the night—because if you are, I shall have to go out. (*He raises the book.*)

LEONARD: I'll make a bargain with you, Mr. Elliott. (*pouring himself a drink*) I will stay only until your friend comes. (*He takes another glass and pours some whisky in it.*)

(*From behind his book* SIMON *brings his watch up to his face.*)

SIMON: My friend won't be coming—so one of us will have to go.

(LEONARD *puts some more silver down by the drinks and picks up the two glasses.*)

LEONARD (*going to the divan*): Since you are not expecting anyone, Mr. Elliott, why not have a drink with me? (*He stands there with a glass in each hand.*)

SIMON (*from behind his book*): You just carry on drinking by yourself, Mr. Leonard. (*waving a hand towards the drinks*) Empty all the bottles and drink yourself into a stupor. Then I can call an ambulance and have you removed painlessly.

LEONARD: Mr. Elliott, if I just wanted to drink I would have headed for the nearest bar. The drink is something to do with my hands, and a mild and rather pleasant form of anaesthesia. (*Gently*) I would just like to talk to you.

SIMON (*putting the book down and sitting up*): But you talk in riddles, Mr. Leonard! You've talked in riddles ever since you came into my apartment. What do you *suggest* we talk about?

LEONARD: We could draw some comparisons, perhaps—between your life and mine. The life of an old man and the life of a young man.

SIMON: What is this—market research?

LEONARD: Not for the market—just a little research of my own. What it's like to be a young bachelor in an apartment like this. I've forgotten, you see.

SIMON: Well, I'm terribly sorry, but . . .

LEONARD (*holding out the glass*): Have a drink, Simon, and talk to me.

(*There is a slight pause.* SIMON'S *expression alters. He looks slightly puzzled, as if some chord from the past had been struck.*)

SIMON (*taking the glass*): You said that—as if you knew me very well.

(LEONARD *goes and fetches the soda syphon and offers it to* SIMON. SIMON *shakes his head.*)

LEONARD (*putting soda in his own glass, then returning the syphon to the bookcase top*): But I do know you very well. I've *been* you, or somebody like you, a long time ago. (*He walks back and sits beside* SIMON *on the divan.*) The gay days—just out of university—fit as a fiddle. My first job—my first apartment—my first mistress . . . (*He looks at* SIMON. SIMON *blushes and drinks hurriedly.*) They happened to me too, you know. (*He sighs.*) I sometimes think the young think the old have always been old. (SIMON, *embarrassed, knocks his drink back quickly.*) I envy you, you see. Your clean-cut looks, your nice healthy liver. I used to knock a whisky back neat like that, when I was your age. (*He looks at his glass and takes a sip.*) Now I have to dilute it. (*He takes* SIMON'S *empty glass, rises, and moves to the drinks.*) I have to dilute everything. (*pouring another whisky into* SIMON'S *glass*) You'll have to, when you get older. (*filling up his own with soda*) Diluted pleasures. (*He goes back to* SIMON *and gives him his neat whisky, sitting beside him as before.*) What do you do, Simon? I mean, what is your job?

SIMON: I work in a publisher's.

LEONARD: Do you enjoy it?

SIMON (*guardedly*): Ye-es. It's all right.

LEONARD: But you're not crazy about it? You'd rather be driving about the Côte d'Azur in a nice white sports car. Or red—do you prefer red? (SIMON *grins boyishly.*) All that can be arranged, Simon, if you'd like to go.

SIMON (*sceptically*): Hah!

LEONARD: I remember my first sports car—well. Drop-head coupe, they called them then. I drove all the way from Nice to Ventimiglia on the wrong side of the road.(*He smiles.*) Of course, there wasn't much traffic in those days. Suicide now.

(SIMON *is not really listening. He looks thoughtful.*)

SIMON (*suddenly looking at* LEONARD): Do you know my father? (LEONARD *looks somewhat bewildered.*) I just suddenly wondered if you knew my father?

LEONARD: As far as I know, I've never had the pleasure.

SIMON: I thought he might have sent you here to—er—check up or something.

LEONARD: No. Why? Doesn't he trust you?

SIMON: I don't know, really. It just struck me that it was the sort of thing the old boy might do.

LEONARD: It's a tendency fathers have, I suppose. (*He pauses.*) Well, would you like to go abroad, all expenses paid?

SIMON: I've had my holidays.

LEONARD: Have another one.

SIMON: With you? (*He gives* LEONARD *a curious look.*) Is this some kind of proposition?

LEONARD: Not in the sense you're thinking of. (*He smiles.*) I wouldn't be going.

SIMON: Some kind of job? (*He takes a drink.*) Because I can assure you my father wouldn't . . . (*He drinks again, finishing the glass.*) Well, he placed me in this publisher's, and he'd be furious . . .

LEONARD: Not a job. Just a free holiday. (*He takes* SIMON'S *glass.*) Let me give you another drink—on me. (*He rises and goes to the drinks.*)

SIMON: Look, have I won some sort of competition? Because if I have, I'd rather have the money. (*He lies back on the bed and contemplates the ceiling.*) I'm thinking of getting married, you see.

LEONARD (*pouring the whiskies; his voice is sombre*): Some soda this time?

SIMON: No. *Have* I won some competition?

LEONARD (*putting more money down with the rest and moving back to the divan*): Well, that remains to be seen—but the offer is entirely from me. (*He holds out the glass.*)

SIMON (*sitting up and taking it*): You're so cryptic. Everything you say is so cryptic! I mean—why should you offer me a holiday abroad, all expenses paid? Why *me,* a complete stranger? You must want something in return.

LEONARD (*lightly*): I tell you what, Simon. If you tell me about your "suicide," I'll tell you what I really want with you. (*He sits beside him.*)

SIMON: Oh, that! That was just a joke. Can't think why you're interested.

LEONARD: Rather a macabre joke, wasn't it?

SIMON: I suppose so.

LEONARD: The young lady might have died of fright.

(*There is a slight pause.*)

SIMON (*mocking*): How do you know it was a "young lady"?

LEONARD: Well, now, Simon, you don't look to me the sort of young man who'd go to all that trouble for anybody else. May I ask what it was you hoped to gain?

SIMON (*after drinking*): It's quite simple, really. I wanted her to get a divorce. (*He takes another drink.*) It sounds silly, but I thought if she saw I was prepared to die for her . . .

LEONARD: But you weren't prepared to die for her—were you, Simon?

SIMON: We—ell . . . (*He grins ruefully and slightly drunkenly.*)

LEONARD: There are very few young men today who are prepared to die for love, are there? If I thought that what I had discovered on entering this apartment had been anything but a little mock charade, our association might have been rather different.

SIMON (*puzzled*): What association?

LEONARD: No matter. Tell me about this young lady of yours. Where did you meet?

SIMON: The Tate Gallery. I went in one day in the lunch hour, and she was there. She . . .

LEONARD: Dropped her gloves?

SIMON (*scornfully*): *That* went out with Queen Victoria.

LEONARD (*murmuring*): Forgive me, I'm old-fashioned. (*He rises, moves to the table and puts down his glass.*)

SIMON: We both happened to be looking at the same picture.

LEONARD: "Woman Taken in Adultery"?

SIMON (*ignoring this*): It was a Picasso. And I just simply said to her, "Do you like Picasso?" and she said she did.

LEONARD: Ah, now that's something a young man can get away with—and an old man can't. If I went up to a young girl in similar circumstances and said, "Do you like Picasso?" she'd either look round for the attendant or use one of those modern phrases like "Get lost, Grandpa!" (*He smiles sadly.*) Anyway—you went on from there.

SIMON (*flippantly*): Never looked back. (*He lies back.*)

(*There is a pause.* LEONARD *moves to the window, then turns.*)

LEONARD: Tell, me Simon, how did you manage to conduct this *liaison dangereuse* without the young woman's husband finding out? I do remember, in my youth, that used to be one of my problems.

SIMON: Well, it was a bit difficult. We got fed up with the lunch hour.

LEONARD (*smiling*): Such a rush, isn't it?

SIMON (*sleepily*): Anyway, he used to go to his club every Friday night, so we started meeting then.

LEONARD: And that wasn't enough? You wanted to see her all the time?

SIMON: Well, it was a bit of a nuisance—being tied down to one evening a week —and Friday used to be my squash night.

LEONARD (*looking at him in some astonishment*): You know, I can't understand what any woman can see in a young man like yourself.

SIMON (*sitting up*): I beg your pardon?

LEONARD: You're so selfish. (*He moves to* SIMON.) I mean, we older men are so much more appreciative, so much more grateful for small mercies. We're not interested in sports evenings and nights with the boys.

SIMON: I say—look here . . .

LEONARD: But then we lose out physically every time, don't we? Receding hair —false teeth—tired legs . . . Not to be compared with a young man in his prime.

SIMON: But it's not just a physical thing. I'm perfectly serious about wanting her to get a divorce.

LEONARD: Are you sure she wouldn't lose just a little of her attraction if she did?

SIMON (*looking a little glassy-eyed*): Perfectly sure.

LEONARD: And why won't she get a divorce?

SIMON: Well—(*He swallows his drink.*) she married him when she was sixteen, you see—(*holding out his glass to* LEONARD) and she won't leave him—

(LEONARD *takes both glasses to the bookcase and pours two more drinks, putting down further money.*)

(SIMON's *voice a little slurred*)—father image, I suppose. You don't have to keep paying for those drinks, you know.

(LEONARD *returns with the drinks.*)

Anyway—(*swinging his legs off the divan and sitting up*) she's married to this old fuddy-duddy—impotent, boring, falling-asleep-in-the-chair type. (*He takes the drink from* LEONARD. *As he does so, a faint kind of realization comes to him as to who* LEONARD *might be, but he cannot quite seem to sort out his thoughts. He drinks.*)

(LEONARD *moves away and sits above the table.*)

I said to her, "He's an old man—" he's quite well off, I believe, "—he can get a housekeeper." But she's sentimental. . . . (*He looks oddly at* LEONARD, *and blinks his eyes curiously a few times, as if there was something wrong with his vision again.*)

LEONARD: And she didn't turn up today.

SIMON (*yawning*): No. It's the first time—for ages. (*He blinks again.*) I ought to ring her and find out—but I can't—because of . . . (*He yawns.*)

LEONARD: Him?

SIMON: Yes. But I can't understand—she's always managed. . . . (*He takes a drink.*)

LEONARD: Perhaps he locked her in somewhere.

SIMON: Yes, that's more than likely. (*He wipes his hand across his brow.*) The old . . .

LEONARD: Buzzard?

SIMON (*grinning*): Yes. If I could only—I'd like to take her to the—you know what you were saying—the Côte—I'd like to take . . . (*He yawns again and blinks his eyes.*) Wouldn't go—on my own.

LEONARD: There are some lovely girls there, Simon.

SIMON: Yes, but not like her—not like—(*after the slightest pause*) Monica. (*Beads of sweat appear on his brow. He rises.*) I think I'd like more soda—(*He looks down at his glass.*) with my . . . (*He sways, as if unable to walk, then holds out his glass.*) Would you . . .?

LEONARD (*rising*): Certainly. (*He takes the glass and moves to the drinks.*)

SIMON: You know—(*He sways again.*) you don't have to keep paying for all those drinks—you really don't. (*He takes a step or two and falls on his knees on the polar bear rug.*)

LEONARD: Is there something wrong?

SIMON (*muttering*): Dizzy—I feel—dizz . . .

LEONARD (*putting the glasses back on the tray*): You shouldn't play games with gas, Simon.

SIMON: Yes—it's the gas. The gas—and the drink—on top. (*He makes an effort to pull himself up, and keels over.*)

LEONARD (*crossing*): I am sorry. Let me help you. (*He tries rather ineffectually to get* SIMON *up.*)

SIMON: I feel so sleepy. I want to go to sleep ...

LEONARD: Yes, well, if we could get you to the bed ... (*He cannot succeed in getting* SIMON *to his feet.*)

SIMON: It's no use. (*He slumps down on the rug again.*) Let me go to sleep—please. ... (*He lies full-length on the rug, his head upstage.*)

(LEONARD *looks at him for a moment, then turns.*)

LEONARD: I'll get you some cushions. (*He brings the cushions from the divan.*) Make you more comfortable. (*He puts them under* SIMON'*s head, and straightens out his legs.*) There, that's better, isn't it?

(SIMON *looks at him glassily.*)

(*Straightening up and looking down at* SIMON). Do you feel a little cold? I'll shut the window. (SIMON *makes a feeble gesture, but* LEONARD *ignores it and moves to the window.*) It's getting dark anyway, isn't it? (*He shuts the window and closes the curtains, then turns on a small lamp on the mantelpiece and tilts the light deliberately towards* SIMON.) Not in your eyes, I hope?

SIMON (*blinking*): What time is it? (*His voice is far away.*) Is it time to go to sleep?

LEONARD (*gently*): It soon will be. Just lie quietly. Or would you like your book? (*He takes the book from the divan and gives it to* SIMON. *The book slips from* SIMON'*s fingers, half on, half off his chest.* LEONARD *moves to the table and picks up his bowler and umbrella.*) A little quiet read ...

(SIMON'*s eyes half close, then open again. They follow* LEONARD *glassily.*)

SIMON: Are you going? Where—are—you ... ?

LEONARD (*putting on his bowler*): Somewhere warm and sunny—like I was telling you about. You know, when I first came in I thought I might persuade you to go there. I even thought I might live here in your place. (*He goes to the mirror.*) Take over your existence. (*He gazes at his reflection—an elderly man with bowler and umbrella.*) But then, I don't look right, do I? (*He turns.*) Do you think they'll ever find the secret of eternal youth, Simon? (*He crosses and stands above* SIMON.) But then that sort of thought doesn't really worry you, does it? Youth is curiously uncurious about age. (*He looks down at him.*)

(SIMON's *eyes stare. His body gives a slight shiver.* LEONARD *takes a pair of gloves from his pocket and puts them on.*)

(*Moving round above* SIMON). Would you like the fire on, Simon? (*He bends down and turns on the gas tap, but does not light the fire. The gas hisses faintly.* LEONARD *turns and looks down at* SIMON.) I'm going now.

SIMON (*in blurred speech*): You haven't . . .

LEONARD: I haven't . . . ?

SIMON (*his eyes beginning to close*): You haven't told me . . .

(*The gas hisses.*)

You never—told me—what—you want?

(*There is a pause.*)

(LEONARD *leans over him. His voice is more reminiscent of earlier on.*)

LEONARD: Mr. Elliott, I don't believe you could take it in.

(SIMON's *eyelids flutter slightly and then slowly close. He lies very still. There is a pause, then* LEONARD *walks to the wastepaster basket and takes out the rose and the envelope. He puts the rose sadly to his nose, then gently places it on* SIMON's *chest. He looks at the envelope for a moment, then folds it over and puts it in his pocket. With his hat on and his umbrella over his arm, he turns and walks out of the room as—*

THE CURTAIN FALLS

Coming Through the Rye

WILLIAM SAROYAN

Characters

The Voice
Butch, *age 9*
Carroll, *age 70*
Steve, *age 27*
Miss Quickly
Roosevelt, *age 3*
Alice, *age 5*
Larry, *age 7*
Pedro Gonzalez, *age 8*
Johnny Gallanti, *age 9*
Henrietta, *age 13*
Hastings, *age 27*
Peggy

Reading Guides

1. *Coming Through the Rye* is, in one sense, a fantasy. Therefore, the place is unreal. It is important to remember that, while the characters are someplace, they are also no place.

2. When the play begins, the characters are as they were when they died. Yet, they are about to be born. When they are born, they are born as babies.

Coming Through the Rye

A LARGE ROOM, *beyond which is visible, in varying degrees of light and movement, infinite space. Sun, moon, planets, stars, constellations, and so on.*

The room is one of many. It is The American Room, and is so marked.

Each person here has been conceived and is waiting to be born. Each possesses his ultimate physical form and ego. Ultimate, that is, in the sense that here, in this waiting room, he is the way he shall be the day he begins to die, or the day he dies, in the world.

The faces of the unconceived appear to be a white cloud of a summer afternoon.

A solemn but witty VOICE *speaks.*

THE VOICE: OK, people. Your time has come. You are now going to enter the world. You'll find it a strange place. There are no instructions. You know your destiny now, but the moment you are in the world, breathing, you shall forget it. You can thank God for that, let me tell you. Good things, and bad, are ahead for each of you. The world is still new, and the idea of sending you out there for a visit has not yet proved itself to be a good one. It may in time, though. Your destination is America. (*a phrase of patriotic music*) It's an interesting place. No better and no worse than any other place, except of course superficially, which the Americans make a good deal of, one way or the other. The climate's fair everywhere, excellent here and there. Everything you do, you shall imagine is your own doing. You can thank God for that, too. You shall live as long as you shall. No more. You will find noise and confusion everywhere, even in your sleep. Sometimes in sleep, however, you shall almost, but not quite, return to this place. Nothing in the world is important. Nothing is unimportant. Many things shall *seem* important. Many shall seem *unimportant.* In a moment you shall begin to be human. You have waited here nine months of the world's time. A few of you a little less. From now on you shall be alone in body, apparently cut off from everything. You shall also *seem* to be alone in spirit. That, however, is an illusion. Each of you is the continuation of two others, each of whom was a continuation of two others, each of whom—and so on. (*blithely*) I could go on talking for two or three years, but it wouldn't mean anything. OK, now, here you go! Take a deep breath! (*dramatically*) Hold it! You will exhale in the world. OK, Joe, let 'em out!

(*A few chords of music. Some* PEOPLE *go out.* BUTCH, *a boy of nine, and* MR. CARROLL, *a man of seventy, come in.* BUTCH *is thoughtfully bouncing an old tennis ball.*)

BUTCH: Well, we're next, Mr. Carroll. Do you like the idea of being born?

CARROLL: Why, yes, of course, Butch. There's nothing like getting born and being alive.

BUTCH: I don't know whether I'm lucky or unlucky. Steve says I'm lucky because I don't have to stay in the world very long, and Miss Quickly—she says it ain't fair.

CARROLL: What *ain't?*

BUTCH: Me having to get born, just for nine years. Before I get a chance to turn around I'll have to come back, so what's the use going? I'm the way I'm going to be when I die, and you're the way you're going to be when you die. I'm nine, and you're an old man.

CARROLL: Butch, my boy, those nine years are going to be wonderful.

BUTCH: Maybe. Miss Quickly says it'll take me five or six years just to begin. Gosh, that only leaves three. I won't even get a chance to see any big league baseball games.

CARROLL: Maybe you will.

BUTCH: Heck no. How am I going to get from a little town in Texas to New York?

CARROLL: It may happen.

BUTCH: Boy, I *hope* it does, but Miss Quickly—she told Steve it wasn't fair.

CARROLL: What wasn't?

BUTCH: My father dying before I'm born and my mother being poor, and dying a year later. She says I may have to go to an institution. What the heck's an institution?

CARROLL: That's an orphanage, I guess. Now, listen, Butch, don't you go worrying about anything. Everything's wonderful out there.

BUTCH: How's it really going to be?

CARROLL: Well, the minute you're out there you're alive, the same as here, only different. Out there you begin right away.

BUTCH: Begin what?

CARROLL: Living—and dying. They're both beautiful, Butch. (*happily*) Living and dying in the world. That great big little tiny place. And from the first breath you take you begin being somebody: *yourself.*

BUTCH: I'm myself right now.

CARROLL: That's because you're here waiting. You've started at last. It takes a long time to get started. It took me—well, I don't know how long exactly in the world's time—but it was a long time.

BUTCH: Steve says the world stinks.

CARROLL: Now, Steve is a young fellow with ideas. He's a nice boy, but he's wrong about the world. It's the only place for us, and any of us who get to go out there are mighty lucky.

BUTCH: What happens when we leave the world?

CARROLL: We come back.

BUTCH: Here? And wait some more?

CARROLL: Not *here,* exactly. We wait *here, after* we've started. When we leave the world we go back to where we were before we came here.

BUTCH: Where the heck's that?

CARROLL: It's not exactly *any* place, Butch. And it's not exactly waiting either. *This* is where we *wait.*

BUTCH: Oh, well, I guess it'll be all right. But nine years. What the heck chance will I have to see anything?

CARROLL: Butch, one day out there is a long time, let alone nine years. Twenty-four hours every day. Sixty minutes every hour.

BUTCH: What are you going to be out there, Mr. Carroll?

CARROLL (*laughing*): Oh, a lot of things, one after another.

BUTCH: Well, *what?*

CARROLL: Well, let's see. (*He brings out a paper and studies it.*) It says here, Thomas Carroll. Mother: Amy Wallace Carroll. Father: Jonathan Carroll. Will be, at birth: Son, brother, nephew, cousin, grandson, and so on.

BUTCH: Brother?

CARROLL: Yes. I guess I've got a sister or a brother out there, maybe a couple of sisters and a couple of brothers.

BUTCH: I thought we were all brothers. I thought everybody was related to everybody else.

CARROLL: Oh, yes, of course, but this kind of brotherhood is closer. Whoever my brother is, he has my father and mother for *his* father and mother.

BUTCH: Well, what the heck's the difference? I thought we were all the same.

CARROLL: Oh, we are, really, but in the world there are families. They're still all really one family, but in the world the family is broken down to the people you come from, and the people that come from you. It gets pretty complicated.

BUTCH: But everybody *is* one family just the same, though, ain't they?

CARROLL: Well, yes, but in the world everybody forgets that for a while.

BUTCH (*bringing out his paper, which is a good deal smaller than* CARROLL'S): What the heck. I never looked at this. What do I get to be? (*reading the card*) James Nelson, also called Butch. By gosh, there it is right there. Also called Butch, but my real name is James Nelson. Let's see what I get to be. (*reading*) Son. Newsboy. Schoolboy. (*reflectively*) Son. No brothers?

CARROLL: Well, I guess not, Butch.

BUTCH: Why the heck not?

CARROLL: There will be all sorts of kids out there in Texas. They'll *all* be your brothers.

BUTCH: Honest?

CARROLL: Sure.

BUTCH (*reading*): Newsboy. What's that?

CARROLL: Well, I guess you'll sell papers.

BUTCH: Is that good?

CARROLL: Now don't you worry about anything, Butch.

BUTCH: OK. The heck with it. (*He puts the paper away.*)

CARROLL (*affectionately*): Give me a catch, Butch.

BUTCH (*delighted*): No fooling?

CARROLL: Why, sure, I'm going to play second base for the New Haven Orioles.

BUTCH (*throwing the ball, which* CARROLL *tries to catch*): Who the heck are they?

CARROLL: A bunch of kids in my neighborhood. (*He throws the ball back.*)

(STEVE: *comes in. About twenty-seven, sober, serious, but a drunkard.* BUTCH *holds the ball and watches* STEVE. *Then goes to him.*)

BUTCH: Steve? Tell him about the war—and all that stuff.

STEVE (*scarcely noticing* BUTCH, *absorbed in thought*): Tell *who, what?*

BUTCH: Mr. Carroll. About the war.

STEVE (*looking at* CARROLL, *smiling*): I was talking to the old lady—

BUTCH: He means Miss Quickly.

STEVE: Yeah.

BUTCH (*to* CARROLL): If everybody is everybody else's brother, what the heck do they have a war for?

CARROLL: Well, now, Butch—

STEVE (*laughing solemnly*): I'm afraid you won't be able to find a good answer for that question, Doc.

BUTCH (*delighted*): Honest, Steve?

CARROLL: Now, Steve, you know the world is a wonderful place.

STEVE (*simply*): I'm sorry, but I think it stinks. I think the human race is unholy and disgusting. I think putting people in the world is a dirty trick.

CARROLL: No. No. No, it isn't, Steve.

STEVE: What is it, then? You're called out, everybody's a stranger, you suffer every kind of pain there is, and then you crawl back. A little tiny place that got sidetracked in space and began to fill up with terrible unclean animals in clothes.

CARROLL: Those *animals* have created several magnificent civilizations, and right now they're creating another one. It's a privilege to participate.

BUTCH (*delighted*): You mean the World Series?

STEVE (*wearily*): OK, Doc. Anything you say.

CARROLL: Excuse me, Steve. Can I ask you a question?

STEVE: Anything at all.

CARROLL: What's ahead for you?

STEVE: A number of things.

CARROLL: Won't you tell me what they are?

STEVE: (*to* BUTCH) How about it, kid? Come back in a few minutes.

BUTCH: Ah, shucks. I want to listen. I'm not born yet.

STEVE: This is nothing. I'll be seeing you.

BUTCH (*obedient, going to one side*): OK, Steve.

CARROLL: What is your destiny, Steve?

STEVE (*pause*): Murder.

CARROLL (*amazed*): Murder?

STEVE (*slowly*): Yes. *I am going to murder* another human being.

CARROLL: Oh, I'm sorry, Steve.

STEVE: He's here, too.

CARROLL: Here? Who is he?

STEVE: I don't know if you've noticed him. *I* have. His name is Hastings.

CARROLL (*shocked*): Ralph Hastings?

STEVE: That's right.

CARROLL: Why, he's a nice young fellow. Are you sure it's not a mistake?

STEVE: No, it's not a mistake.

CARROLL: Well, good Lord. This is awful. But why? Why do you do it?

STEVE: It's a lot of nonsense.

CARROLL: What do you mean, Steve?

STEVE: You know he's rich. Well, he does a number of things that I think wreck the lives of poor people, so I—— If he's going to wreck lives of people, what's he born for? If all I'm supposed to do is kill him, what am *I* born for?

CARROLL: I'm sorry, Steve. Of course you'll never know once you're out there.

STEVE: That'll help some, of course, but I just don't like the idea. What do *you* do, Doc?

CARROLL: Oh, nothing really.

STEVE: Do *you* kill anybody?

CARROLL: No, I don't, Steve. I do a lot of ordinary things.

STEVE: Do you raise a family?

CARROLL (*delighted, but shyly*): Oh, yes. Three sons. Three daughters. All kinds of grandchildren.

STEVE (*sincerely*): That's swell. That'll help a little.

CARROLL: Help? Help what?

STEVE: Help balance things.

CARROLL: Do *you* marry, Steve?

STEVE: Not exactly.

CARROLL (*a little shocked but sympathetic*): Oh?

STEVE: I get a lot of women, but not a *lot* of them. I get a year of one, though. That's toward the end. She's here. (*smiling*) I'm a little ashamed of myself.

CARROLL: Why should you be ashamed?

STEVE: Well, she's Peggy.

CARROLL (*shocked*): Peggy?

STEVE: She'll probably be all right for me by that time.

CARROLL: Peggy's really a good girl, I suppose, but she seems so—

STEVE: I don't know her very well.

(MISS QUICKLY *enters, with* SEVEN KIDS, *ranging in age from 3 to 13*: ROOSEVELT, *black, aged 3.* ALICE, *aged 5.* LARRY, *aged 7.* PEDRO GONZALEZ, *Mexican, aged 8.* JOHNNY GALLANTI, *Italian, aged 9.* BUTCH. HENRIETTA, *aged 13.*)

MISS QUICKLY: Now, children, what'll it be? Singing or play-acting?

SOME: Singing.

SOME: Play-acting.

ROOSEVELT (*emphatically, as if with a grudge*): Nothing.

MISS QUICKLY: Nothing, Roosevelt? Now, really, you want to sing, don't you?

ROOSEVELT: No.

MISS QUICKLY: You want to act in a play, don't you?

ROOSEVELT: No.

MISS QUICKLY: You want to—

ROOSEVELT: No. I don't want to do nothing.

MISS QUICKLY: But *why,* Roosevelt?

ROOSEVELT: Because.

MISS QUICKLY: Because, what?

ROOSEVELT: Because I don't.

MISS QUICKLY: Don't you want to have fun?

ROOSEVELT: No.

MISS QUICKLY (*patiently*): But why, child?

ROOSEVELT: Because.

MISS QUICKLY: Oh, dear.

STEVE (*calling*): Come here, Roosevelt.

ROOSEVELT (*going to* STEVE): She's always making us do stuff.

MISS QUICKLY (*Gaily, to* STEVE): Oh, thank you, Steve. All right, children, we'll sing.

ROOSEVELT (*getting up into* STEVE's *arms*): They're going to sing! She's *always* making people sing, or something. (*looking at* MISS QUICKLY) Shame on you!

STEVE: You stick with me, pardner.

ROOSEVELT: Wants 'em to play act.

MISS QUICKLY (*sharply*): All right, children! (*She blows the pitch.*) *Beautiful Dreamer* by Stephen Foster. Ready. One, two, three: Sing!

(MISS QUICKLY *and the* CHILDREN *sing the song.*)

That was fine, children. Now, Roosevelt, don't you want to sing?

ROOSEVELT (*opening his eyes*): Shame on you—talk to me that way!

MISS QUICKLY: My gracious! Come along, children!

(*They go to one side.* RALPH HASTINGS *comes in, looks around. He is a well-dressed, decent sort of fellow, same age as* STEVE, *but younger looking. He looks at* ROOSEVELT, *runs his hand through the kid's hair.*)

HASTINGS: How's the boy?

ROOSEVELT: No.

HASTINGS (*laughing*): No, what?

ROOSEVELT: No, everything.

STEVE (*comforting him*): OK, kid.

ROOSEVELT (*with anger*): Only Steve's *my* pardner.

HASTINGS: Sure.

ROOSEVELT: Steve's the best man everywhere.

HASTINGS (*smiling at* STEVE): Sure, he is.

CARROLL (*studying the two young men sadly*): Well, Mr. Hastings, here we are.

HASTINGS: By the grace of God, here we wait for the first mortal breath. Are you pleased, Mr. Carroll?

CARROLL: I can't wait to begin.

HASTINGS: You, Steve?

STEVE (*simply*): I'm here.

HASTINGS: And so am I. (*pause*) Well—

STEVE: Look. I don't know if you know, but if you do—

HASTINGS: As a matter of fact, I *do* know, but what the hell—!

STEVE: I want you to know—

HASTINGS (*cheerfully*): It's all right.

CARROLL (*thoughtfully*): There must be some mistake.

HASTINGS: No, there's no mistake. Everything's in order. I'm sorry, Steve. I'll have it coming to me, I suppose.

STEVE: I don't think so.

HASTINGS: These things all balance. I *must* have it coming to me.

STEVE: That's why I say the world stinks.

HASTINGS: It depends, I guess.

STEVE (*sincerely*): Thanks. (*to* CARROLL) Right now he's the way he is the day he dies, and I'm the way I am that day. It's obvious it's not him, and not me, so it *must* be the world.

HASTINGS: We're not human yet.

STEVE: You mean we're not inhuman yet.

CARROLL: Now, boys.

HASTINGS (*cheerfully*): Of course, Mr. Carroll. (*to* STEVE) I have a lot of fun, after a fashion, as long as it lasts. How about you?

STEVE (*laughs, stops*): It's OK.

(PEGGY *comes in, looks around, comes over to the three men. She simply stands near them.*)

You know—I like you, Peggy. Even here, you're lost.

PEGGY: Oh, it's boring—that's what burns me up. Nothing to do. No excitement. I want to get started, so I can get it over with. I want to dance . . .

(CARROLL *and* HASTINGS *move away.*)

STEVE: Ah, now, Peggy—sure you do.

PEGGY: All I want to do is get it over with. I'm in a hurry. When do we start?

STEVE (*He puts* ROOSEVELT *with the other kids.*): Any time, now—any minute. They just got rid of another mob. We're next. (*pause, while he smiles at her*) Near you, Peggy, I'm in a hurry myself.(*He takes her by the shoulders.*)

PEGGY (*shocked a little*): Here?

STEVE: What's the difference? I've waited a long time for you. (*He takes her and kisses her.*) You see, Peggy, you're no good, and I love you for it. Because I'm no good, too. I don't know why, but it's so. Now, before we know it, we'll be separated, and I won't be seeing you again for a long time. Remember me, so that when we *do* meet again, you'll know who I am.

PEGGY: I've got a poor memory, but I guess I'll know you just the same.

STEVE (*kissing her again*): You'll remember, don't worry.

(*They stand, kissing.*)

THE VOICE: OK, people! Here we go again! I'm not going to go through the whole speech. You're going out whether you like it or not, so get going, and good luck to you!

(*Everybody goes. Only* STEVE *and* PEGGY *stand together, kissing.*)

OK, you two—get going!

(PEGGY *tries to move, but* STEVE *won't let her go.*)

Come on, come on, you American lovers, get going!

(PEGGY *struggles.* STEVE *holds her. She falls. He holds her terribly.*)

PEGGY (*whispering*): Let me go—please let me go!

(*They struggle passionately for some time.*)

THE VOICE: What's *this?* What goes on around here?

(*A whistle is blown, like a police whistle, but* STEVE *clings to* PEGGY. *At last* PEGGY *breaks away from him, gets to her feet, turns and runs.* STEVE *gets up and looks around, smiling wisely. He straightens out. As he stands, a newborn babe begins to bawl, as if it were himself being born. He looks around, turns easily, and walks out.*)

STEVE: OK, OK. I'm going.

The Long Fall

CARROLL V. HOWE

Characters

IRONWORKER
JOE LARKIN
JAMES O'MALLEY
NICK BRUNO
SWEDE
BILL MORGAN
CHARLIE MORGAN
BLAND

Reading Guides

1. Read the beginning of *The Long Fall* carefully to be sure to understand the family relationships, for they are important to the eventual emotional impact.
2. The weather conditions are very important in this play. Be sure that you have a clear idea of *time, place,* and *circumstance.*

The Long Fall

THE SCENE *is the exterior of a shack at the base of a bridge in the process of construction. The shack itself, wooden, weather-stained, with a sloping roof, is located right; it begins about stage center and extends off right. It is raised off the ground. Two steps lead to the door in the left wall of the shack. One window is set in the right wall; two more in the upstage wall. A large sign hangs on the edge of the roof: MORGAN AND O'MALLEY CONSTRUCTION COMPANY. The downstage wall of the shack is open to the audience. Inside, there is a potbellied stove, a desk, a drafting table, and a coatrack.*

At left, the base of a bridge extends upwards, before a sky background. A dock overlooking the river, center, is approached between the shack and the base of the bridge. A large, perforated, metal barrel for fire stands up center. A large, empty reel for wire rope is down left. Dirty snow covers the ground, and there is a general impression of cold and bleakness. It is winter, about eleven o'clock in the morning.

JOE LARKIN, *a small, neat, nervous man of about forty-five, dressed in a faded gray shirt, black leather tie, dark gray working trousers, and a leather jacket, is standing inside the office looking up at the bridge through one of the upstage windows. An* IRONWORKER *is standing beside the fire barrel, warming his hands, and also looking up at the bridge. There is a quality of apprehension in the attitudes of both men. After a moment, the* IRONWORKER *turns, picks up a pair of wire rope slings resting against the steps of the shack, and goes off left. The telephone in the shack rings; after a pause* LARKIN *turns to answer it.*

LARKIN (*into phone*): Morgan and O'Malley Construction Company. Who's this? . . . Who? . . . Oh, *Evening Ledger,* huh? . . . I'm Joe Larkin, the timekeeper. What do you want? . . . Oh . . . Yeah, yeah, that's right. About an hour ago. His name was Duke Morgan. . . . No, they haven't found him yet; the current washed him under the ice. . . . Nobody's at fault. Usually when a man falls, it's nobody's fault but his own. . . . Ice? . . . Sure, there's ice; what about it? Men often work in weather like this, ice or no ice. . . . Yeah, the second accident yesterday. . . . Bill Morgan is bossing this job. . . . No, he's not responsible. You might be interested in knowing it was his own brother who got killed! . . . (*vehemently*) Listen, mister, somebody's been giving you the wrong dope; you're dead wrong. . . . Of course you can send a man over; we got nothing to hide! . . . Okay, okay! (LARKIN *slams down the phone, turns, sees* JAMES O'MALLEY, *who has entered from left and come into the shack during the latter part of* LARKIN'S *speech.* O'MALLEY *is a stout, well-dressed man of about fifty.*) Oh, hello, Mr. O'Malley.

O'MALLEY: Hello, Joe. Who was that?

LARKIN: News editor of the *Ledger.* He wanted to know about the accident. He's sending a man over.

O'MALLEY: That's why I'm here, too. Morgan called me a little while ago. What's this about his brother getting killed? He only told me someone had fallen. It wasn't Duke?

LARKIN: Yeah. He fell into the river from one of the towers. The current got him under the ice, and they haven't found him yet.

O'MALLEY: Christ, that's awful! (*after a pause*) How's Morgan taking it?

LARKIN: I don't know. He hasn't said a damn thing. You know how he is; never shows nothing.

O'MALLEY: Did his boy, Charlie, start this morning?

LARKIN: Yeah. He'll only be here for a couple of weeks, though. Then he goes back to school. He's home for Christmas.

O'MALLEY: I know. He's a nice lad.

LARKIN: Helluva nice lad. I broke him in last summer—on the Crocker job.

O'MALLEY (*after a pause*): What did you tell the *Ledger* was the wrong dope?

LARKIN (*reluctantly*): It was—uh—it was about our outfit.

O'MALLEY: What was it?

LARKIN: This guy wanted to know if it was true that more men get killed on Morgan–O'Malley jobs than with any other contractors.

O'MALLEY (*after a pause*): When the reporter gets here, send him to me. I don't want him nosing around the job, trying to stir up trouble.

LARKIN: Yes, sir.

O'MALLEY: Where's Mr. Morgan?

LARKIN: He's over the other shack, drawing up a report to turn in to the union.

O'MALLEY: Find him, and tell him I'd like to see him. Have the blueprints for the center span arrived?

LARKIN: Yes, sir. They're on the table.

O'MALLEY (*pauses before the drafting table*): How do the men feel about it?

LARKIN: Not so good. Two men have fallen since yesterday. You know how it is: a lot of times these things seem to run in threes. No one likes to work with that hanging over him.

O'MALLEY: Nonsense. Two accidents don't necessitate a third. Ironworkers are like children—believe in old wives' tales. (*pause*) Did anyone quit?

LARKIN: No. They're sticking because of the extra money. Mr. Morgan gave the Duke's gang the rest of the day off; they were pretty shaken up. (*pause*) Then there's the ice! The men don't like that.

O'MALLEY: I know it, but there's nothing we can do. If we could only get a break with this damn weather . . . (*shrugs*) Well, tell Mr. Morgan I'd like to see him. I'll wait here.

LARKIN: Okay, Mr. O'Malley.

(*He exits from the shack, and starts to cross right.* NICK BRUNO *enters from left, followed by* SWEDE. NICK *is a dark, muscular, intense man of thirty-five.* SWEDE *is tall, blonde, slow-moving, about five years younger. Both are wearing working clothes.*)

NICK (*calling to* LARKIN): Joe! Hey, Joe!

LARKIN (*turning*): Nick! What are you guys doing here? I thought Morgan gave you the rest of the day off.

NICK: Swede and I decided to stick around for awhile. Have any new guys been hired during the last couple of days?

LARKIN: Sure, why?

NICK: Who are they?

LARKIN: A couple of punks. Dutch van Riper's gang was a man short after Georgie fell yesterday and—say, what's this all about, anyway?

SWEDE (*slowly*): Duke landed on a scaffold on the lower level first, then rolled off into the river. Nick saw some guy down there, only about ten feet away from Duke, but he didn't do nothing—just stood there and watched him fall. Nick saw the guy, clear, but didn't recognize him.

NICK: I saw him, all right. His face even looked familiar. But I know I ain't seen him before on this job.

SWEDE: So we thought it might be a new man, if anybody's been hired.

NICK: Dutch's gang worked the lower level this morning, didn't they?

LARKIN (*slowly*): Yeah, they did, but on the other side. They were on the other side of the river.

NICK: Well, this other punk—where was he working?

LARKIN (*hesitantly*): Uh—I don't know. He—uh—I think they put him on the lift. Yeah, that's right. I remember now. He'd never done this work before, so they put him on the lift.

SWEDE: Then he couldn't have been there when Duke fell.

LARKIN: I guess not.

NICK: This don't add up! Who is this guy, anyway?

LARKIN (*hesitates again*): Ah—I don't know. I'd never seen him before. Mr. Morgan called up the union hall; they sent him over this morning.

SWEDE: And those two are the only new men on the job?

LARKIN: That's right. (*a pause; to* NICK, *placatingly*) You're all jazzed up, Nick. Why don't you go home and relax? Maybe you just imagined you saw this guy.

NICK (*angrily*): I'm not imagining it. Wasn't I there? I remember it all. Swede's passing; I'm on the gun; Duke's catching. Swede throws this rivet—I guess Duke isn't ready—he makes a phony pass, and it takes him on the chest. He yells and falls over backwards. I nearly go over myself making a grab for him. (*with mounting intensity; reliving it*) He lands on a scaffold about twenty feet down—starts to pull himself up—real slow, like he's punch . . . I yell, "Don't move!" Then I see this other guy, standing there only ten feet from Duke . . . "For Christ's sake, run over and grab him!" . . . Bastard don't move. (*approaching hysteria*) Duke on his knees, hanging on the edge, crawling right off . . . keeps turning over in the air . . . then he hits, two hundred feet down! . . . Sound of ice breaking comes back up —seems about a year later. (*long pause. He comes back to himself.*) I lay down on the edge, shaking. I covered my eyes. When I looked again, there was only a hole in the ice, and this other guy was gone. I've been looking for the son of a bitch ever since.

(*His voice breaks. He is trembling with remembrance.*)

SWEDE (*calming him down*): Take it easy, Nick. You're just making it worse.

LARKIN: You ought to go home, Nick. You aren't doing yourself any good going around like this.

NICK: I'm not leaving till I find that guy. (*in a burst*) Damn it, the Duke could still be alive! (*pause*) Come on, Swede, let's look around some more.

(NICK *exits left.*)

SWEDE (*turning before he exits*): I think you're stalling us, Larkin. If you know who this guy is, tell him to get the hell out of here. The way Nick is jazzed up, he'll kill him.

(*Follows* NICK *out.* LARKIN *turns, starts to cross right.* O'MALLEY *appears at the door of the shack.*)

O'MALLEY: Larkin, have you seen Mr. Morgan yet?

LARKIN: I'm sorry, Mr. O'Malley. I got held up. I'll go right over. (*He starts offstage right, stops.* BILL MORGAN *enters from right. He is a tall, muscular, athletic man of fifty. He moves purposefully, with an easy sense of power. His features are rough and impassive; there is about them the tough unyielding quality of weathered granite.*) Hello, Mr. Morgan.

MORGAN: Larkin, have you seen Charlie anywhere around?

LARKIN: No, I haven't, Mr. Morgan. I'm looking for him myself.

MORGAN: I haven't seen him since the accident. Look around the job for him, will you? Tell him I want to see him.

LARKIN: Okay, Mr. Morgan. (*starts to cross*) Oh, Mr. O'Malley wants to see you. He's in the office.

MORGAN: Thanks. (*He crosses to the shack, enters.*) Hello, Jim.

O'MALLEY: Hello, Bill. Larkin told me about your brother; you didn't say who it was. I'm sorry as hell. If there's anything I can do . . .

MORGAN: There's nothing anyone can do. What's done is done.

O'MALLEY (*after a moment*): Bill, I think we ought to knock off the job until the weather clears.

MORGAN: What?

O'MALLEY: I said, "We ought to knock off the job until the weather clears."

MORGAN: Are you crazy? We can't do that. We've got every cent we own tied up in this. We've waited years for this break; if we flub it, we're finished. You know that as well as I do.

O'MALLEY: I know, but . . .

MORGAN: The state highway department is all over my back. We're a month behind schedule now.

O'MALLEY: If they'd clear our priorities through, without all this red tape we'd . . .

MORGAN: We took this job with the understanding we'd handle the priorities ourselves. We got a tough break when Donaldson wasn't reelected, but we can do it—with a little luck.

O'MALLEY: Yes, but these accidents . . .

MORGAN: Accidents happen. That's part of the game.

O'MALLEY: But working in this weather—the ice . . .

MORGAN: The men are getting time and a half for it, aren't they? They don't have to work if they don't want to.

O'MALLEY: But I thought that with your brother . . .

MORGAN: Sentiment has no part in business. That's something else.

O'MALLEY (*after a pause*): All right, then. What do you want to do?

MORGAN: Work the rest of the week out, anyway. Once we get the center span connected, it'll be clear sailing. The weather may break any day. We'll wait and see. All right?

O'MALLEY (*reluctantly*): I guess it has to be.

(CHARLIE MORGAN *enters from up center right. He is like his father, tall, muscular, but of slighter build. He is about twenty-three. He is dressed in working clothes. He goes into the shack.*)

CHARLIE: Hello, Dad. I heard over the other shack you were looking for me. Hello, Mr. O'Malley.

O'MALLEY: Hello, Charlie. I'm terribly sorry about your uncle.

MORGAN (*He is obviously very fond and proud of* CHARLIE.): I was looking for you after the accident. Where have you been?

CHARLIE: I didn't feel so good. I've been sitting out on the dock, looking at the ice. They've sent a diver down.

MORGAN: I know. You all right now?

CHARLIE: I'm all right now.

MORGAN: Where were you when Duke fell?

CHARLIE (*after a short pause*): On the lower level.

MORGAN: Did you see him fall?

CHARLIE: No. N-no, I didn't. Someone yelled over, there'd been an accident. Then I found out it was Duke.

O'MALLEY: You don't look so good, Charlie. Maybe you'd better take the rest of the day off.

CHARLIE: I'm all right. I walked over and looked at them diving for him. It made me sick for awhile, thinking about it. But I'm all right now.

O'MALLEY: This is your first day at this work?

CHARLIE: I worked at it last summer, but on the ground—rodman. I'm having trouble with the height.

O'MALLEY: Everyone goes through that—you'll get used to it. It just takes time.

CHARLIE: Yeah, I guess so.

O'MALLEY: Bill, I think I'll go back uptown. I'm supposed to meet Bradley about the girder shipment for the center span. (*pause*) By the way, the *Ledger* is sending a reporter to cover the accident. Take care of him, will you? Don't let him get too nosey.

MORGAN: Okay. I'll call you if anything develops.

O'MALLEY: I'll stop back again this evening. (*To* CHARLIE) Goodbye, Charlie. Try not to let what happened this morning get on your nerves. And extend to your uncle's family my deepest sympathy.

CHARLIE: I'll do that, Mr. O'Malley.

O'MALLEY: See you later, Bill.

MORGAN: See you. (O'MALLEY *exits left. Father and son turn and look at each other.* MORGAN *speaks.*) Well, son?

CHARLIE: It seems sort of hard to realize that—Duke's dead—doesn't it?

MORGAN: Yes—it does.

CHARLIE: Have you told—Clara?

MORGAN: No. Not yet. I thought we'd do it together—tonight. (*pause*) I'm afraid she'll take it hard. They're just buying a new house.

CHARLIE: Dad, I . . . (*hesitates*)

MORGAN: What?

CHARLIE: I want to quit.

MORGAN: What!

CHARLIE: I don't think I'm going to be any good at this.

MORGAN: Nonsense. You're upset. It's the accident.

CHARLIE: Ever since it happened, I've been walking around down here, trying to get up nerve to go back up.

MORGAN: Why don't you?

CHARLIE: I started to—a couple of times. But I couldn't. To tell the truth, I'm scared. I'm scared I'll fall, too. (*hesitates*) Maybe I can try it again another time.

MORGAN: You think it's as simple as that—that it will be easier another time?

CHARLIE: I don't know. It might be.

MORGAN: I'll tell you; it won't be. It will be worse another time, because you'll spend from now to then thinking about it. It will magnify itself. You've got to get over these things quickly. Face your fear, beat it out of you, and you'll be all right. But if you let it go, you'll never be able to get rid of it.

CHARLIE (*after a moment*): But suppose I should fall?

MORGAN: You won't fall. Get that idea out of your head! Accidents happen on all jobs. Just watch yourself! The new man never falls; he's too careful. It's only the oldtimers, like Paul; they get careless. Or sometimes a wise kid, trying to show off, trying to impress the others. But even that's rare.

CHARLIE: It's more than just being careful. I can't move around right up there. My muscles freeze up; they don't function. I get a sort of paralysis.

MORGAN: That's because you're thinking about it. Concentrate on what you're doing—don't worry about anything else—and everything will be all right. (*pause*) If you want to take the rest of the day off, you'll probably feel better tomorrow.

CHARLIE: It'll be worse tomorrow; you just said that yourself. (*pause*) Damn it, I can't help being afraid of height.

MORGAN: You flew a P-40 during the war.

CHARLIE: That was different. I had a plane around me. Here there's nothing but a little beam hanging in space. I can't take it!

MORGAN: All right, then! If you want to quit, quit. When a man feels as you do, there's no use forcing him.

CHARLIE: I said I'll work the day out. Maybe I'll get over it. If I do, I'll stick with it.

MORGAN: You make up your own mind. I have work to do.

(MORGAN *turns to his desk.* CHARLIE *looks at his back for a moment.*)

CHARLIE: I'm sorry, Dad.

(*He turns and exits from the shack, starts off right, as* LARKIN *comes in from left.*)

LARKIN: Hey, Charlie!

CHARLIE (*turning*): What?

LARKIN: Listen, kid, were you working around Duke's gang this morning?

CHARLIE: Yeah—earlier. I was following them up, painting rivet heads. Why?

LARKIN: On the lower level?

CHARLIE: At first. They finished, and went up on top.

LARKIN: And you stayed down below?

CHARLIE: I wasn't finished with the section.

LARKIN: Where were you when it happened?

CHARLIE (*after a short pause*): You mean the accident?

LARKIN: Yeah.

CHARLIE: I was over by the lift. I—uh—I'd run out of paint. I went back to get some more.

LARKIN: You sure?

CHARLIE: Of course I'm sure. I was by the lift when someone yelled over, there'd been an accident.

LARKIN: Then you weren't near Duke when he fell?

CHARLIE: No. (*after a moment*) What's this all about, anyway?

LARKIN: Nick Bruno's looking for you—there might be trouble.

CHARLIE: Who's Nick Bruno?

LARKIN: The riveter in Duke's gang. It's a wonder he hasn't already found you.

CHARLIE: What does he want me for?

LARKIN: He's all jazzed up from the accident. He was there when it happened —has some crazy idea you had a chance to grab Duke from a scaffold on the lower level.

CHARLIE (*carefully*): What makes him think that?

LARKIN: Like I said, he's all keyed up. He probably saw you working there earlier, and thought you were still there when Duke fell. (*pause*) You sure you weren't there?

CHARLIE: I've told you twice! I was over by the lift.

LARKIN: Okay, okay! I'd rather believe you; it makes a cleaner story. Nobody gets involved. But you'd better get out of here—just to be safe. Nick might come around here any minute.

CHARLIE: So?

LARKIN: He'll probably try to beat hell out of you—and one of you will get hurt. He and Duke were pretty close; they worked together on a lot of jobs.

CHARLIE: Suppose I stay on the job!

LARKIN: It'll cause a lot of trouble. Why bring on headaches? Be smart; your old man can get you somewhere else.

CHARLIE: Thanks. I appreciate this, Joe. But I think I'll stick around, anyway.

LARKIN: You're crazy. Besides, Nick has a good story. You were working up there. Word might get around you were there when it happened. If it did, it would be worse on your old man than you; the men aren't too happy about the accidents, as it is.

CHARLIE: But if I wasn't there?

LARKIN: If you weren't there, you know it. Things are bad enough as they are. Why make them worse?

CHARLIE: You think it'd be better if I shoved off?

LARKIN: I know it would. I been in this game a good many years; I know the way things work.

(NICK *and* SWEDE *enter from left during* LARKIN'S *speech.* CHARLIE'S *back is turned to them.*)

CHARLIE: Maybe you're right. I'll think it over and ...

NICK (*calling to* LARKIN): Hey, Larkin, we been look all over the job for that guy. I'm beginning to think I didn't even ... (CHARLIE *turns and looks at* NICK, *who sees him.*) There he is, Swede! (*Crosses to* CHARLIE, *starts to push him, feeding his own anger.*) Listen, you yellow bastard, what the hell's the idea of standing there like a piece of tripe when my buddy fell?

CHARLIE: What do you mean?

NICK (*pushing harder*): You know what I mean! You saw me plain enough.

CHARLIE: You've got the wrong idea, fella. I ...

(NICK *lashes out viciously with a hard left to the stomach;* CHARLIE *doubles and* NICK *rabbit punches him to the ground.*)

LARKIN (*crosses to* NICK, *and pushes him back*): Nick, Nick, wait a minute! Maybe he can explain ...

(SWEDE *crosses to* LARKIN, *and drags him away from* NICK.)

SWEDE: Okay, Larkin! Now Nick's found the guy, let him get it out of his system!

(NICK, *free from* LARKIN, *crosses back to* CHARLIE, *who is still prostrate on the ground. He takes a spud wrench from his belt, and starts to swing it down on* CHARLIE, *who is on his knees. The door to the shack flies open, and* MORGAN *comes out. He grabs* NICK *from behind, gets the wrench from him, and throws him to the ground.*)

MORGAN: What the hell's going on here? (*No one answers.*) You, Bruno! What are you trying to do?

NICK (*sullenly, climbing to his feet*): Ask that son of a bitch!

MORGAN (*to* CHARLIE): What's the trouble?

CHARLIE (*who has risen, groggily*): Forget it. I can fight my own battles. You've nothing to do with it.

MORGAN (*after a long look at* CHARLIE): You, Pete! What's this all about?

LARKIN (*temporizing*): Well, Mr. Morgan, Nick here . . .

NICK (*interrupting*): I'll tell you what it's all about. You know this guy? (*indicates* CHARLIE)

MORGAN: He's my son.

NICK (*incredulously*): Your what?

MORGAN: I said he's my son! Now what's the trouble?

NICK: I didn't know he was your son.

MORGAN: He is. Now what's this all about?

NICK (*uncomfortably*): I—uh—I guess I made a mistake. I—I thought I saw him standing on the lower level, near where Duke landed before he went on into the river. (*pause*) But I—I guess it couldn't have been—if he's Duke's nephew.

MORGAN: Where were you when you thought you saw him?

NICK: On the upper level, where he fell from.

SWEDE: Now wait a minute. (*crosses to* CHARLIE) Where were you when he fell?

CHARLIE: Over by the lift.

SWEDE: What were you doing there?

CHARLIE: I was getting more paint. It ran out.

SWEDE: You were following us up, weren't you?

CHARLIE: Yes.

SWEDE: We only did one section on the lower level this morning. Why did you go back for more paint after only one section?

CHARLIE: Why—I—uh . . .

SWEDE: You had a full bucket when you started, didn't you?

CHARLIE: I—I guess some of it spilled. I—I was pretty nervous this morning.

SWEDE: So nervous you can't remember if any spilled?

CHARLIE: I—uh—it must have . . . I . . .

SWEDE (*intensely*): So nervous you can't remember if any spilled!

(*There is a pause. All the men look at* CHARLIE.)

CHARLIE (*finally*): All right. I was there. But I can explain . . .

MORGAN (*looking at* CHARLIE *unbelievingly*): This isn't true, Charlie! (CHARLIE *does not answer.*) It isn't true! You weren't there!

CHARLIE: I've already said I was. But if you'll give me a chance . . .

NICK (*moving in*): You let your own uncle drop two hundred feet without moving an inch to save him. You lousy yellow . . .

MORGAN (*pushing* NICK *back*): All right, Bruno! I'll handle this.

NICK: You say! I worked with Duke nine years. I'm supposed to let this punk get away with it, just like that?

MORGAN: He's closer than you.

NICK: Let us alone. I'll give him what's coming to him.

MORGAN: Bruno! Get your gear together, and get off the job! I told you to shove off this morning. Now beat it!—if you still want to work here.

NICK: Who says? You're a hot one, the big boss! You ain't firing me. And I'm not going yet. I got some business to settle first with this stinking . . .

MORGAN (*reaches out, grabs* NICK *by the front of his jacket, swings him in close*): That's enough! (*He shoves* NICK *roughly over toward* SWEDE.) Take him off the job, Swede, before he gets himself into trouble. Bring him back tomorrow; he'll probably have snapped out of it.

SWEDE (*after a moment, crosses to* MORGAN): I don't like the way you're handling this, Morgan.

MORGAN: You don't? You want to do something about it?

(*There is a pause.*)

SWEDE (*finally*): Come on, Nick, let's go.

NICK: But . . .

SWEDE: I said, "Let's go!"

(NICK *crosses to* MORGAN, *picks up the wrench at* MORGAN'S *feet. He and* SWEDE *exit right.*)

MORGAN (*to* LARKIN): Joe—make sure they get out of here.

LARKIN: Sure, Mr. Morgan. (*He exits right.*)

MORGAN (*to* CHARLIE): Then it's true. You were there.

CHARLIE: Yes, but—Dad, Dad, there's more to it than that.

MORGAN: How can there be more to it? You stood there and let a man fall, just like that! Your own blood you let fall, just like that!

CHARLIE: I—I tried . . . I—I couldn't do anything.

MORGAN (*intensely*): You could; you could! No man just stands there and lets another man fall, and doesn't do anything!

CHARLIE: I—I wanted to move. I tried to move.

MORGAN (*more intensely*): That isn't true. It can't be true. Ten years ago Paul jumped across eight feet of air, from beam to beam, to save me—I wouldn't be here now. Then my own son lets him fall. How could you do that?

CHARLIE: I'm telling you I tried. But I couldn't move. (*points to the bridge, speaks hysterically*) Look, look—there's ice on the beams! We'd both have fallen. Wouldn't you rather see me alive?

MORGAN (*after a pause, deliberately*): All my life I've lived by rules of my own making. I thought if anyone would live up to them, you would. (*in a burst*) Damn it, even if you did fall, you should have tried!

CHARLIE (*frantically*): You don't see it. Dad, Dad—all morning I crept around, hardly able to breathe. All morning I was froze up—my knees shook every time I had to move. I couldn't have saved him if he'd been two feet away, much less ten. (*reliving it*) I heard a scream, short, choked, like an animal. Then he landed, ten feet away. I didn't know who he was. When he fell, I started to fall. I grabbed the truss and held—the whole bridge was shaking—my hands acted like they weren't mine—grabbing that truss so tight—flattening me against it. Then he was gone, and I heard the smash of breaking ice. (*pause; in a monotone*) Then it was quiet, and I knew it was all over, and I was standing there shaking and still holding on to the truss. . . . And I came down.

MORGAN (*harshly*): Then you came and lied to me. Duke only just killed, and you came and lied to me.

CHARLIE (*brokenly*): What could I do—tell you? I didn't think anyone had seen me. I didn't think anyone would know about it. (*after a moment*) What —what do you want me to do?

MORGAN: I don't know. I only know what you should have done. Now it's too late. (*pause*) You'd better get off the job. This is no place for you. Go home. I'll see you this evening.

CHARLIE: What will have changed by this evening?

MORGAN: I don't know. All I know is, you're no good around here. (*in a burst*) God, why did this have to happen?

CHARLIE: Dad, I . . .

MORGAN (*turning in fury*): Get out of here! Go home; go back to school; go anywhere, but get away from me, you . . . (*Sick with grief and pride, he strikes* CHARLIE *heavily across the mouth. They look at each other a moment, then* CHARLIE *turns and runs off left. After a moment,* MORGAN *crosses after him, calling.*) Charlie! (*pause*) Charlie!

(*There is no answer. Head bowed,* MORGAN *crosses back toward the shack.* LARKIN *comes in from the right.*)

LARKIN: They're gone, Mr. Morgan.

MORGAN (*dully*): Who:

LARKIN: Nick and the Swede.

MORGAN: Oh.

LARKIN (*after a moment*): Mr. Morgan . . .

MORGAN: Yes?

LARKIN: I'm awfully sorry this had to happen.

MORGAN: Yes.

LARKIN: We've been in this game a long time. Maybe we've forgotten how it was at first. I remember when I started, I was afraid to move up there.

MORGAN: But to save a man's life . . .

LARKIN: Even that. Your muscles play tricks on you. It's hard to do what maybe you want to do.

MORGAN: But to keep a man from falling . . .

LARKIN: I had a chance to grab a guy who fell once, when I first started. But I couldn't move, just like your boy. I stood there—like I was paralyzed. He didn't die, but I had a bad time. Later on, I did prove myself, on another job. It was only then I knew that I'd always had the guts, but couldn't use them.

MORGAN: You had the guts, but couldn't use them?

LARKIN: That's right. (*coaxingly*) Tell you what, Mr. Morgan. Let me go after your boy and talk to him. He's no different than any of the other guys —just got a tough break at the wrong time. So I'll just go and talk to him. Okay?

MORGAN (*after a moment*): All right, Joe.

(LARKIN *exits left.* MORGAN *enters the shack.* O'MALLEY *and* BLAND *enter from right, and go into the shack.* BLAND *is a reporter type.*)

O'MALLEY (*to* MORGAN): Bill, Bland here is from the *Ledger.* I met him on my way out. I've been telling him about the accident. (*to* BLAND) This is Mr. Morgan.

BLAND: Glad to meet you, Mr. Morgan.

MORGAN (*with an effort*): Anything I can do for you?

BLAND: Just a little information about the accident. What time did it take place?

MORGAN: About ten-fifteen this morning.

BLAND: What was the man's name who fell?

MORGAN: Paul Morgan. He was called "Duke."

BLAND: He was your brother?

MORGAN: That's right.

BLAND: Too bad. Were there any witnesses to the accident?

MORGAN: Two. I gave them the rest of the day off.

BLAND (*a statement*): This is the second fatality in two days.

MORGAN: Yes.

BLAND: That's a pretty high mortality rate.

MORGAN: It all depends—I suppose it is—pretty high.

BLAND: Any idea what might be causing these accidents?

MORGAN: No—they just happen.

BLAND: This is rather treacherous weather to work in.

O'MALLEY (*interceding, after an uneasy glance at* MORGAN): The men work in all sorts of weather, depending on commitments.

BLAND: Oh! And who makes the commitments?

O'MALLEY: In this instance—we have.

BLAND: You mean you two?

O'MALLEY: That's right.

BLAND: I see. (*pause*) How long has this bridge been under construction?

O'MALLEY: About nine months. We started . . . (*The alarm whistle blows off stage left, loud and piercing.*) Oh, my God! (O'MALLEY *runs to the door of the shack.*)

BLAND: What's that?

O'MALLEY: Accident. (*goes down stairs*) We'd better go and see what it is.

BLAND: Mind if I come along?

O'MALLEY: No, I don't suppose so. Come on, Bill!

(O'MALLEY *runs off left, followed by* BLAND.)

BLAND (*as they exit*): What provisions are made for families in accidents of this sort?

(*They exit.* MORGAN *leaves the shack, crosses to the fire barrel, looking up at the bridge. After a moment* LARKIN *runs in from left.*)

LARKIN: Mr. Morgan!

MORGAN (*a statement*): It's Charlie.

LARKIN (*after a moment*): Yes.

MORGAN: He's . . .

(LARKIN *does not answer. After a moment,* MORGAN *bows his head. When he raises it, he is suddenly older—the vitality is gone.*)

LARKIN: I saw it. He climbed to where Duke fell from. I'd gone up on the lift. I yelled and ran across towards him. He started to cross an I-beam near the edge. He slipped—it must have been the ice. I didn't see him after he fell. He didn't yell or anything.

(*long pause.* MORGAN *raises his head.*)

MORGAN: Then he's . . . he's . . . (LARKIN *says nothing.* MORGAN *starts to cross right.*) Joe—I'm going home. Tell O'Malley to call up the union hall for two new men—and to write a report of the accident. . . . I'll be back in the morning. (*He stops, looks up at bridge.*) It took nerve for him to go up there—so soon . . .

LARKIN: More than I've got.

MORGAN (*still looking up at the bridge, the one thing he comprehends*): My son—he has a lot of guts, doesn't he?

LARKIN (*slowly*): He sure—does, Mr. Morgan.

MORGAN (*still looking up, his pride somehow fulfilled*): Yes—he sure does.

(*Both men look to the bridge.*)

CURTAIN

About Alienation

Alienation and *alien* have a common Latin root and are similar in meaning. *Alien* indicates not only a difference in geography but also a difference in culture, religion, and philosophy. In one sense, therefore, alienation can be interpreted as a condition which occurs when a person travels from one emotional world (youth) to another (adulthood) During the course of this travel, he discards some ideas and attitudes and adopts others. And although there may be a considerable amount of conflict, he usually arrives at adulthood with basic concepts which do not differ greatly from his fellow adults. There are those people who, as they make this journey, develop ideas and attitudes which are unique. Their vision of reality is so different that all of their lives they are aliens in a world not of their making. There are others, however, who refuse for both noble and selfish reasons to modify their youthful attitudes, and they also become strangers, foreigners.

We see tangible evidence of the second form of alienation all around us: beards and beads, miniskirts and bell-bottoms, revolution and riot. These things are not new, only more visible. They are the result of a difficult, confusing, frustrating trip. They are the result of a difference in ideas and attitudes between one generation and another. This could be called *social alienation.* There are other kinds.

The plays in this section are all concerned with some kind of alienation. The people in the following plays are confronted with an alien world. And, in one way or another, they are strangers. Thus, conflict arises.

The Rope deals with parental alienation. *Crawling Arnold* deals with parental alienation as well as with political alienation. *The Bridge* deals with total alienation—to the point of suicide.

The Rope

EUGENE O'NEILL

Characters

ABRAHAM BENTLEY
ANNIE, *his daughter*
PAT SWEENEY, *her husband*
MARY, *their child*
LUKE BENTLEY, *Bentley's son by a second marriage*

Reading Guides

1. *The Rope* is written in several dialects. It may be hard to understand because O'Neill has attempted to recreate the sound of a language. Spelling does not matter in this case. Thus, you may be forced to read parts aloud. Also, you will find that some of the phrases and words are strange because of the different mode of speech.

2. This is a violent play—physically and emotionally. The violence, for a short time, is held in check by each of the characters, but it is the violence that generates the action. You should make every attempt to visualize what the characters are doing. Mary does not say much, but her presence on stage is critical to the resolution. Keep her in mind.

The Rope

SCENE. *The interior of an old barn situated on top of a high headland of the seacoast. In the rear, to the left, a stall in which lumber is stacked up. To the right of it, an open double doorway looking out over the ocean. Outside the doorway, the faint trace of what was once a road leading to the barn. Beyond the road, the edge of a cliff which rises sheer from the sea below. On the right of the doorway, three stalls with mangers and hayracks. The first of these is used as a woodbin and is half full of piled-up cordwood. Near this bin, a chopping block with an ax driven into the top of it.*

The left section of the barn contains the hayloft, which extends at a height of about twelve feet from the floor as far to the right as the middle of the doorway. The loft is bare except for a few scattered mounds of dank-looking hay. From the edge of the loft, half-way from the door, a rope about five feet long with an open running noose at the end is hanging. A rusty plow and various other farming implements, all giving evidence of long disuse, are lying on the floor near the left wall. Farther forward an old cane-bottomed chair is set back against the wall.

In front of the stalls on the right stands a long, roughly constructed carpenter's table, evidently homemade. Saws, a lathe, a hammer, chisel, a keg containing nails and other tools of the carpentry trade are on the table. Two benches are placed, one in front, one to the left of it.

The right side of the barn is a bare wall.

It is between six and half-past in the evening of a day in early spring. At the rising of the curtain some trailing clouds near the horizon, seen through the open doorway, are faintly tinged with gold by the first glow of the sunset. As the action progresses, this reflected light gradually becomes brighter, and then slowly fades into a smoky crimson. The sea is a dark slate color. From the rocks below the headland sounds the muffled monotone of breaking waves.

As the curtain rises MARY *is discovered squatting cross-legged on the floor, her back propped against the right side of the doorway, her face in profile. She is a skinny, overgrown girl of ten, with thin, carroty hair worn in a pigtail. She wears a shabby gingham dress. Her face is stupidly expressionless. Her hands flutter about aimlessly in relaxed, flabby gestures.*

She is staring fixedly at a rag doll which she has propped up against the doorway opposite her. She hums shrilly to herself.

At a sudden noise from outside she jumps to her feet, peeks out, and quickly snatches up the doll, which she hugs fiercely to her breast. Then, after a second's fearful hesitation, she runs to the carpenter's table and crawls under it.

As she does so ABRAHAM BENTLEY *appears in the doorway and stands, blinking into the shadowy barn. He is a tall, lean, stoop-shouldered old man of sixty-five. His thin legs, twisted by rheumatism, totter feebly under him as he shuffles slowly along by the aid of a thick cane. His face is gaunt, chalky-white, furrowed with wrinkles, surmounted by a shiny bald scalp fringed with scanty wisps of white hair. His eyes peer weakly from beneath bushy, black brows. His mouth is a sunken line drawn in under his large, beaklike nose. A two weeks' growth of stubby patches of beard covers his jaws and chin. He has on a threadbare brown overcoat but wears no hat.*

BENTLEY (*comes slowly into the barn, peering around him suspiciously. As he reaches the table and leans one hand on it for support,* MARY *darts from underneath and dashes out through the doorway.* BENTLEY *is startled; then shakes his cane after her.*): Out o' my sight, you Papist brat! Spawn o' Satan! Spyin' on me! They set her to it. Spyin' to watch me! (*He limps to the door and looks out cautiously. Satisfied, he turns back into the barn.*) Spyin' to see—what they'll never know. (*He stands staring up at the rope and taps it testingly several times with his stick, talking to himself as he does so.*) It's tied strong—strong as death—(*He cackles with satisfaction.*) They'll see, then! They'll see! (*He laboriously creeps over to the bench and sits down wearily. He looks toward the sea and his voice quavers in a doleful chant.*) "Woe unto us! for the day goeth away, for the shadows of the evening are stretched out." (*He mumbles to himself for a moment—then speaks clearly.*) Spyin' on me! Spawn o' the Pit! (*He renews his chant.*) "They hunt our steps that we cannot go in our streets: our end is near, our days are fulfilled; for our end is come."

(*As he finishes* ANNIE *enters. She is a thin, slovenly, worn-out-looking woman of about forty with a drawn, pasty face. Her habitual expression is one of a dulled irritation. She talks in a high-pitched, singsong whine. She wears a faded gingham dress and a torn sunbonnet.*)

ANNIE (*comes over to her father but warily keeps out of range of his stick*): Paw! (*He doesn't answer or appear to see her.*) Paw! You ain't fergittin' what the doctor told you when he was here last, be you? He said you was to keep still and not go a-walkin' round. Come on back to the house, Paw. It's gittin' near suppertime and you got to take your medicine b'fore it, like he says.

BENTLEY (*his eyes fixed in front of him*): "The punishment of thine iniquity is accomplished, O daughter of Zion: he will visit thine iniquity, O daughter of Edom; he will discover thy sins."

ANNIE (*waiting resignedly until he has finished—wearily*): You better take watch on your health, Paw, and not be sneakin' up to this barn no more. Lord sakes, soon 's ever my back is turned you goes sneakin' off agen. It's enough to drive a body outa their right mind.

BENTLEY: "Behold, every one that useth proverbs shall use this proverb against thee, saying, As is the mother, so is her daughter!" (*He cackles to himself.*) So is her daughter!

ANNIE (*her face flushing with anger*): And if I am, I'm glad I take after her and not you, y' old wizard! (*scornfully*) A fine one you be to be shoutin' Scripture in a body's ears all the livelong day—you that druv Maw to her death with your naggin', and pinchin', and miser stinginess. If you've a mind to pray, it's down in the medder you ought to go, and kneel down by her grave, and ask God to forgive you for the meanness you done to her all her life.

BENTLEY (*mumbling*): "As is the mother, so is her daughter."

ANNIE (*enraged by the repetition of this quotation*): *You* quotin' Scripture! Why, Maw wasn't cold in the earth b'fore you was down in the port courtin' agen—courtin' that harlot that was the talk o' the whole town! And then you disgraces yourself and me by marryin' her—*her*—and bringin' her back home with you; and me still goin' every day to put flowers on Maw's grave that you'd fergotten. (*She glares at him vindictively, pausing for breath.*) And between you you'd have druv me into the grave like you done Maw if I hadn't married Pat Sweeney so's I could git away and live in peace. Then you took on so high and mighty 'cause he was a Cath'lic —*you* gittin' religion all of a moment just for spite on me 'cause I'd left —and b'cause she egged you on against me; *you* sayin' it was a sin to marry a Papist, after not bein' at Sunday meetin' yourself for more'n twenty years!

BENTLEY (*loudly*): "He will visit thine iniquity—"

ANNIE (*interrupting*): And the carryin's-on you had the six years at home after I'd left you—the shame of the whole county! Your wife, indeed, with a child she *claimed* was your'n, and her goin' with this farmer and that, and even men off the ships in the port, and you blind to it! And then when she got sick of you and ran away—only to meet her end at the hands of God a year after—she leaves you alone with that—*your* son, Luke, *she* called him—and him only five years old!

BENTLEY (*babbling*): Luke? Luke?

ANNIE (*tauntingly*): Yes, Luke! "As is the mother, so is her son"—that's what you ought to preach 'stead of puttin' curses on me. You was glad enough to git me back home agen, and Pat with me, to tend the place, and help bring up that brat of hers. (*jealously*) You was fond enough of him all them years—and how did he pay you back? Stole your money and ran off and left you just when he was sixteen and old enough to help. Told you to your face he'd stolen and was leavin'. He only laughed when you was took crazy and cursed him; and he only laughed harder when you hung up that silly rope there (*she points*) and told him to hang himself on it when he ever came home agen.

BENTLEY (*mumbling*): You'll see, then. You'll see!

ANNIE (*wearily—her face becoming dull and emotionless again*): I s'pose I'm a bigger fool than you be to argy with a half-witted body. But I tell you agen that Luke of yours ain't comin' back; and if he does he ain't the kind to hang himself, more's the pity. He's like her. He'd hang *you* more likely if he s'pected you had any money. So you might 's well take down that ugly rope you've had tied there since he run off. He's probably dead anyway by this.

BENTLEY (*frightened*): No! No!

ANNIE: Them as bad as him comes to a sudden end. (*irritably*) Land sakes, Paw, here I am argyin' with your lunatic notions and the supper not ready. Come on and git your medicine. You can see no one ain't touched your old rope. Come on! You can sit 'n' read your Bible. (*He makes no movement. She comes closer to him and peers into his face—uncertainly.*) Don't you hear me? I do hope you ain't off in one of your fits when you don't know nobody. D'you know who's talkin'? This is Annie—your Annie, Paw.

BENTLEY (*bursting into senile rage*): None o' mine! Spawn o' the Pit! (*With a quick movement he hits her viciously over the arm with his stick. She gives a cry of pain and backs away from him, holding her arm.*)

ANNIE (*weeping angrily*): That's what I git for tryin' to be kind to you, you ugly old devil! (*The sound of a man's footsteps is heard from outside, and* SWEENEY *enters. He is a stocky, muscular, sandy-haired Irishman dressed in patched corduroy trousers shoved down into high laced boots and a blue flannel shirt. The bony face of his bullet head has a pressed-in appearance except for his heavy jaw, which sticks out pugnaciously. There is an expression of mean cunning and cupidity about his mouth and his small, round, blue eyes. He has evidently been drinking, and his face is flushed and set in an angry scowl.*)

SWEENEY: Have ye no supper at all made, ye lazy slut? (*seeing that she has been crying*) What're you blubberin' about?

ANNIE: It's all his fault. I was tryin' to git him home but he's that set I couldn't budge him; and he hit me on the arm with his cane when I went near him.

SWEENEY: He did, did he? I'll soon learn him better. (*He advances toward* BENTLEY *threateningly.*)

ANNIE (*grasping his arm*): Don't touch him, Pat. He's in one of his fits and you might kill him.

SWEENEY: An' good riddance!

BENTLEY (*hissing*): Papist! (*chants*) "Pour out thy fury upon the heathen that know thee not, and upon the families that call not on thy name: for they have eaten up Jacob, and devoured him, and consumed him, and made his habitation desolate."

SWEENEY (*instinctively crosses himself—then scornfully*): Spit curses on me till ye choke. It's not likely the Lord God'll be listenin' to a wicked auld sinner the like of you. (*to* ANNIE) What's got into him to be roamin' up here? When I left for the town he looked too weak to lift a foot.

ANNIE: Oh, it's the same crazy notion he's had ever since Luke left. He wanted to make sure the rope was still here.

BENTLEY (*pointing to the rope with his stick*): He-he! Luke'll come back. Then you'll see. You'll see!

SWEENEY (*nervously*): Stop that mad cacklin', for the love of heaven! (*with a forced laugh*) It's great laughter I should be havin' at you, mad as you are, for thinkin' that thief of a son of yours would come back to hang himself on account of your curses. It's five years he's been gone, and not a sight of him; an' you cursin' an' callin' down the wrath o' God on him by day an' by night. That shows you what God thinks of your curses—an' Him deaf to you!

ANNIE: It's no use talkin' to him, Pat.

SWEENEY: I've small doubt but that Luke is hung long since—by the police. He's come to no good end, that lad. (*his eyes on the rope*) I'll be pullin' that thing down, so I will; an' the auld loon'll stay in the house, where he belongs, then, maybe. (*He reaches up for the rope as if to try and yank it down.* BENTLEY *waves his stick frantically in the air, and groans with rage.*)

ANNIE (*frightened*): Leave it alone, Pat. Look at him. He's liable to hurt himself. Leave his rope be. It don't do no harm.

SWEENEY (*reluctantly moves away*): It looks ugly hangin' there open like a mouth. (*The old man sinks back into a relieved immobility.* SWEENEY *speaks to his wife in a low tone.*) Where's the child? Get her to take him out o' this. I want a word with you he'll not be hearin'. (*She goes to the door and calls out.*) Ma-ry! Ma-ry! (*A faint, answering cry is heard, and a moment later* MARY *rushes breathlessly into the barn.* SWEENEY *grabs her roughly by the arm. She shrinks away, looking at him with terrified eyes.*) You're to take your grandfather back to the house—an' see to it he stays there.

ANNIE: And give him his medicine.

SWEENEY (*As the child continues to stare at him silently with eyes stupid from fear, he shakes her impatiently.*): D'you hear me, now? (*to his wife*) It's soft-minded she is, like I've always told you, an' stupid; and you're not too firm in the head yourself at times, God help you! An' look at him! It's the curse is in the wits of your family, not mine.

ANNIE: You've been drinkin' in town or you wouldn't talk that way.

MARY (*whining*): Maw! I'm skeered!

SWEENEY (*lets go of her arm and approaches* BENTLEY): Get up out o' this, ye auld loon, an' go with Mary. She'll take you to the house. (BENTLEY *tries to hit him with the cane.*) Oho, ye would, would ye? (*He wrests the cane from the old man's hands.*) Bad cess to you, you're the treach'rous one! Get up, now!

(*He jerks the old man to his feet.*) Here, Mary, take his hand. Quick now! (*She does so tremblingly.*) Lead him to the house.

ANNIE: Go on, Paw! I'll come and git your supper in a minute.

BENTLEY (*stands stubbornly and begins to intone*): "O Lord, thou hast seen my wrong; judge thou my cause. Thou hast seen all their vengeance and all their imaginations against me—"

SWEENEY (*pushing him toward the door.* BENTLEY *tries to resist.* MARY *pulls at his hand in a sudden fit of impish glee, and laughs shrilly*): Get on now an' stop your cursin'.

BENTLEY: "Render unto them a recompense, O Lord, according to the work of their hands."

SWEENEY: Shut your loud quackin'! Here's your cane. (*He gives it to the old man as they come to the doorway and quickly steps back out of reach.*) An' mind you don't touch the child with it or I'll beat you to a jelly, old as ye are.

BENTLEY (*resisting* MARY'S *efforts to pull him out, stands shaking his stick at* SWEENEY *and his wife*): "Give them sorrow of heart, thy curse unto them. Persecute and destroy them in anger from under the heavens of the Lord."

MARY (*tugging at his hand and bursting again into shrill laughter*): Come on, Gran'paw. (*He allows himself to be led off, right.*)

SWEENEY (*making the sign of the cross furtively—with a sigh of relief*): He's gone, thank God! What a snake's tongue he has in him! (*He sits down on the bench to the left of table.*) Come here, Annie, till I speak to you. (*She sits down on the bench in front of table.* SWEENEY *winks mysteriously.*) Well, I saw him, sure enough.

ANNIE (*stupidly*): Who?

SWEENEY (*sharply*): Who? Who but Dick Waller, the lawyer, that I went to see. (*lowering his voice*) An' I've found out what we was wishin' to know. (*with a laugh*) Ye said I'd been drinkin'—which was true; but 'twas all in the plan I'd made. I've a head for strong drink, as ye know, but he hasn't. (*He winks cunningly.*) An' the whiskey loosened his tongue till he'd told all he knew.

ANNIE: He told you—about Paw's will?

SWEENEY: He did. (*disappointedly*) But for all the good it does us we might as well be no wiser than we was before. (*He broods for a moment in silence—then hits the table furiously with his fist.*) God's curse on the auld miser!

ANNIE: What did he tell you?

SWEENEY: Not much at the first. He's a cute one, an' he'd be askin' a fee to tell you your own name, if he could get it. His practice is all dribbled away from him lately on account of the drink. So I let on I was only payin' a friendly call, havin' known him for years. Then I asked him out to have a drop o' drink, knowin' his weakness; an' we had rashers of them, an'

I payin' for it. Then I come out with it straight and asked him about the will—because the auld man was crazy an' on his last legs, I told him, an' he was the lawyer made out the will when Luke was gone. So he winked at me an' grinned—he was drunk by this—an' said: "It's no use, Pat. He left the farm to the boy." "To hell with the farm," I spoke back. "It's mortgaged to the teeth; but how about the money?" "The money?" an' he looks at me in surprise, "What money?" "The cash he has," I says. "You're crazy," he says. "There wasn't any cash—only the farm." "D'you mean to say he made no mention of money in his will?" I asked. You could have knocked me down with a feather. "He did not—on my oath," he says. (SWEENEY *leans over to his wife—indignantly.*) Now what d'you make o' that? The auld divil!

ANNIE: Maybe Waller was lyin'.

SWEENEY: He was not. I could tell by his face. He was surprised to hear me talkin' of money.

ANNIE: But the thousand dollars Paw got for the mortgage just before that woman ran away—

SWEENEY: An' that I've been slavin' me hands off to pay the int'rist on!

ANNIE: What could he have done with that? He ain't spent it. It was in twenty-dollar gold pieces he got it, I remember Mr. Kellar of the bank tellin' me once.

SWEENEY: Divil a penny he's spent. Ye know as well as I do if it wasn't for my hammerin', an' sawin', an' nailin', he'd be in the poorhouse this minute —or the madhouse, more likely.

ANNIE: D'you suppose that harlot ran off with it?

SWEENEY: I do not; I know better—an' so do you. D'you not remember the letter she wrote tellin' him he could support Luke on the money he'd got on the mortgage she'd signed with him; for he'd made the farm over to her when he married her. An' where d'you suppose Luke got the hundred dollars he stole? The auld loon must have had cash with him then, an' it's only five years back.

ANNIE: He's got it hid some place in the house most likely.

SWEENEY: Maybe you're right. I'll dig in the cellar this night when he's sleepin'. He used to be down there a lot recitin' Scripture in his fits.

ANNIE: What else did Waller say?

SWEENEY: Nothin' much; except that we should put notices in the papers for Luke, an' if he didn't come back by sivin years from when he'd left—two years from now, that'd be—the courts would say he was dead an' give us the farm. Divil a lot of use it is to us now with no money to fix it up; an' himself ruinin' it years ago by sellin' everythin' to buy that slut new clothes.

ANNIE: Don't folks break wills like his'n in the courts?

SWEENEY: Waller said 'twas no use. The auld divil was plain in his full senses when he made it; an' the courts cost money.

ANNIE (*resignedly*): There ain't nothin' we can do then.

SWEENEY: No—except wait an' pray that young thief is dead an' won't come back; an' try an' find where it is the auld man has the gold hid, if he has it yet. I'd take him by the neck an' choke him till he told it, if he wasn't your father. (*He takes a full quart flask of whiskey from the pocket of his coat and has a big drink.*) Aahh! If we'd on'y the thousand we'd stock the farm good an' I'd give up this dog's game (*He indicates the carpentry outfit scornfully.*) an' we'd both work hard with a man or two to help, an' in a few years we'd be rich; for 'twas always a payin' place in the auld days.

ANNIE: Yes, yes, it was always a good farm then.

SWEENEY: He'll not last long in his senses, the doctor told me. His next attack will be very soon an' after it he'll be a real lunatic with no legal claims to anythin'. If we on'y had the money— 'Twould be the divil an' all if the auld fool should forget where he put it, an' him takin' leave of his senses altogether. (*He takes another nip at the bottle and puts it back in his pocket—with a sigh.*) Ah, well, I'll save what I can an' at the end of two years, with good luck in the trade, maybe we'll have enough. (*They are both startled by the heavy footsteps of someone approaching outside. A shrill burst of* MARY'S *laughter can be heard and the deep voice of a man talking to her.*)

SWEENEY (*uneasily*): It's Mary; but who could that be with her? It's not himself. (*As he finishes speaking* LUKE *appears in the doorway, holding the dancing* MARY *by the hand. He is a tall, strapping young fellow about twenty-five with a coarse-featured rather handsome face bronzed by the sun. What his face lacks in intelligence is partly forgiven for his good-natured, half-foolish grin, his hearty laugh, his curly dark hair, a certain devil-may-care recklessness and irresponsible youth in voice and gesture. But his mouth is weak and characterless; his brown eyes are large but shifty and acquisitive. He wears a dark blue jersey, patched blue pants, rough sailor shoes, and a gray cap. He advances into the stable with a mocking smile on his lips until he stands directly under the rope. The man and woman stare at him in petrified amazement.*)

ANNIE: Luke!

SWEENEY (*crossing himself*): Glory be to God—it's him!

MARY (*hopping up and down wildly*): It's Uncle Luke, Uncle Luke, Uncle Luke! (*She runs to her mother, who pushes her away angrily.*)

LUKE (*regarding them both with an amused grin*): Sure, it's Luke—back after five years of bummin' round the rotten old earth in ships and things. Paid off a week ago—had a bust-up—and then took a notion to come out here—bummed my way—and here I am. And you're both of you tickled to death to see me, ain't yuh?—like hell! (*He laughs and walks over to* ANNIE.) Don't yuh even want to shake flippers with your dear, long-lost brother, Annie? I remember you and me used to git on so fine together—like hell!

ANNIE (*giving him a venomous look of hatred*): Keep your hands to yourself.

LUKE (*grinning*): You ain't changed, that's sure—on'y yuh're homelier'n ever. (*He turns to the scowling* SWEENEY.) How about you, brother Pat?

SWEENEY: I'd not lower myself to take the hand of a—

LUKE (*with a threat in his voice*): Easy goes with that talk! I'm not so soft to lick as I was when I was a kid; and don't forget it.

ANNIE (*to* MARY, *who is playing catch with a silver dollar which she has had clutched in her hand—sharply*): Mary! What have you got there? Where did you get it? Bring it here to me this minute! (MARY *presses the dollar to her breast and remains standing by the doorway in stubborn silence.*)

LUKE: Aw, let her alone! What's bitin' yuh? That's on'y a silver dollar I give her when I met her front of the house. She told me you was up here; and I give her that as a present to buy candy with. I got it in Frisco—cartwheels, they call 'em. There ain't none of them in these parts I ever seen, so I brung it along on the voyage.

ANNIE (*angrily*): I don't know or care where you got it—but I know you ain't come by it honest. Mary! Give that back to him this instant! (*As the child hesitates, she stamps her foot furiously.*) D'you hear me? (MARY *starts to cry softly, but comes to* LUKE *and hands him the dollar.*)

LUKE (*taking it—with a look of disgust at his half-sister*): I was right when I said you ain't changed, Annie. You're as stinkin' mean as ever. (*to* MARY, *consolingly*) Quit bawlin', kid. You 'n' me'll go out on the edge of the cliff here and chuck some stones in the ocean same's we useter, remember? (MARY's *tears immediately cease. She looks up at him with shining eyes, and claps her hands.*)

MARY (*pointing to the dollar he has in his hand*): Throw that! It's flat 'n' it'll skip.

LUKE (*with a grin*): That's the talk, kid. That's all it's good for—to throw away; not buryin' it like your miser folks'd tell you. Here! You take it and chuck it away. It's your'n. (*He gives her the dollar and she hops to the doorway. He turns to* PAT *with a grin.*) I'm learnin' your kid to be a sport, Tightwad. I hope you ain't got no objections.

MARY (*impatiently*): Come on, Uncle Luke. Watch me throw it.

LUKE: Aw right. (*to* PAT) I'll step outside a second and give you two a chanct to git all the dirty things yuh're thinkin' about me off your chest. (*threateningly*) And then I'm gointer come and talk turkey to you, see? I didn't come back here for fun, and the sooner you gets that in your beans, the better.

MARY: Come on and watch me!

LUKE: Aw right, I'm comin'. (*He walks out and stands, leaning his back against the doorway, left.* MARY *is about six feet beyond him on the other side of the road.*

She is leaning down, peering over the edge of the cliff and laughing excitedly.)

MARY: Can I throw it now? Can I?

LUKE: Don't git too near the edge, kid. The water's deep down there, and you'd be a drowned rat if you slipped. (*She shrinks back a step.*) You chuck it when I say three. Ready, now! (*She draws back her arm.*) One! Two! Three! (*She throws the dollar away and bends down to see it hit the water.*)

MARY (*clapping her hands and laughing*): I seen it! I seen it splash! It's deep down now, ain't it?

LUKE: Yuh betcher it is! Now watch how far I kin chuck rocks. (*He picks up a couple and goes to where she is standing. During the following conversation between* SWEENEY *and his wife he continues to play this way with* MARY. *Their voices can be heard but the words are indistinguishable.*)

SWEENEY (*glancing apprehensively toward the door—with a great sigh*): Speak of the divil an' here he is! (*furiously*) Flingin' away dollars, the dirty thief, an' us without—

ANNIE (*interrupting him*): Did you hear what he said? A thief like him ain't come back for no good. (*lowering her voice*) D'you s'pose he knows about the farm bein' left to him?

SWEENEY (*uneasily*): How could he? An' yet—I dunno— (*with sudden decision*) You'd best lave him to me to watch out for. It's small sense you have to hide your hate from him. You're as loony as the rist of your breed. An' he needs to be blarneyed round to fool him an' find out what he's wantin'. I'll pritind to make friends with him, God roast his soul! An' do you run to the house an' break the news to the auld man; for if he seen him suddin it's likely the little wits he has left would leave him; an' the thief could take the farm from us tomorrow if himself turned a lunatic.

ANNIE (*getting up*): I'll tell him a little at a time till he knows.

SWEENEY: Be careful, now, or we'll lose the farm this night. (*She starts towards the doorway.* SWEENEY *speaks suddenly in a strange, awed voice.*) Did you see Luke when he first came in to us? He stood there with the noose of the rope almost touchin' his head. I was almost wishin'— (*He hesitates.*)

ANNIE (*viciously*): I was wishin' it was round his neck chokin' him, that's what I was—hangin' him just as Paw says.

SWEENEY: Ssshh! He might hear ye. Go along, now. He's comin' back.

MARY (*pulling at* LUKE'*s arm as he comes back to the doorway*): Lemme throw 'nother! Lemme throw 'nother!

LUKE (*enters just as* ANNIE *is going out and stops her*): Goin' to the house? Do we get any supper? I'm hungry.

ANNIE (*glaring at him but restraining her rage*): Yes.

LUKE (*jovially*): Good work! And tell the old man I'm here and I'll see him in a while. He'll be glad to see me, too—like hell! (*He comes forward.* ANNIE *goes off, right.*)

MARY (*in an angry whine, tugging at his hand*): Lemme throw 'nother. Lemme—

LUKE (*shaking her away*): There's lots of rocks, kid. Throw them. Dollars ain't so plentiful.

MARY (*screaming*): No! No! I don' wanter throw rocks. Lemme throw 'nother o' them.

SWEENEY (*severely*): Let your uncle in peace, ye brat! (*She commences to cry.*) Run help your mother now or I'll give ye a good hidin'. (MARY *runs out of the door, whimpering.* PAT *turns to* LUKE *and holds out his hand.*)

LUKE (*looking at it in amazement*): Ahoy, there! What's this?

SWEENEY (*with an ingratiating smile*): Let's let bygones be bygones. I'm harborin' no grudge agen you these past years. Ye was only a lad when ye ran away an' not to be blamed for it. I'd have taken your hand a while back, an' glad to, but for her bein' with us. She has the divil's own tongue, as ye know, an' she can't forget the rowin' you an' her used to be havin'.

LUKE (*still looking at* SWEENEY'S *hand*): So that's how the wind blows! (*with a grin*) Well, I'll take a chanct. (*They shake hands and sit down by the table,* SWEENEY *on the front bench and* LUKE *on the left one.*)

SWEENEY (*pulls the bottle from his coat pocket—with a wink*): Will ye have a taste? It's real stuff.

LUKE: Yuh betcher I will! (*He takes a big gulp and hands the bottle back.*)

SWEENEY (*after taking a drink himself, puts bottle on table*): I wasn't wishin' herself to see it or I'd have asked ye sooner. (*There is a pause, during which each measures the other with his eyes.*)

LUKE: Say, how's the old man now?

SWEENEY (*cautiously*): Oh, the same as ivir—older an' uglier, maybe.

LUKE: I thought he might be in the bughouse by this time.

SWEENEY (*hastily*): Indeed not; he's foxy to pritind he's loony, but he's his wits with him all the time.

LUKE (*insinuatingly*): Is he as stingy with his coin as he used to be?

SWEENEY: If he owned the ocean, he wouldn't give a fish a drink; but I doubt if he's any money left at all. Your mother got rid of it all I'm thinkin'. (LUKE *smiles a superior, knowing smile.*) He has on'y the farm, an' that mortgaged. I've been payin' the int'rist an' supportin' himself an' his doctor bills by the carpentryin' these five years past.

LUKE (*with a grin*): Huh! Yuh're slow. Yuh oughter get wise to yourself.

SWEENEY (*inquisitively*): What d'ye mean by that?

LUKE (*aggravatingly*): Aw, nothin'. (*He turns around and his eyes fix themselves on the rope.*) What the hell— (*He is suddenly convulsed with laughter and slaps his thigh.*) Haha! If that don't beat the Dutch! The old nut!

SWEENEY: What?

LUKE: That rope. Say, has he had that hangin' there ever since I skipped?

SWEENEY (*smiling*): Sure; an' he thinks you'll be comin' home to hang yourself.

LUKE: Hahaha! Not this chicken! And you say he ain't crazy! Gee, that's too good to keep. I got to have a drink on that. (SWEENEY *pushes the bottle toward him. He raises it toward the rope.*) Here's how, old chum! (*He drinks.* SWEENEY *does likewise.*) Say, I'd almost forgotten about that. Remember how hot he was that day when he hung that rope up and cussed me for pinchin' the hundred? He was standin' there shakin' his stick at me, and I was laughin' 'cause he looked so funny with the spit dribblin' outa his mouth like he was a mad dog. And when I turned round and beat it he shouted after me: "Remember, when you come home again there's a rope waitin' for yuh to hang yourself on, yuh bastard!" (*He spits contemptuously.*) What a swell chanct. (*His manner changes and he frowns.*) The old slave driver! That's a hell of a fine old man for a guy to have!

SWEENEY (*pushing the bottle toward him*): Take a sup an' forgit it. 'Twas a long time past.

LUKE: But the rope's there yet, ain't it? And he keeps it there. (*He takes a large swallow.* SWEENEY *also drinks.*) But I'll git back at him aw right, yuh wait 'n' see. I'll git every cent he's got this time.

SWEENEY (*slyly*): If he has a cent. I'm not wishful to discourage ye, but— (*He shakes his head doubtfully, at the same time fixing* LUKE *with a keen glance out of the corner of his eye.*)

LUKE (*with a cunning wink*): Aw, he's got it aw right. You watch me! (*He is beginning to show the effects of the drink he has had. He pulls out tobacco and a paper and rolls a cigarette and lights it. As he puffs he continues boastfully.*) You country jays oughter wake up and see what's goin' on. Look at me. I was green as grass when I left here, but bummin' round the world, and bein' in cities, and meetin' all kinds, and keepin' your two eyes open —that's what'll learn yuh a cute trick or two.

SWEENEY: No doubt but you're right. Us country folks is stupid in most ways. We've no chance to learn the things a travelin' lad like you'd be knowin'.

LUKE (*complacently*): Well, you watch me and I'll learn yuh. (*He snickers.*) So yuh thinks the old man's flat broke, do yuh?

SWEENEY: I do so.

LUKE: Then yuh're simple; that's what—simple! Yuh're lettin' him kid yuh.

SWEENEY: If he has any, it's well hid, I know that. He's a sly old bird.

LUKE: And I'm a slyer bird. D'yuh hear that? I c'n beat his game any time. You watch me! (*He reaches out his hand for the bottle. They both drink again.* SWEENEY *begins to show signs of getting drunk. He hiccoughs every now and then and his voice grows uncertain and husky.*)

SWEENEY: It'd be a crafty one who'd find where he'd hidden it, sure enough.

LUKE: You watch me! I'll find it. I betcher anything yuh like I find it. You watch me! Just wait till he's asleep and I'll show yuh—ternight. (*There is a noise of shuffling footsteps outside and* ANNIE'S *whining voice raised in angry protest.*)

SWEENEY: Ssshh! It's himself comin' now. (LUKE *rises to his feet and stands, waiting in a defensive attitude, a surly expression on his face. A moment later* BENTLEY *appears in the doorway, followed by* ANNIE. *He leans against the wall, in an extraordinary state of excitement, shaking all over, gasping for breath, his eyes devouring* LUKE *from head to foot.*)

ANNIE: I couldn't do nothin' with him. When I told him *he'd* come back there was no holdin' him. He was a'most frothin' at the mouth till I let him out. (*whiningly*) You got to see to him, Pat, if you want any supper. I can't—

SWEENEY: Shut your mouth! We'll look after him.

ANNIE: See that you do. I'm goin' back. (*She goes off, right.* LUKE *and his father stand looking at each other. The surly expression disappears from* LUKES'S *face, which gradually expands in a broad grin.*)

LUKE (*jovially*): Hello, old sport! I s'pose yuh're tickled to pieces to see me—like hell! (*The old man stutters and stammers incoherently as if the very intensity of his desire for speech had paralyzed all power of articulation.* LUKE *turns to* PAT.) I see he ain't lost the old stick. Many a crack on the nut I used to get with that.

BENTLEY (*suddenly finding his voice—chants*): "Bring forth the best robe, and put it on him; and put a ring on his hand, and shoes on his feet: And bring hither the fatted calf, and kill it; and let us eat and be merry: For this my son was dead, and is alive again; he was lost, and is found." (*He ends up with a convulsive sob.*)

LUKE (*disapprovingly*): Yuh're still spoutin' the rotten old Word o' God same's ever, eh? Say, give us a rest on that stuff, will yuh? Come on and shake hands like a good sport. (*He holds out his hand. The old man totters over to him, stretching out a trembling hand.* LUKE *seizes it and pumps it up and down.*) That's the boy!

SWEENEY (*genuinely amazed*): Look at that, would ye—the two-faced auld liar. (BENTLEY *passes his trembling hand all over* LUKE, *feeling of his arms, his chest, his back. An expression of overwhelming joy suffuses his worn features.*)

LUKE (*grinning at* SWEENEY): Say, watch this. (*with tolerant good-humor*) On the level I b'lieve the old boy's glad to see me at that. He looks like he was tryin' to grin; and I never seen him grin in my life, I c'n remember. (*As* BENTLEY *attempts to feel of his face.*) Hey, cut it out! (*He pushes his hand away, but not roughly.*) I'm all here, yuh needn't worry. Yuh needn't be scared I'm a ghost. Come on and sit down before yuh fall down. Yuh ain't got your sea legs workin' right. (*He guides the old man to the bench at left of ta-*

ble.) Squat here for a spell and git your wind. (BENTLEY *sinks down on the bench.* LUKE *reaches for the bottle.*) Have a drink to my makin' port. It'll buck yuh up.

SWEENEY (*alarmed*): Be careful, Luke. It might likely end him.

LUKE (*holds the bottle up to the old man's mouth, supporting his head with the other hand.* BENTLEY *gulps, the whiskey drips over his chin, and he goes into a fit of convulsive coughing.* LUKE *laughs.*): Hahaha! Went down the wrong way, did it? I'll show yuh the way to do it. (*He drinks.*) There yuh are—smooth as silk. (*He hands the bottle to* SWEENEY, *who drinks and puts it back on the table.*)

SWEENEY: He must be glad to see ye or he'd not drink. 'Tis dead against it he's been these five years past. (*shaking his head*) An' him cursin' you day an' night! I can't put head or tail to it. Look out he ain't meanin' some bad to ye underneath. He's crafty at pretendin'.

LUKE (*as the old man makes signs to him with his hand*): What's he after now? He's lettin' on he's lost his voice again. What d'yuh want? (BENTLEY *points with his stick to the rope. His lips move convulsively as he makes a tremendous effort to utter words.*)

BENTLEY (*mumbling incoherently*): Luke—Luke—rope—Luke—hang.

SWEENEY (*appalled*): There ye are! What did I tell you? It's to see you hang yourself he's wishin', the auld fiend!

BENTLEY (*nodding*): Yes—Luke—hang.

LUKE (*taking it as a joke—with a loud guffaw*): Hahaha! If that don't beat the Dutch! The old nanny goat! Aw right, old sport. Anything to oblige. Hahaha! (*He takes the chair from left and places it under the rope. The old man watches him with eager eyes and seems to be trying to smile.* LUKE *stands on the chair.*)

SWEENEY: Have a care, now! I'd not be foolin' with it in your place.

LUKE: All out for the big hangin' of Luke Bentley by hisself. (*He puts the noose about his neck with an air of drunken bravado and grins at his father. The latter makes violent motions for him to go on.*) Look at him, Pat. By God, he's in a hurry. Hahaha! Well, old sport, here goes nothin'. (*He makes a movement as if he were going to jump and kick the chair from under him.*)

SWEENEY (*half starts to his feet—horrified*): Luke! Are ye gone mad?

LUKE (*stands staring at his father, who is still making gestures for him to jump. A scowl slowly replaces his good-natured grin.*): D'yuh really mean it—that yuh want to see me hangin' myself? (BENTLEY *nods vigorously in the affirmative.* LUKE *glares at him for a moment in silence.*) Well, I'll be damned! (*to* PAT) An' I thought he was only kiddin'. (*He removes the rope gingerly from his neck. The old man stamps his foot and gesticulates wildly, groaning with disappointment.* LUKE *jumps to the floor and looks at his father for a second. Then his face grows white with a vicious fury.*) I'll fix your hash, you stinkin' old murderer! (*He grabs the chair by its back and swings it over his head as if he were going to crush* BENTLEY'S *skull with it. The old man cowers on the bench in abject terror.*)

SWEENEY (*jumping to his feet with a cry of alarm*): Luke! For the love of God! (LUKE *hesitates; then hurls the chair in back of him under the loft, and stands menacingly in front of his father, his hands on his hips.*)

LUKE (*grabbing* BENTLEY'S *shoulder and shaking him—hoarsely*): Yuh wanted to see me hangin' there in real earnest, didn't yuh? You'd hang me yourself if yuh could, wouldn't yuh? And you my own father! Yuh damned son-of-a-gun! Yuh would, would yuh? I'd smash your brains out for a nickel! (*He shakes the old man more and more furiously.*)

SWEENEY: Luke! Look out! You'll be killin' him next.

LUKE (*giving his father one more shake, which sends him sprawling on the floor*): Git outa here! Git outa this b'fore I kill yuh dead! (SWEENEY *rushes over and picks the terrified old man up.*) Take him outa here, Pat! (*His voice rises to a threatening roar.*) Take him outa here or I'll break every bone in his body! (*He raises his clenched fists over his head in a frenzy of rage.*)

SWEENEY: Ssshh! Don't be roarin'! I've got him. (*He steers the whimpering, hysterical* BENTLEY *to the doorway.*) Come out o' this, now. Get down to the house! Hurry now! Ye've made enough trouble for one night! (*They disappear off right.* LUKE *flings himself on a bench, breathing heavily. He picks up the bottle and takes a long swallow.* SWEENEY *reenters from rear. He comes over and sits down in his old place.*) Thank God he's off down to the house, scurryin' like a frightened hare as if he'd never a kink in his legs in his life. He was moanin' out loud so you could hear him a long ways. (*with a sigh*) It's a murd'rous auld loon he is, sure enough.

LUKE (*thickly*): The damned son-of-a-gun!

SWEENEY: I thought you'd be killin' him that time with the chair.

LUKE (*violently*): Serve him damn right if I done it.

SWEENEY: An' you laughin' at him a moment sooner! I thought 'twas jokin' ye was.

LUKE (*suddenly*): So I was kiddin'; but I thought he was tryin' to kid me, too. And then I seen by the way he acted he really meant it. (*banging the table with his fist*) Ain't that a hell of a fine old man for yuh!

SWEENEY: He's a mean auld swine.

LUKE: He meant it aw right, too. Yuh shoulda seen him lookin' at me. (*with sudden lugubriousness*) Ain't he a hell of a nice old man for a guy to have? Ain't he?

SWEENEY (*soothingly*): Hush! It's all over now. Don't be thinkin' about it.

LUKE (*on the verge of drunken tears*): How kin I help thinkin'—and him my own father? After me bummin' and starvin' round the rotten earth, and workin' myself to death on ships and things—and when I come home he tries to make me bump off—wants to see me a corpse—my own father, too! Ain't he a hell of an old man to have? The rotten son-of-a-gun!

SWEENEY: It's past an' done. Forgit it. (*He slaps* LUKE *on the shoulder and pushes the bottle toward him.*) Let's take a drop more. We'll be goin' to supper soon.

LUKE (*takes a big drink—huskily*): Thanks. (*He wipes his mouth on his sleeve with a snuffle.*) But I'll tell yuh something you can put in your pipe and smoke. It ain't past and done, and it ain't goin' to be!(*more and more aggressively*) And I ain't goin' to fergit it, either! Yuh kin betcher life on that, pal. And *he* ain't goin' to ferget it—not if he lives a million—not by a damned sight! (*with sudden fury*) I'll fix his hash! I'll git even with him, the old skunk! You watch me! And this very night, too!

SWEENEY: How'd you mean?

LUKE: You just watch me, I tell yuh! (*banging the table*) I said I'd git even and I will git even—this same night, with no long waits, either! (*frowning*) Say, you don't stand up for him, do yuh?

SWEENEY (*spitting—vehemently*): That's child's talk. There's not a day passed I've not wished him in his grave.

LUKE (*excitedly*): Then we'll both git even on him—you 'n' me. We're pals, ain't we?

SWEENEY: Sure.

LUKE: And yuh kin have half what we gits. That's the kinda feller I am! That's fair enough, ain't it?

SWEENEY: Surely.

LUKE: I don't want no truck with this rotten farm. You kin have my share of that. I ain't made to be no damned dirt-puncher—not me! And I ain't goin' to loaf round here more'n I got to, and when I goes this time I ain't never comin' back. Not me! Not to punch dirt and milk cows. You kin have the rotten farm for all of me. What I wants is cash—regular coin yuh kin spend—not dirt. I want to show the gang a real time, and then ship away to sea agen or go bummin' agen. I want coin yuh kin throw away—same's your kid chucked that dollar of mine overboard, remember? A real dollar, too! She's a sport, aw right!

SWEENEY (*anxious to bring him back to the subject*): But where d'you think to find his money?

LUKE (*confidently*): Don't yuh fret. I'll show yuh. You watch me! I know his hidin' places. I useter spy on him when I was a kid—Maw used to make me—and I seen him many a time at his sneakin'. (*indignantly*) He used to hide stuff from the old lady. What d'yuh know about him—the mean skunk.

SWEENEY: That was a long time back. You don't know—

LUKE (*assertively*): But I do know, see! He's got two places. One was where I swiped the hundred.

SWEENEY: It'll not be there, then.

LUKE: No; but there's the other place; and he never knew I was wise to that. I'd have left him clean on'y I was a kid and scared to pinch more. So you watch me! We'll git even on him, you 'n' me, and go halfs, and yuh kin start the rotten farm goin' agen and I'll beat it where there's some life.

SWEENEY: But if there's no money in that place, what'll you be doin' to find out where it is, then?

LUKE: Then you 'n' me 'ull make him tell!

SWEENEY: Oho, don't think it! 'Tis not him'd be tellin'.

LUKE: Aw, say, you're simple! You watch me! I know a trick or two about makin' people tell what they don't wanter. (*He picks up the chisel from the table.*) Yuh see this? Well, if he don't answer up nice and easy we'll show him! (*A ferocious grin settles over his face.*) We'll git even on him, you 'n' me—and he'll tell where it's hid. We'll just shove this into the stove till it's red-hot and take off his shoes and socks and warm the bottoms of his feet for him. (*savagely*) He'll tell then—anything we wants him to tell.

SWEENEY: But Annie?

LUKE: We'll shove a rag in her mouth so's she can't yell. That's easy.

SWEENEY (*his head lolling drunkenly—with a cruel leer*): 'Twill serve him right to heat up his hoofs for him, the limpin' auld miser! —if ye don't hurt him too much.

LUKE (*with a savage scowl*): We won't hurt him—more'n enough. (*suddenly raging*) I'll pay him back aw right! He won't want no more people to hang themselves when I git through with him. I'll fix his hash! (*He sways to his feet, the chisel in his hand.*) Come on! Let's git to work. Sooner we starts the sooner we're rich. (SWEENEY *rises. He is steadier on his feet than* LUKE. *At this moment* MARY *appears in the doorway.*)

MARY: Maw says supper's ready. I had mine. (*She comes into the room and jumps up, trying to grab hold of the rope.*) Lift me, Uncle Luke. I wanter swing.

LUKE (*severely*): Don't yuh dare touch that rope, d'yuh hear?

MARY (*whining*): I wanter swing.

LUKE (*with a shiver*): It's bad, kid. Yuh leave it alone, take it from me.

SWEENEY: She'll get a good whalin' if I catch her jumpin' at it.

LUKE: Come on, pal. T'hell with supper. We got work to do first. (*They go to the doorway.*)

SWEENEY (*turning back to the sulking* MARY): And you stay here, d'you hear, ye brat, till we call ye—or I'll skin ye alive.

LUKE: And termorrer mornin', kid, I'll give yuh a whole handful of them shiny, bright things yuh chucked in the ocean—and yuh kin be a real sport.

MARY (*eagerly*): Gimme 'em now! Gimme 'em now, Uncle Luke. (*as he shakes his head—whiningly*) Gimme one! Gimme one!

LUKE: Can't be done, kid. Termorrer. Me 'n' your old man is goin' to git even now—goin' to make him pay for—

SWEENEY (*interrupting—harshly*): Hist with your noise! D'you think she's no ears? Don't be talkin' so much. Come, now.

LUKE (*permitting himself to be pulled out the doorway*): Aw right! I'm with yuh. We'll git even—you 'n' me. The damned son-of-a-gun! (*They lurch off to the right.*)

(MARY *skips to the doorway and peeps after them for a moment. Then she comes back to the center of the floor and looks around her with an air of decision. She sees the chair in under the loft and runs over to it, pulling it back and setting it on its legs directly underneath the noose of the rope. She climbs and stands on the top of the chair and grasps the noose with both her upstretched hands. Then with a shriek of delight she kicks the chair from under her and launches herself for a swing. The rope seems to part where it is fixed to the beam. A dirty gray bag tied to the end of the rope falls to the floor with a muffled, metallic thud.* MARY *sprawls forward on her hands and knees, whimpering. Straggly wisps from the pile of rank hay fall silently to the floor in a mist of dust.* MARY, *discovering she is unhurt, glances quickly around and sees the bag. She pushes herself along the floor and, untying the string at the top, puts in her hand. She gives an exclamation of joy at what she feels and, turning the bag upside down, pours its contents in her lap. Giggling to herself, she gets to her feet and goes to the doorway, where she dumps what she has in her lap in a heap on the floor just inside the barn. They lie there in a glittering pile, shimmering in the faint sunset glow—fifty twenty-dollar gold pieces.* MARY *claps her hands and sings to herself: "Skip—skip—skip." Then she quickly picks up four or five and runs out to the edge of the cliff. She throws them one after another into the ocean as fast as she can and bends over to see them hit the water. Against the background of horizon clouds still tinted with blurred crimson she hops up and down in a sort of grotesque dance, clapping her hands and laughing shrilly. After the last one is thrown she rushes back into the barn to get more.*)

MARY (*picking up a handful—giggling ecstatically*): Skip! Skip! (*She turns and runs out to throw them as the* CURTAIN *falls.*)

Crawling Arnold

JULES FEIFFER

Characters

BARRY ENTERPRISE
GRACE ENTERPRISE
MISS SYMPATHY
MILLIE
ARNOLD ENTERPRISE

Reading Guides

1. *Crawling Arnold* takes place in an exaggerated situation with exaggerated characters; you should takes these facts into account. You should realize, however, that the characters are based on reality.

2. There is a political situation involved in this play that is never mentioned directly. You should be aware that various things are going on outside—in the world—that affect the behavior of the characters in the play.

ABOUT ALIENATION

THE CURTAIN *rises on a projection: an enormous color slide of a smiling baby. The stage is dark, and voices come out of the darkness. Everybody "oohs" and "ahhhs" at the projection.*

BARRY: That's little Will at six months.

GRACE: Eight months, dear. Even little Will wasn't that big at six months.

BARRY: Seven months, then. What a big bad bandit of a boy, eh, Miss Sympathy?

MISS SYMPATHY: An alert child.

BARRY (*clicks slide changer*): Next slide please. (*The projection changes.*) There he is at only one year! Did you ever see such a rough and tough customer, Miss Sympathy?

GRACE: Fourteen months, dear.

BARRY: Thirteen months.

MISS SYMPATHY: He does seem like an alert child.

BARRY: Alert? You should see him crawl around down in the shelter. Arnold just goes down when the siren sounds and sits there. But little Will! He has to touch everything. Won't keep out of anything—the oxygen tank, the gas masks, the plastic bombs—

MISS SYMPATHY: The shelter? (*The lights come up slowly to reveal the expensively bedecked patio of the* ENTERPRISE *home.* BARRY *and* GRACE ENTERPRISE, *a vigorous, athletic couple in their seventies, are sitting with* MISS SYMPATHY, *a young and pretty social worker, in deck chairs facing the slide screen. The projector is behind them, being operated by* MILLIE, *the Negro maid. She, expressionlessly, begins to wheel it off.*)

BARRY: Our *fallout* shelter! Wait till you see it! (*to* MILLIE) You can serve our helmets now, Millie.

(MILLIE *coolly exits.* BARRY *and* GRACE *look hostilely after her.*)

GRACE: It's the only shelter in the country that has a television set and a whatayoucall them, dear?

BARRY: Stereo rig.

GRACE: Stereo rig. (*She begins to fuss with the baby, making small gurgling noises at it.*)

MISS SYMPATHY: A television set? But what good would a—

BARRY: It's not a real television set. It's the frame of one, and then I have a sixteen-millimeter movie projector and a library of films—*Tim McCoy, Our Gang*—a variety of fare. The idea, you understand, is that under enemy attack the family can survive down there for *weeks,* while being able to simulate normal conditions of living. For example, I've had cards made up with the names of our favorite shows, and at the time they would ordinarily go on, we run a picture—a slide picture on the screen showing the title of the show—

GRACE: *Lassie—Ben Casey—*

BARRY: And during the half-hours those shows normally run, we sit and reminisce about our favorite episodes.

MISS SYMPATHY: You've *done* this?

BARRY: Several times. Before Little Will was born, Mrs. Enterprise and I—*and Arnold*—used to spend many happy weeks—many happy weeks in our shelter.

GRACE: One gets to *know* Ben Casey so much more deeply after one has talked about him in a fallout shelter for two weeks.

(MILLIE *enters with four air-raid helmets on a serving tray. There is evident tension between herself and the* ENTERPRISES. BARRY *and* GRACE *each sullenly take a helmet.*)

You may serve cocktails now, Millie. (GRACE *places a helmet in baby carriage.* MISS SYMPATHY *quietly demurs.*)

BARRY: You're making a mistake, Miss Sympathy. Today's drill begins pretty soon.

(MILLIE *exits, with* MISS SYMPATHY *looking after her, curiously.*)

You should see our library down there! Four years' worth of back copies of the *Reader's Digest.* I didn't know how long we'd be down there, so I wanted to get articles of *lasting* interest. (*He takes the baby carriage from* GRACE *and begins to fuss with the baby, making small gurgling noises.*)

GRACE (*proudly*): It's the only shelter in the country to be written up in *Good Housekeeping.*

MISS SYMPATHY: Little Will is how old?

GRACE (*proudly*): He'll be—

BARRY (*jealously*): He'll be two in September. (*He buries his face in the blankets of the carriage, muffling the sound of his voice.*) Isn't this the biggest, baddest, toughest little fellow who ever lived? I'll tell the world this is the biggest, baddest, toughest little fellow who ever lived!

MISS SYMPATHY (*peering into the carriage*): My, he's a *large* baby.

BARRY: Arnold was half his size at that age. Arnold couldn't crawl until he was almost *two.* Little Will's been crawling for four months now. *Four* months.

MISS SYMPATHY: And Arnold?

BARRY (*nervously*): Wasn't Millie supposed to bring us some drinks?

GRACE: Well, that's why we asked you to come, Miss Sympathy.

BARRY (*embarrassed*): Yes. Arnold is crawling again too. For four months.

GRACE (*sadly*): Regressed.

MISS SYMPATHY (*taking out a pad and making notes*): That sometimes happens when the first child feels overcompetitive with the second child. *Sibling rivalry.*

GRACE: Crawl. As soon as he enters the house he falls on all fours and crawls, crawls, crawls. I say to him, "Arnold, you *know* you can walk beautifully. At business you walk beautifully—"

MISS SYMPATHY: At business?

BARRY (*embarrassed*): Arnold is thirty-five. (*He fusses with the carriage.*)

MISS SYMPATHY (*making a long note*): *Advanced* sibling rivalry.

GRACE (*distressed*): That's what we wanted to talk to you about. I know there's nothing seriously wrong with Arnold. He's always been a good boy. Done everything we told him. Never talked back. Always well-mannered. Never been a show-off.

MISS SYMPATHY (*taking notes*): He's never had any previously crawling history?

GRACE: I'm afraid he took the news of Little Will's birth rather hard. I imagine when one has been raised as an only child and has lived happily all one's years in one's parents' home, it's hard to welcome a little stranger.

BARRY (*buries his head in the blankets, muffling his voice*): Who's Daddy's brave big bandit of a man! Little Will's Daddy's brave big bandit of a man.

GRACE: Please, dear. Don't talk with your mouth full.

(MILLIE *enters with three drinks on a platter. A coolness immediately settles on the patio.* BARRY *and* GRACE *lapse into a sullen silence.* GRACE *coldly receives her drink.*)

Thank you, Millie.

(BARRY *grumbles something under his breath as he receives his.* MISS SYMPATHY *is obviously perturbed.*)

MISS SYMPATHY (*whispers to* MILLIE *as she is served her drink*): I strongly sympathize with the aspirations of your people.

(MILLIE *exits.*)

BARRY (*rocking the carriage*): A nationwide alert! All the American people mobilized as one, sitting it out in shelters all over the country. That's what I'd like Little Will to grow up to see. I guess it's just an old man's dream.

GRACE: Here's Arnold! Please, Miss Sympathy, don't tell him you're here because we asked—

ARNOLD (*enters crawling. He is an attractive young man in his thirties. He wears a hat and a business suit and carries an attaché case*): Father—Mother—(*He notices* MISS SYMPATHY, *sizes her up for a long moment, then cooly turns to his mother.*) Company?

GRACE: Arnold, dear, this is Miss Sympathy, this is our son, Arnold Enterprise.

MISS SYMPATHY: I'm pleased to meet you.

ARNOLD (*turning away*): That's O.K. (*to his mother*) Dinner ready?

BARRY: You're being damned rude, Arnold!

ARNOLD: I apologize. I have things on my mind. Are you having drinks?

GRACE: Oh, I'm sorry, dear. With you on the floor that way I forgot that you drink.

ARNOLD: Occasionally to excess. (*Crawls around.*) Did anyone see my coloring book?

GRACE: Millie!

(ARNOLD *crawls around. There is an awkward pause.* MILLIE, *finally, enters with a drink.* MISS SYMPATHY *leans forward, examining everyone's reaction.*)

ARNOLD (*accepting the drink*): It's got an olive in it!

GRACE: Please, dear.

ARNOLD (*to* MILLIE): You know I drink martinis with a lemon peel!

GRACE (*placating*): Millie—would you mind—

(MILLIE *coolly takes back the glass and starts off.*)

MISS SYMPATHY (*whispers to* MILLIE *as she exits*): I have great regard for the aspirations of your people!

GRACE (*to* ARNOLD): Did you have to—

ARNOLD (*to himself*): When I began drinking martinis ten years ago I ordered them with an olive. I didn't know any better, I guess. They always came back with a lemon peel. (*to* MISS SYMPATHY) There was something so garbagey about a lemon peel lying at the bottom of my martini.

BARRY (*angry*): Arnold! I'm sorry, Miss Sympathy.

MISS SYMPATHY (*waving* BARRY *off*): No. No. I understand. (*to* ARNOLD) Please go on.

ARNOLD (*shrugs*): There's nothing to go on. I got used to it. I got to like it. I got to *want* lemon peels in my martinis. It still looked garbagey, but I found that *exciting!* I've always been surrounded by lots of money, cut off from life. That lemon peel floating there in its oil slick that way was to me my only contact with The People. It reminded me of East *River* movies—the Dead End Kids. Remember the Dead End Kids?

MISS SYMPATHY: No, I'm afraid not—

ARNOLD (*suspiciously*): What do you *do?*

(BARRY *and* GRACE *look distressed.* MISS SYMPATHY *warns them off with her eyes.*)

MISS SYMPATHY: I'm a social worker.

ARNOLD (*astonished*): And you don't remember the Dead End Kids?

MISS SYMPATHY: A *psychiatric* social worker.

ARNOLD: Oh, *you'd* remember Ingrid Bergman movies. Where's my coloring book, Mother?

GRACE: Where did you leave it yesterday, dear?

ARNOLD (*restlessly*): I've got to find my coloring book. I feel in the mood for coloring.

GRACE: I'll help you look, Arnold, if you'll just tell me where you think you left it.

(ARNOLD, *perturbed, crawls around the patio looking for his coloring book.* GRACE *follows him anxiously.* BARRY, *flushed with embarrassment, rocks the baby carriage almost violently.*)

BARRY: That's a good boy, Little Will; that's a nice, big good boy, Little Will.

ARNOLD: I found it! (*He crawls off in a corner with the coloring book.* GRACE *follows him. As he begins coloring, she looks over his shoulder.*)

BARRY (*miserably, to* MISS SYMPATHY): I've tried to know that boy.

MISS SYMPATHY: Communications between the generations is never easy, Mr. Enterprise.

BARRY: We wrote away to Dear Abby about him. She was snotty.

MISS SYMPATHY: I'm not sure you acted wisely. She's not licensed, you know.

BARRY: I tried in every way to get close to him, like a father should.

MISS SYMPATHY: Perhaps if you had been a bit more patient—

BARRY: I've tried, believe me, I've tried. I introduced him into my way of life —my friends—I even got him accepted into my athletic club, and they don't usually take Jews.

MISS SYMPATHY: Arnold's Jewish?

BARRY: *That* week. It's not worth discussing. The next week he converted to Buddhism. They don't take Buddhists at my club either. But I got him in. It didn't do any good. All he ever did was go down to the gym and ride one of those vibrating horses for hours. He'd just sit there and ride till closing time. And he'd have a faraway look in his eyes. It became the scandal of the club.

GRACE (*to* ARNOLD): The sky is blue, dear. Not red; *blue.*

ARNOLD: Picasso colors it red.

GRACE: Picasso is an artist, dear. Artists can color the sky red because they *know* it's blue. Those of us who aren't artists must color things the way they really are or people might think we're stupid.

BARRY (*flushed, strides over to* ARNOLD): For Christ's sake, stop embarrassing us in front of the woman! Color the goddamn sky blue! (*He glares over* ARNOLD's *shoulder.* GRACE *flutters nervously over to* MISS SYMPATHY.)

GRACE: Another drink perhaps, Miss Sympathy?

MISS SYMPATHY: I'm fine, thank you. You mustn't allow yourself to get too depressed, Mrs. Enterprise.

GRACE (*hopefully*): I manage to keep myself busy. Organizational work. I'm the block captain of the "Let's Be a Friend of Our Children Society." It's made up of mothers who've had somber histories with their children and are trying to profit others with their experience.

MISS SYMPATHY: That sounds very ambitious.

GRACE: And I'm chairman of the Gratification Committee of the Husband's Fulfillment League. We prepare and distribute many useful pamphlets based on lessons learned from many somber experiences with fulfillment. And, of course, there's still tennis.

MISS SYMPATHY: It all sounds very ambitious.

GRACE: But primarily my life has been my husband's. When he's happy, I try to be happy. When he's unhappy, I try to be unhappy. When he wants me, I try to want him. The key to a successful marriage is giving. *I've* given. Everything.

(MILLIE *enters and serves* ARNOLD *his drink.*)

ARNOLD: That's it. A lemon peel! (*He drops coloring book and examines the martini.*) I can't tolerate a martini without a lemon peel. (*to* MILLIE) Have you been back to the UN, Millie?

MILLIE (*coolly*): Not since last time.

ARNOLD (*to* MISS SYMPATHY): Millie was on television at the UN. We all watched her.

MISS SYMPATHY (*interested*): Oh, what were you doing there?

(GRACE *and* BARRY *writhe uncomfortably.*)

MILLIE: Rioting. (*She exits.*)

BARRY (*furious*): I swear we've got to replace that girl.

GRACE: It doesn't do any good. Any of the girls you get these days, they're all the same. One time or another they've *all* rioted at the UN.

MISS SYMPATHY: I, naturally, don't agree with her means, but if we examine her motivation we should be able to understand why she may have felt that such a form of protest was in order. A misguided protest, I admit, but—

BARRY: She wants her own shelter!

MISS SYMPATHY: What?

BARRY: When I started work on the shelter, I was going to build two of them. One for us and one for Millie and any friends she'd want to invite. Same dimensions, same material, exactly like ours in every way.

GRACE: Millie resented the idea.

BARRY: That girl has been with us ten years, hardly a peep out of her in all that time. Before her, the girl we used to take in was Millie's mother. When Millie's mother was ill, her *grandmother* would come in to clean.

GRACE: Millie's grandmother was a *good* girl.

BARRY: We never had any trouble before. But when I tell Millie I'm building her a shelter—same dimensions, same material, exactly like ours in every way—she nearly quits!

MISS SYMPATHY: I sympathize with her aspirations. She wanted to share *your* shelter of course.

BARRY (*outraged*): *Yes!*

MISS SYMPATHY: You see, while on the surface it would seem that the two shelters are alike in every way, the simple fact that Millie is excluded from one of them can have a devastating psychological effect on her. I have always been opposed to separate but equal fallout shelters.

BARRY: But now she *wants* one!

MISS SYMPATHY: Oh?

BARRY: She comes back from the UN and we're having a practice air-raid drill —and you understand we're all Americans here, *we* accept the law of the land—so we invite Millie into our shelter. And she refuses! Suddenly she wants her *own* shelter!

MISS SYMPATHY: But why? For what reason?

GRACE (*distraught*): She says she's a neutralist!

ARNOLD: She's a hypocrite. A real neutralist wouldn't take shelter at all.

BARRY: Do you hear that kid? He's worse than she is!

MISS SYMPATHY: Are you a neutralist, Arnold?

ARNOLD: No, the neutralists are too extreme. I'm neutral.

GRACE (*maneuvering to leave* MISS SYMPATHY *alone with* ARNOLD): Barry, dear, don't you think we should make a final check of the shelter? The drill should start any time now.

BARRY: Good thinking. I wonder what the delay is. The block captain mentioned last week that they were having a little trouble with the siren.

(*They exit wheeling the baby carriage.*)

MISS SYMPATHY (*There is an awkward silence. She decides to get right to it.*): Don't you know how to walk?

ARNOLD: That's a funny question. Why do you ask?

MISS SYMPATHY: Well, you're not walking.

ARNOLD: I'm not smoking, either. Why don't you ask me if I know how to smoke?

MISS SYMPATHY (*containing herself*): That's very good. (ARNOLD *shrugs.*) Do you mind if I crawl with you?

ARNOLD (*hotly*): Yes, I do!

MISS SYMPATHY: But *you* do it!

ARNOLD: I do it because I believe in it. You do it because you think you're being therapeutic. You're not. You're only being patronizing. I realize that in your field it's sometimes difficult to tell the difference.

MISS SYMPATHY (*with difficulty*): That's very good.

ARNOLD: If you really feel the urge to crawl with me—*really* feel it, I mean—then you'll be most welcome. Not any more welcome or unwelcome than you are now by the way. I am by no means a missionary. Did you see my coloring book?

MISS SYMPATHY: When anyone says anything you don't like, you retreat into that coloring book.

ARNOLD: I admit it's rude. I shouldn't do it unless I have a coloring book for you too. (*He studies her.*) Do you wear glasses?

MISS SYMPATHY: Contact lenses.

ARNOLD (*suddenly shy*): You'd be prettier with glasses. Or rather *I* think you'd be prettier with glasses. I like the way a girl looks with glasses. It makes her face look—less undressed.

MISS SYMPATHY: You think contact lenses make me look naked?

ARNOLD: I think the more people have on, the better they get along with each other. If everybody in the world wore big hats, thick glasses, and dark overcoats they'd all pass each other by thinking, "What an interesting person must be inside all that." And they'd be curious, but they wouldn't ask questions. Who'd dare ask questions like "What are you really like?" to a person in a big hat, thick glasses, and a dark overcoat? The desire to invade privacy rises in direct proportion to the amount of clothing a person takes off. It's what we call "communication." Take off the big hat, and they say, "Good morning, sir!" Take off the thick glasses, and they say, "My, don't you have *haunted* eyes!" Take off the overcoat, and they say, "Tell me *everything!*" So there you have intimacy, followed by understanding, followed by disillusion, followed by—(*shrugs*). If only everybody wore more clothing, we wouldn't have wars.

MISS SYMPATHY: You're saying you'd like to wear an overcoat with me. Is that it?

ARNOLD: I'd feel better if one of us at least wore a big hat. Do you ever have fantasies?

MISS SYMPATHY: Aren't you getting intimate?

ARNOLD: *You* decided to wear the contact lenses.

MISS SYMPATHY: Everybody has fantasies.

ARNOLD: What are yours about?

MISS SYMPATHY: Being a better social worker.

ARNOLD: Dear God.

MISS SYMPATHY (*sadly*): I used to have fantasies about Adlai Stevenson. But that's all over now.

ARNOLD: I have fantasies all the time. When I'm awake, when I'm asleep, I *live* with them. I embellish them. Polish them day after day. You cultivate a good fantasy long enough, and soon it can seep out into the real world. Do you know how old my parents are?

MISS SYMPATHY: I hadn't thought of it. Middle fifties?

ARNOLD: They're both over seventy.

MISS SYMPATHY: And they had a *baby?*

ARNOLD (*shrugs, reaches for the coloring book, changes his mind*): My father doesn't look very much older than me, does he?

MISS SYMPATHY (*evasive*): I don't know if I noticed.

ARNOLD: You're kind. But that's how it's been always. They're both alert, involved, aggressive people. So while I'm out trying, unsuccessfully, to make it with a girl and I come home, mixed up and angry and feeling like not much of anything, what are they waiting up proudly to tell me? *They're* having a baby. I'll try to say this in as uninvolved and unneurotic a way as I know how—it's hard to face a daily series of piddling, eroding defeats and, in addition, have the fact thrown in your face that your *father* at *age seventy* can still do better than you can.

(*There is a long pause.* ARNOLD *fishes a ball out from under a chair and tosses it to* MISS SYMPATHY. *She one-hands it.*)

You catch pretty good.

(*She cocks her arm back.* ARNOLD *throws out one hand defensively.*)

No, don't throw it. I'm not ready to compete yet.

MISS SYMPATHY: These fantasies—were any of them about crawling?

ARNOLD: In my fantasies, it was everyone else who crawled. For instance, in one of them I had this uncle. Uncle Walter—

(*A weak siren begins to wail erratically.*)

BARRY (*enters, running with the baby carriage*): That's it! The alert! Down to the shelter, everyone!

GRACE (*enters with a fire extinguisher and shopping bag*): Oh, it's so exciting! It's so exciting!

(BARRY *switches on a transistor radio.*)

RADIO VOICE: Stay tuned to this frequency. All other frequencies have left the air. This is Conelrad!

BARRY (*listening intently*): I met that fellow down at civil-defense headquarters once. You'd be surprised. He's just like you and me.

(GRACE *is in a sudden, heated conversation with* ARNOLD.)

GRACE: But you *have* to go down! You went down with us last year!

RADIO VOICE: It is the law that everyone on the street take shelter—

ARNOLD: We're *not* on the street. We're on the patio.

BARRY (*exasperated*): You think the Russians give a damn we're not on the street?

GRACE: It's the spirit of the law one should follow, dear.

BARRY: Arnold, I've had enough of this nonsense! Downstairs! That's a parental order!

ARNOLD (*hotly*): I colored the sky blue, didn't I? Why don't *you* ever meet *me* halfway?

BARRY (*exits wheeling the baby carriage*): *I* can't do anything with him.

GRACE: We can't leave our oldest out on the patio!

BARRY (*reenters with the baby carriage*): He's the one who's breaking the law. Let's go! (*He exits with the carriage.*)

GRACE: You'd better follow me, Miss Sympathy. It's dark in the basement.

MISS SYMPATHY (*weakly, to* ARNOLD): It *is* the law.

ARNOLD: I told you I'm not asking for converts.

GRACE: For the last time, won't you come, Arnold? It's not going to be any fun without you.

ARNOLD: I'm doing something *else,* Mother.

BARRY (*reenters with the baby carriage*): The hell with him. The law doesn't mean a thing to *our* son. Come on!

(*He exits with the baby carriage.* GRACE *exits.*)

MISS SYMPATHY (*to* ARNOLD): I, as do you, question the sense of such a drill, but objecting to this law by defying it robs *all* laws of their meaning. Now, I can see working for its reform while continuing to *obey* it, but to be both against it and defy it at the same time seems to me to weaken your position.

ARNOLD: They're all downstairs. You'd better go.

MISS SYMPATHY (*starting away*): You do understand?

ARNOLD (*dryly*): I think I hear planes.

(*She exits running. Sound of offstage pounding*)

BARRY (*offstage*): Goddamit, Millie! What are you doing in there? Unlock the door!

GRACE (*offstage*): That's not nice, Millie! Let us into our fallout shelter!

(*sound of pounding*)

BARRY (*offstage*): Millie! There is such a thing as the laws of trespass! You're in *my* shelter!

(*Sound of pounding.* MISS SYMPATHY *enters.*)

ARNOLD (*grinning*): Millie locked herself in the shelter?

MISS SYMPATHY: She says, "Let the white imperialists wipe each other out."

ARNOLD (*laughs*): I can appreciate her sensitivity and support her aspirations, but I reject the extremes to which she's gone. (*brightly*) But I do understand her motivations.

(*sound of pounding*)

BARRY (*offstage*): Millie, you're not playing fair!

ARNOLD: You really shouldn't be up here, you know.

MISS SYMPATHY: I thought we were having an all-clear by default.

ARNOLD: I doubt it.

BARRY (*offstage*): All right, Millie. We'll stay down here anyway! We'll use the basement as our shelter! Down on your stomach, Grace. Where's Miss Sympathy? Miss Sympathy!

MISS SYMPATHY (*yelling*): Upstairs! I thought it was over!

BARRY (*offstage*): The law's the law, Miss Sympathy. We can't come up till we hear the all-clear. Otherwise we'd be making Khrushchev happy!

ARNOLD: It *is* the law.

MISS SYMPATHY: What if I lay on my stomach up here? It's so dusty down there.

ARNOLD: I guess that would be *semi*-compliance.

MISS SYMPATHY: Does it seem within the spirit of the law to you?

ARNOLD: Well, I know lying on your stomach *is* the accepted crisis position. I don't imagine you'd be penalized because of location.

(*She lies on her stomach.* ARNOLD *views her with wry amusement.*)

Don't you know how to stand?

MISS SYMPATHY (*dryly*): That's quite witty. You were telling me about your fantasy.

ARNOLD: Which one?

MISS SYMPATHY: Your uncle. (*Checks notes.*) Walter.

ARNOLD: Well, in a fantasy it's you who are in control, isn't it? So you can make things any way you want them. So I wanted an uncle. I guess I was eight or nine at the time. So I made him up. Uncle Walter. Uncle Walter was a mess. His eyes were very bad, and he wore big, thick bifocals—about this size—half the size of his face, and he had a beard. Hair all over. I mean it started with his nose hairs and blended with his ear hairs and went all the way down to his chest hairs. Except I never saw his chest. He was frail and he always wore a scarf. And a big heavy black overcoat. Even inside the house. It used to shed. *He* used to shed. My mother and father were always embarrassed when he came to visit. And I was too—but for *them,* not for him. I kept hoping Uncle Walter would understand that I was as normal as he was and that it wasn't my fault my parents were a little strange. He would never let me near him. He *hated* children. So *I* hated children. Anything Uncle Walter did I wanted to do. I tried to get bad eyes. I'd let them blur out of focus until they'd tear. I began seeing my parents as Uncle Walter saw them. I don't mean I began to understand them the way Uncle Walter did. I mean I *became* Uncle Walter looking at my parents. I became Uncle Walter looking at *me!* Then—I don't know how it happened—my father talked Uncle Walter into joining his athletic club. I thought it was a big joke—that in a week Uncle Walter would have them all wearing overcoats, bifocals, and beards—(*mimes sign*) "The Unhealthy Athletic Club." But all that happened was that Uncle Walter got healthy. He got rid of his overcoat. He shaved his beard. He took pills for his vitamin deficiency, and his eyes became twenty-twenty. He began to smile at me and say, "Howsa boy!" He talked business with the family. It was *my* fantasy, and he had sold me out! He died a month later. Never trust a grown-up.

MISS SYMPATHY: Will you tell me why you're crawling?

(ARNOLD *crawls over to* MISS SYMPATHY.)

ARNOLD: I find that in crawling like a child I begin to act like a child again.

MISS SYMPATHY: Is that why you started?

ARNOLD: Possibly. I did a very childlike thing on the way home. I never would have thought of doing such a thing before I crawled. As an adult my values encompassed a rigid good, a rigid evil, and a mushy everything-in-between. As a child I've rediscovered one value I had completely forgotten existed.

MISS SYMPATHY: What's that?

ARNOLD: Being naughty.

MISS SYMPATHY: You did something naughty on the way home. Is that what you're telling me?

ARNOLD: I don't think I want to talk about it right now. I want to enjoy it by myself for a little while longer.

MISS SYMPATHY (*exasperated*): God, you're as hard to reach as a child! (*quickly*) I understand why, of course.

ARNOLD: Why?

MISS SYMPATHY: First you tell me what you did today that was naughty.

ARNOLD: First you tell me why I'm as hard to reach as a child.

MISS SYMPATHY (*as if to a child*): First you tell me what you did that was naughty.

ARNOLD (*kidding*): You first.

MISS SYMPATHY (*as if to a child*): Oh, no, you!

ARNOLD (*kidding*): I asked you first.

MISS SYMPATHY (*as if to a child*): Then will you tell me?

ARNOLD (*trying to withdraw*): Yes.

MISS SYMPATHY (*very arch*): Promise?

ARNOLD (*serious*): Yes.

MISS SYMPATHY (*very arch*): Cross your heart and hope to die?

ARNOLD (*stares at her, unbelieving*): I can understand why you have trouble reaching children.

BARRY (*off stage*): Hey, up there. Have you heard the all-clear sound yet?

MISS SYMPATHY (*yelling angrily*): No, it hasn't, Mr. Enterprise!

BARRY (*offstage*): Funny. It should have sounded by now.

GRACE (*offstage*): I'm getting a chill lying on my stomach this way.

BARRY (*offstage*): It's the proper position, Grace.

GRACE (*offstage*): Can't we go up soon, Barry?

BARRY (*offstage*): When the all clear sounds we'll go up. That's the law. Is that Millie yelling something?

GRACE (*offstage*): Yell louder, Millie. We can't hear you—(*pause*) She wants to know if the all clear sounded yet.

BARRY (*offstage*): Tell her to go to hell.

ARNOLD (*after a long study of* MISS SYMPATHY): Do you really want me to get up?

MISS SYMPATHY (*petulantly*): It's not what *I* want. It's what's best for yourself.

ARNOLD: You mean if I got up I'd be doing it for myself.

MISS SYMPATHY (*petulantly*): Not for me. Not for your mother. Not for your father. Strictly for yourself.

ARNOLD: That's too bad. I don't care much about getting up for myself. I would have liked to have done it for you, though.

MISS SYMPATHY (*with sudden warmth*): I *would* be very pleased.

ARNOLD: If I got up right now?

MISS SYMPATHY (*warmly*): Yes.

ARNOLD (*begins to rise*): Okay.

MISS SYMPATHY (*tackles him*): No.

ARNOLD: But you said—

MISS SYMPATHY: Now *now. Later!* (*Whispers.*) It's against the law!

ARNOLD (*shrugs; returns to his crawling position*): Did you see my coloring book?

MISS SYMPATHY (*furious*): You're not being *honest!* You blame me for accepting the rules of society. Well, without those rules we'd have anarchy. Every mature person has to operate within the warp and woof of society. You want to operate outside that warp and woof, to return to a *child's* world —to start all over again!

ARNOLD (*appreciatively*): Yeah! (*From his pocket he plucks a lollipop.*)

MISS SYMPATHY (*impatiently*): Well, you *can't* start all over again. It will all come out the *same way!*

ARNOLD (*sucking the lollipop*): Then I'll start all over again, again.

MISS SYMPATHY: But it will all come out the same way *again!*

ARNOLD: Then I'll start all over again, again, again. It's *my* game. (*He takes a long, loud suck on the lollipop.*)

BARRY (*offstage*): Wasn't that the all-clear?

MISS SYMPATHY: I'm afraid not, Mr. Enterprise.

GRACE (*offstage*): I'm catching cold.

BARRY (*offstage*): Let me put my jacket under you.

GRACE (*offstage*): I'm *tired* of this.

BARRY (*offstage*): But it's only a few minutes. We've spent over two weeks in our shelter.

GRACE (*offstage*): But we had television.

BARRY (*offstage*): The law is there for the citizens to obey. If *we* are irresponsible, how can we attack *others* for being irresponsible?

MISS SYMPATHY (*coldly, to* ARNOLD): You have a very irresponsible attitude.

ARNOLD: "Naughty" is the word I prefer.

MISS SYMPATHY: You were going to tell me something.

ARNOLD: I forgot.

MISS SYMPATHY: What you did on the way home from work—(*with sarcasm*) Something *naughty.*

ARNOLD: Do you find me attractive, Miss Sympathy?

MISS SYMPATHY (*a long pause. She begins to sniffle*): Yes, I do.

ARNOLD (*surprised*): You can say it just like that?

MISS SYMPATHY (*barely restraining tears*): Because I do. I know I do. You're the kind of person I find attractive *always.* From previous examples I know you fall into my spectrum of attractiveness. Actually, it's because I find you so attractive that I'm having trouble with you. If I didn't find you attractive I could explain your problem without the slightest difficulty.

ARNOLD: Everything's so complicated.

MISS SYMPATHY: We live in a complex world.

ARNOLD: *Children* are complex. Adults are just complicated.

MISS SYMPATHY: Why did you ask if I found you attractive?

ARNOLD: Because we've been alone for a while and we'll be alone for a while longer. I thought it was the right thing to say.

MISS SYMPATHY: We have a time limit. The all-clear will probably sound any minute.

ARNOLD: Four months ago you wouldn't have found me attractive.

MISS SYMPATHY: Why do you say that?

ARNOLD: Because four months ago I didn't crawl. Crawling has made me a more attractive person.

MISS SYMPATHY: It has? How?

ARNOLD: Well, for one thing I'm conspicuous now. I never used to be. There's a certain magnetism conspicuous men have for women. (*more cautiously*) I *think* conspicuous men have for women.

MISS SYMPATHY: No, don't stop. In some ways you're right.

ARNOLD: I'm more assertive now. Everybody used to have *their* road. My mother, my father, my friends, Millie—with me the question was Whose road would I take? Whose side was I on? Now I have *my* road, *my* side.

MISS SYMPATHY: You're terribly sweet. Do you mind if I crawl over to you?

ARNOLD: I'd like it.

(*She does. For a while they stare wistfully at each other. Then* ARNOLD *drops to his stomach and kisses her.*)

I'm on my stomach now.

MISS SYMPATHY: Yes.

ARNOLD: I'm not even crawling any more. That's *real* regression.

MISS SYMPATHY: Yes. (*He kisses her.*) Before we do anything I want to tell you—

ARNOLD: What?

MISS SYMPATHY: Before—when I was feeling sorry for you—I felt you'd rejoin society if you were only made to feel like a man.

ARNOLD: An expert analysis.

MISS SYMPATHY: I was going to offer to go to bed with you to make you feel like a man. I couldn't offer myself in that spirit now.

ARNOLD: I'm glad you told me. The social worker my folks had in last month went to bed with me because she wanted to make me feel like a man. I think she got more out of it than I did.

MISS SYMPATHY: How many have there been?

ARNOLD: One a month for four months. My parents keep bringing them around. They're very nervous about me.

MISS SYMPATHY (*doubtfully*): You're not just using me, Arnold—

ARNOLD: We're using each other, Miss Sympathy. That's what using's for. (*He beings to unbutton the back of her blouse.*)

MISS SYMPATHY: The all-clear—What if the all-clear should sound?

ARNOLD: It won't. It's broken. That's what I did that was naughty today. (*They embrace as lights dim.*)

BARRY (*offstage*): Was that the all-clear?

CURTAIN

The Bridge

MARIO FRATTI

Characters

PABLO, *thirty-five years old; a Puerto Rican living in New York*
JOSEPH, *a policeman assigned to rescue work*
LIEUTENANT, *Joseph's commanding officer*

Reading Guides

1. You must spend some time visualizing the setting of *The Bridge,* for it is important to feel the danger that Pablo and Joseph face. This danger underlies the actions of the two characters; yet in reading the play, one tends to forget the action.

2. In one sense this is a difficult play because the reader must figure out when Joseph means what he says and when he does not. Possibly an actor could make this clear to you, but you do not have an actor; you have only your imagination. Use it.

The Bridge

SCENE. *The top of Brooklyn Bridge, a place not uncommon for suicides.*

TIME. *Today.*

PABLO *is standing in the middle of the double span. He is looking down, apparently about to jump.*

Down at the foot of the bridge we imagine a curious crowd.

PABLO, *lost and bewildered, looks around. He is surrounded only by the blue sky.*

PABLO (*to someone who is evidently trying to reach him*): It's no use. You're wasting your time, my friend. . . . Don't! Or I will jump right away. . . . There is no use. . . . It's too late now. (*backing up*) I warn you. . . . If you come too close. . . . Go away! Go back to them! (*He points to the crowd down below.*) Or do you want this "show" to get going?

(*He backs up to the very edge, wavering.*)

I'm warning you. . . . Don't come near or I'll . . .

(JOSEPH, *the policeman, appears at the opposite side of the span. He is out of breath and sweating. He sits down to catch his breath.*)

I'm not joking. I mean it!

JOSEPH: I know.

PABLO: One more move and . . .

JOSEPH: I know.

PABLO: What do you know?

JOSEPH: That you're not joking.

PABLO: Then why are you up here? (JOSEPH *shrugs his shoulders.*)

JOSEPH: Let me catch my breath.

PABLO: You have all the time you want.

JOSEPH: I know.

PABLO: If you don't move.

JOSEPH: I know.

PABLO: If you try to—

JOSEPH (*interrupting*): I know.

PABLO: You know too much.

JOSEPH: That's my job.

PABLO: Then you know there's nothing you can do about me.

JOSEPH: I know.

PABLO: Then why are you up here?

JOSEPH: It's my duty.

PABLO (*with some surprise and curiosity*): Just "duty"?

JOSEPH: And the bonus. There's extra money for such trips.

PABLO: If you save me.

JOSEPH: That's not necessary. Just climbing up here is considered "special duty." And we get double pay.

PABLO (*after a silence*): How many have you seen up here?

JOSEPH: Nine.

PABLO: How many have you . . . saved?

JOSEPH: Eight.

PABLO: A good record. I'm sorry to spoil it. I've made up my mind.

JOSEPH: I know.

PABLO: Eight saved; two lost. It's still a good average. Eighty percent.

JOSEPH: Ninety percent.

PABLO: Why ninety?

JOSEPH: Nine saved; one lost.

PABLO: Why do you say "nine"?

JOSEPH: I always tell the truth.

PABLO: Do you think you can . . . ? (*He includes himself with a gesture.*)

JOSEPH: Absolutely.

PABLO (*incredulous*): Are you including me?

JOSEPH: Yes.

PABLO: Are you serious?

JOSEPH: I'm serious.

PABLO: Do you really think . . . you'll save me?

JOSEPH: As true as there's a God.

PABLO: You must be an atheist. It's unusual, for a cop.

JOSEPH: On the contrary, I'm very religious.

PABLO (*incredulous*): And you're sure that—"as true as there's a God," you'll save me?

JOSEPH: Don't take the name of the Lord in vain. (*He makes the sign of the cross.*)

PABLO: You started.

JOSEPH: I'm on the side of the law.

PABLO: I forget. You're permitted everything.

JOSEPH: Not only because I'm a man of the law, but also because I'm not about to commit a mortal sin. I've just come from church. (*He wipes off his perspiration.*)

PABLO (*ironically*): I apologize if this trip made you lose the holy perfume of the incense. I'm so sorry you're perspiring because of me.

JOSEPH: It doesn't matter. Thanks to you I get a day off tomorrow. There can be some advantage to a calamity.

PABLO: Am I the "calamity"?

JOSEPH: I'd say so.

PABLO: What a way of consoling one's fellow brother! Did you talk to the others like this?

JOSEPH: What others?

PABLO: Those nine—(*He does not utter the word "suicides" but so indicates with a gesture of jumping.*)

JOSEPH: Yes.

PABLO (*more and more intrigued*): To all of them?

JOSEPH: To all of them.

PABLO: Even to the one . . . you didn't save?

JOSEPH: That one, too. A thick skinned Jew.

PABLO: I see. You're one of those who consider the Jews to be different. . . . An inferior race, maybe.

JOSEPH: Insensitive.

PABLO (*reflecting*): Insensitive . . . to what? (*ironically*) To what you said?

JOSEPH: To that too.

PABLO: Which is what you're telling me.

JOSEPH: More or less.

PABLO: Maybe he was *too* sensitive and preferred to—(*He makes the gesture of jumping.*)

JOSEPH: Are you Jewish by any chance?

PABLO: No. I'm a Catholic. Like you, I guess.

JOSEPH (*with tolerance*): There's always something in common, alas!

PABLO: Alas?

JOSEPH: You can't avoid it.

PABLO: Is that bad?

JOSEPH: In a street, in an office, in a prison—people always find that they have something in common. Same religion, political opinion, race . . .

PABLO: Same sex.

JOSEPH: You can't avoid it. The chances are fifty-fifty.

PABLO (*ironically*): Yes we have two things in common. We are both Catholics and we are men.

JOSEPH: The only two things we have in common.

PABLO: The only ones, I hope.

JOSEPH: I hope so too.

PABLO (*studying* JOSEPH): Did you tell that Jew you're a Catholic?

JOSEPH: Of course.

PABLO: That's why he jumped.

JOSEPH (*looking straight in his eyes*): Who told you he jumped?

PABLO: You said so yourself.

JOSEPH: Me? You're wrong.

PABLO: You said,—"Eight were saved, and one was lost."

JOSEPH: That's what I said.

PABLO: Well?

JOSEPH: Well what?

PABLO: If you saved eight of them but not the Jew, it means that the Jew jumped.

JOSEPH: You misunderstood me.

PABLO: Evidently. What did you mean?

JOSEPH: I meant—eight saved from the miseries of this world. One—the Jew—asked for a ladder.

PABLO (*surprised*): So that's what you meant when you said that you'd "save" me.

JOSEPH: As true as there's a God. (*He crosses himself.*)

PABLO (*shaken; reflecting*): You're right . . . I've made up my mind . . . But how can you be so sure?

JOSEPH: It's instinct. And experience.

PABLO: I always thought men like you could not be very smart.

JOSEPH: Never underestimate men of law, remember that! We would never be trusted with keeping "Order" if we weren't well schooled and prepared.

PABLO: What did they teach you?

JOSEPH: Everything.

PABLO: Even how to read the minds of other people?

JOSEPH: That's called psychology. It's one of the most important subjects.

PABLO: And with that psychology you never made a mistake?

JOSEPH: With the exception of the Jews. They're unpredictable.

PABLO: All of them?

JOSEPH: All of them.

PABLO: Including the . . . possible suicides?

JOSEPH: Also those. They pretend. They do it to attract attention. Then there's always a rich Jew who comes along and offers them a job at a hundred dollars a week, and they change their minds.

PABLO (*unable to hide his envy*): A hundred dollars a week . . .

JOSEPH: You'd spend every penny of it on whisky.

PABLO: How would *you* know?

JOSEPH: I know your kind. All I have to do is look at your face.

PABLO: What kind of face do you see?

JOSEPH: You Puer– (*He holds back.*) You're all bums.

PABLO (*sadly*): You started to say—You Puerto Ricans.

JOSEPH: I admit it. Did you study psychology, you too?

PABLO: Is a Puerto Rican and a bum the same thing to you?

JOSEPH (*looking straight in his eyes*): The same thing.

PABLO: Then why did you come to our country and take over?

JOSEPH: Me?

PABLO: Your people.

JOSEPH: If it was up to me . . . (*scornfully*) *I* wouldn't touch you people with a ten-foot pole.

PABLO: It's me who wouldn't let one of you touch me.

JOSEPH: Don't worry about *that.* I won't touch you. (*He "washes" his hands.*)

PABLO: Do all you cops feel that way?

JOSEPH: A man in uniform can only speak for himself. *I,* personally, wouldn't touch you with a ten-foot pole. My friends on the Force . . . (*he thinks for a few seconds.*) . . . feel the same way. But that's their business. They can speak for themselves, if they wish. *I* believe in freedom of choice. (*a brief pause*) How about you?

PABLO: So do I. (*pointing below*) Is there any freer choice than this?

JOSEPH: I mean, do you believe in Freedom, in our Democracy?

PABLO: Why do you ask *me* that?

JOSEPH: I don't trust your kind.

PABLO: What kind are we?

JOSEPH: Bums with many kids.

PABLO: What do you know about me? What do you know about my family?

JOSEPH: You're all alike. It's always the same story and complaint.

PABLO: Did I complain?

JOSEPH: That's because I didn't give you a chance to. Please don't tell me your story. I've heard it a thousand times.

PABLO: Then *you* tell me.

JOSEPH: You left your old parents starving in your little village—

PABLO: I'm an orphan.

JOSEPH (*ignoring*): You came to New York full of hope. To make money. Instead, you began making children. The result—starvation for all. Big families always starve.

PABLO: How many children make a "big family," according to you?

JOSEPH: In your case? I saw four. But I'm sure you have more in some dump.

PABLO (*with curiosity*): Where did you see them?

JOSEPH: Down there, with your miserable wife. My buddies are holding them back. They trust me. They know I can "save" you single-handed. (*a silence*)

PABLO (*slowly*): Why did you say . . . she's "miserable"?

JOSEPH: Your wife? Not because you're about to die. That she will be widowed is not a misfortune. It might be a stroke of luck for her. I said she looks "miserable" because . . . (*he takes his time*) You must know how she looks early in the morning! She just got up. And hasn't washed her face!

PABLO (*timidly*): Did she say anything?

JOSEPH: Oh, I forgot!—And I know it's unfair not to report the last words to a dying man.—She told me to tell you that . . . (*he is trying to remem-*

ber.) a certain man by the name of . . . Sanchez—I think I'm right—has a good job for you, with a very good pay. And . . . She also promised not to complain ever again. She's swearing it by one of your Madonnas. (*a silence*)

PABLO (*sadly*): They all lie. . . . Always . . . (*to* JOSEPH) Would *you* believe them?

JOSEPH: Believe what?

PABLO: In a job with "very good" pay; in all the promises . . .

JOSEPH: Sometimes they tell the truth. Sometimes they lie. It depends. There's freedom of opinion in this country.

PABLO (*after a silence*): What else did she say?

JOSEPH (*trying to remember*): —that if I persuade you to come down, I'd be welcomed into your family with gratitude and "love." (*with contempt*) Who needs it? (*reflecting*) Maybe she also meant . . . in bed. Who wants that disgrace?

PABLO (*hurt*): You're a swine!

JOSEPH (*tense*): Come over here and repeat that to my face. (*a silence*) Come on! (*He rises to his feet, aggressively*) If you have the guts to do it. . . . (*a silence. They stare at each other.*)

PABLO: And what about my . . . ? (*He indicates the word "children" with a gesture of his hand.*)

JOSEPH: Your brats? They weren't crying. You're a strange breed. Not even a tear. (*staring at him*) You tell me. Why do you suppose they don't cry? (*a silence.* PABLO *does not have the courage to reply.*)

JOSEPH: Too exhausted maybe? (PABLO *gestures in the negative.*) Sometimes hunger makes you react like that. (PABLO *gestures in the negative.*) Or maybe you people beat them too often?

PABLO (*weakly*): No . . .

JOSEPH: Maybe they're glad to be rid of you. A drunkard isn't a joyful sight to one's children.

PABLO (*who has not heard the last words; deeply moved*): Maria is twelve . . .

JOSEPH: Who's Maria?

PABLO: My daughter. (*with a gesture he indicates her height*) She's a real little lady. She promised me she wouldn't cry. She is not crying.

JOSEPH (*surprised*): Promised? (PABLO *nods.*) You spoke to her about—? (*He makes the gesture of jumping.*)

PABLO: To a wife it's hard to say such things. She laughs in your face; she doesn't believe you . . . A daughter has more respect. . . . She understands . . .

JOSEPH: What did you tell her?

PABLO: That it's better for them . . .

JOSEPH: What's better? Why?

PABLO: When a father dies in this way, everybody becomes generous.

JOSEPH: Who?

PABLO: Everybody . . . And my family will receive a lot of help, and many gifts. . . . They'll be able to go back to San Juan.

JOSEPH: Bon Voyage! But did she really understand? Did she understand that you—? (*He makes the sign of the cross in the air, meaning "death."*)

PABLO: She understood.

JOSEPH: And she didn't cry?

PABLO: When I first told her, she cried. She held me tightly, with her hands clasping my shoulders. Then she began to understand and promised not to cry today . . . to encourage her little brothers.

JOSEPH (*incredulous, with irony*): "To encourage."

PABLO: She has always obeyed me. She loves me.

JOSEPH: And you reward her with—

PABLO (*ignoring*): She always keeps her promise . . . always. My poor baby, not even a tear . . .

JOSEPH: Yes. You *are* a strange breed.

PABLO: Because we learn not to cry?

JOSEPH: Because you know how to exploit even death.

PABLO: What do you mean?

JOSEPH: Your blind belief that "everybody will become generous and will give money."

PABLO: It's true.

JOSEPH: That's why I said, "You know how to exploit even death." But after all, how can you be so sure that we aren't tired of giving you people charity? There's a limit to everything!

PABLO: In the presence of death . . .

JOSEPH: It's practically become a daily occurrence. A dead person on every street corner. No one is upset by it.

PABLO: I'm certain that—

JOSEPH (*ironically*): "Certain"! You people are ridiculous! There's no such word as "certain" anymore.

PABLO: Two years ago a friend of mine attempted suicide and—

JOSEPH (*interrupting*): *Attempted.* That's different.

PABLO: One of you convinced him to give up the idea. With a million promises.

JOSEPH: Not me!

PABLO: I believe that.

JOSEPH: Thanks!

PABLO: You speak your mind. . . .

JOSEPH: Always. I call a spade a spade. And a bum a bum.

PABLO: You've already called me that.

JOSEPH: *Repetita iuvant.* (*to* PABLO *who does not understand*) They teach us even a little Latin at the Police Academy. To impress fools. *Repetita iuvant* means "Explain the truth ten times, to thick heads. Maybe they'll understand." That friend of yours, for instance. Maybe he was convinced because the police officer repeated the same thing ten times. I have no patience.

PABLO: The promises weren't kept, of course . . . No job, no apartment . . .

JOSEPH: That's life. . . .

PABLO: You say that as if it were an insignificant event.

JOSEPH: Is it perhaps a great international event?

PABLO: It's a man's life.

JOSEPH (*raising one finger*): ONE man . . . Don't get carried away. ONE man.

PABLO: Do you know what they did to him, when he came down?

JOSEPH: Are you going to tell me they beat him up? With all those photographers around? I don't believe you.

PABLO: They put him in an insane asylum.

JOSEPH: A few weeks under observation calms the nerves. But what are you trying to prove with the story of your friend?

PABLO: Six months ago he finally did it. From here. His case made headlines. His family returned to Puerto Rico with a lot of money.

JOSEPH: It's the headlines that you want.

PABLO: If it helps my family, Yes.

JOSEPH: The usual excuse. (*ironically*) "For the family." It's the publicity that you guys want. All of you!

PABLO (*with sincerity*): No! Please believe me. And please tell them. Everyone. Repeat our conversation. Tell them I did it only for my family; that I put my hope in the good hearts of . . . anybody who can . . .

JOSEPH: You Latin Americans have a strange mentality. The only thing you want is charity.

PABLO: Only when—

JOSEPH (*interrupting*): You people are real parasites.

PABLO: It isn't me who created the world the way it is. If you're living, they promise you the moon but—

JOSEPH: Not me!

PABLO: —but they don't keep their promises. But if you die, everybody—

JOSEPH (*interrupting*): Not "everybody." Only some with sins on their conscience. Maybe it's a way of feeling absolved. That's their business. But you, why do you pick the easiest way out?

PABLO (*bitterly*): The "easiest"?

JOSEPH: Why do you want strangers to support your children?

PABLO: It's the only way they can be happy. Unfortunately only death brings pity. That friend of mine—

JOSEPH: You already told me.

PABLO: It's not my fault if that's the way the world is.

JOSEPH: But *you're* responsible for the children. You brought them into the world. Stop drinking and take care of them.

PABLO: I've never been drunk in my life.

JOSEPH: I'm sure you have other vices.

PABLO: Did you ever pay a hospital bill?

JOSEPH: Here come the complaints! Get hospital insurance!

PABLO: Do you know what it costs here in America?

JOSEPH: My wife takes care of that.

PABLO: It's half my salary! (*after reflection*) You have a wife too. . . .

JOSEPH: Certainly. Why?

PABLO: I think of you without a family. . . . The way you talk . . . cruel and hateful—

JOSEPH: *Me* cruel! You, who order a twelve-year-old not to cry. Are *you* the model father?

PABLO: Do you have children too?

JOSEPH: Of course. A boy and a girl. Like any respectable family: only two. When the good Lord (*He crosses himself.*) summons my wife and me to Heaven, they will take our place. We don't reproduce like rabbits—we real Americans. Overpopulation leads to Communism. (*a brief silence*) Why did you have so many children if you knew you were going to finish up like this? (*He points down.*)

PABLO: I didn't know then. . . .

JOSEPH: In bed people don't think of suicide, I know. You bums are all alike. Selfish. You're just in for physical satisfaction—as long as you find your wife attractive. But when she is reduced to that state (*He points down*), with four brats hanging on, you decide to commit suicide. Is this your way of ensuring their future? Depending on the charity of strangers? You're a coward!

(*a silence*)

PABLO: I've read a lot about suicide. . . . Some claim that it's cowardice; others say it's an act of courage. What do you think?

JOSEPH (*slowly*): I have no desire to influence you, as you know. What you decide is *your* own damn business. I couldn't care less. But I do have an opinion on suicide.

PABLO: What is it?

JOSEPH: They go into it in our psychology course. We divided ourselves into two groups: Some insisted on calling it courage; others, extreme cowardice. I personally think that it does take courage that fraction of a second when you jump. On the other hand, it's cowardice because it's an escape from life. But let me make this clear to you. I don't want to influence you in one direction or the other. One suicide more, one less . . .

PABLO (*reproachfully*): Why do you talk like that?

JOSEPH: Like what?

PABLO: With such contempt . . .

JOSEPH: It's my point of view. Don't I have the right? This is a free country!

PABLO: It's the way you say it.

JOSEPH: It's the truth. I always tell the truth, that's me. When a bum does away with himself, there's more room for us. It makes our society more secure. In Indonesia, for instance, they have executed nine hundred thousand bums in a few days. Nine hundred thousand Reds less. The world is a little cleaner and safer for that.

PABLO: I'm no Red!

JOSEPH: Unemployed with a big family? Who are you kidding? You can only be a Red.

PABLO: The Church would excommunicate me.

JOSEPH: You mean that's the only reason why you're not a Red? Because you're afraid of the Church? That's an interesting confession!

PABLO: And because I believe in the family.

JOSEPH (*ironically, pointing down*): I can see that!

PABLO: And in freedom.

JOSEPH: What kind of freedom?

PABLO (*pointing vaguely around him*): This . . .

JOSEPH: The freedom to jump?

PABLO: Democratic freedom . . . That's what I've always believed in. Man should be free to do what he wants.

JOSEPH: And women?

PABLO: Women too.

JOSEPH: Are you leaving your wife and daughter the freedom to do what they want?

PABLO (*waveringly*): Yes . . .

JOSEPH: Complete freedom?

PABLO (*unsure*): Yes . . .

JOSEPH: Even if they take to walking the streets, I suppose?

PABLO (*hurt*): They will have money, lots of money and—

JOSEPH: Are you really certain of it?

PABLO: I read about it every day in the paper. There's always some good soul who starts a collection . . . Even Oswald's family. They have lots of money now.

JOSEPH: He killed a *President.* You're only killing a poor, stupid nobody. Yourself. You want to make a bet? They won't collect more than five hundred dollars.

PABLO: Sure if you tell them I'm a Red. Which *isn't* true. Please don't—

JOSEPH: I won't. I'll only say that . . . you had a nervous breakdown.

PABLO: . . . with debts and no job . . .

JOSEPH: That's a social protest. That wouldn't be wise. Anyway, do you want to bet?

PABLO: I've made up my mind and I'm going to jump. Who will pay if I lose the bet?

JOSEPH: You can sign an IOU. If your family gets over five hundred dollars, I'll add a hundred. If they get less, your wife will owe me a hundred. (*He takes a piece of paper and pen.*) Here. Sign here.

PABLO (*uncertain*): Are you so sure they'll . . . get less than five hundred dollars?

JOSEPH: Positive. I can guarantee it. Yours is an ordinary case. There're ten a day like you. People have become callous to it.

PABLO: If you lie and tell them I'm a Red—

JOSEPH (*interrupting*): Keep politics out of it! Do you want to take me up on it?

PABLO: Honestly—would you have the nerve to take their money if they received less than five hundred dollars?

JOSEPH (*ironically*): My friend you're beginning to have doubts, aren't you?

PABLO: My name is Pablo. What's yours?

JOSEPH (*bored*): Joseph.

PABLO: Tell me, Joseph . . . Tell me seriously. Would you have the nerve to take a hundred dollars from them if—?

JOSEPH: I won't be the only one. They'll be at the mercy of everybody down there. Even your friends who loaned you money—

PABLO: No friend of mine ever—

JOSEPH (*interrupting*): All right, enemies then. Like the grocer and the landlord. And don't forget the undertaker. Nowadays a decent funeral costs a thousand dollars.

PABLO (*alarmed*): A thousand dollars? Are you sure?

JOSEPH: Positive. Even gravediggers have families to feed!

PABLO: But that friend of mine, he didn't pay at all—

JOSEPH: *He* didn't, I'm sure.

PABLO: —his family didn't pay anything for the funeral. The City—

JOSEPH (*interrupting*): With the new Mayor the rules are different. Too many of you guys took advantage of free burials. (*He studies him.*) But what's bothering you? Are you worried about something?

PABLO: Nothing. I'm sure you're just trying to frighten me and—

JOSEPH: *Frighten* you? Who gives a damn about you? Whatever you've decided, you've well decided. And I, after all, don't think you should worry so much.

PABLO: Why?

JOSEPH: I'm sure you've considered everything . . . taken everything into account, thought about it.

PABLO: About what?

JOSEPH: Your daughter.

PABLO: What do you mean?

JOSEPH: She's just twelve and . . . already an attractive little figure . . .

PABLO: So what?

JOSEPH: She'll find some rich customers.

PABLO: You're a louse! (JOSEPH *instinctively draws his revolver.*) Shoot! (PABLO *stretches out his arms.*) This way we'll get it over with sooner!

JOSEPH: Nobody calls *me* a louse!

PABLO: I call you that again. Louse! (*He stretches out his arms again, offers himself as a target.*)

(JOSEPH *raises his revolver and aims at* PABLO)

PABLO: Go ahead, shoot!

JOSEPH (*after reflection, lowering his revolver*): You'd like that, wouldn't you? That way the guilt would be on *my* shoulders.

PABLO: You deserve it.

JOSEPH: And you wouldn't have to take that final step. You're a coward.

PABLO: Because I haven't jumped yet?

JOSEPH: And for everything else. I told you Maria would find rich customers because it always ends up that way. I've come across more than one like her.

PABLO: What do you mean, "like her"?

JOSEPH: In a French whorehouse for instance. Years ago. I took a very young girl—same eyes as your daughter. After we were through, we talked for a while. She was the daughter of a Red executed by the Germans.

PABLO (*angry*): I'm *not* a Red! How can I make you understand?

JOSEPH: That's the way all daughters of radicals wind up. In a whorehouse!

PABLO (*furious*): I'm *no* radical!

JOSEPH: All right, then. All daughters of bums. Is that better? In a whorehouse.

PABLO (*upset*): Not Maria . . . They'll go back to Puerto Rico and—

JOSEPH (*interrupting*): She will find customers there too. They'll pay less but—

PABLO: That's enough, you dirty . . . !

JOSEPH: What are you getting so excited about? You're dead and buried. You won't see anything, you won't feel anything.

PABLO: I've never met a bastard like you before!

JOSEPH: *I'm* the bastard? Look who's talking!

PABLO: Damn you! If I had— (*He wrings his hands.*)

JOSEPH: You want my gun? Here! (*He puts it down beside him.*) Only with a gun would you have the guts to face anyone.

PABLO: Put it in the middle of the bridge and then go back to your place.

JOSEPH: I suffer from heights. That's why I sat down here. (*He points to the gun beside him.*) You're as good as dead anyway. So you can risk your useless life.

PABLO: I'm more useful than you! More honest! I've worked all my life!

JOSEPH (*ironical*): That's great! And here's the result. Look at you!

PABLO: I . . . I . . . (*He can't find words.*) I can't believe that you . . .

JOSEPH: That I—what?

PABLO: That you can talk like that. It's inhuman.

JOSEPH: That's psychology. All I need is to look at your face. You, a typical bum. Your daughter, a typical—

PABLO (*violent*): Leave my daughter out of this!

JOSEPH (*suddenly noticing that someone is climbing up*): Take it easy, friend, take it easy! The Lieutenant is coming. (*He buttons up his shirt and puts away his gun. The police* LIEUTENANT *appears near* JOSEPH.)

LIEUTENANT: Well? Where do we stand?

JOSEPH: We were talking about his children, his wife . . . (*to* PABLO) Right? (PABLO *does not answer.*) He's very attached to his family . . . Especially his daughter.

LIEUTENANT: Should we bring her up here?

PABLO (*promptly*): No!

JOSEPH: He's afraid that something might happen to her. He's coming down . . . (*He instinctively gestures a jump; he corrects the gesture to indicate descent.*)

LIEUTENANT: Are you sure?

JOSEPH: I'm doing my best.

LIEUTENANT: Please. If you fail again, I'll be demoted.

JOSEPH: Leave it to me.

LIEUTENANT: Is he difficult?

JOSEPH: Yes and no . . . I'll achieve my purpose, don't worry.

LIEUTENANT: *Our* purpose.

JOSEPH: Of course!

LIEUTENANT (*to* PABLO): Hello, Young Man! (*He waves and smiles.*)

JOSEPH (*to the* LIEUTENANT): His name is Pablo.

LIEUTENANT: Hello Pablo! How're you doing? (PABLO *does not answer.*) We have some cokes down below! Nice and cold! And your family, they're all upset! Come on, like a good sport. (PABLO *ignores him. The* LIEUTENANT *whispers something to* JOSEPH.)

JOSEPH (*to the* LIEUTENANT): You can depend on me.

LIEUTENANT: Please . . . (*He descends, disappears.*)

JOSEPH (*to* PABLO): He's only worried about being demoted. Hypocrite!

PABLO: Less hypocrite than you! You lied to him.

JOSEPH: Me?

PABLO: You made him believe that you were doing your best to . . .

JOSEPH: To what?

PABLO: To get me to come down.

JOSEPH: It's useless with a headstrong fool like you.

PABLO: Why did you lie to him?

JOSEPH: I told him that . . . we talked about your family. That's no lie, is it? And that you're partial to your eldest child. Isn't that right?

PABLO: She isn't my firstborn.

JOSEPH (*surprised*): You never told me that! (*reflecting*) She seemed to be the tallest.

PABLO: My firstborn is a boy. He's fourteen now.

JOSEPH: Your family keeps growing. You see? I was right. The only thing you people know how to do is to manufacture children. Where is he? I didn't see him down there with the rest of them.

PABLO: I left him in Puerto Rico. With his grandfather.

JOSEPH: You should have all remained there. Only ungrateful people and parasites leave their native country.

PABLO: Your Government made me an American citizen.

JOSEPH: Nobody asked for my advice.

PABLO: You come to us with your chewing gum, your Coca-Cola. You give us passports with your American eagle and then—

JOSEPH: What else do you want? New York City?

PABLO: The freedom you promise. The right to travel, to come to America.

JOSEPH: But why do all of you come here? Take a trip in your own country. You must have some interesting sights there too!

PABLO: If Rome conquers a neighbor, the neighbor goes to Rome. It's natural.

JOSEPH: Conquests would stop if all the slaves descended on the Capital.

PABLO: This is not the Capital.

JOSEPH: It is. This city pays the highest salaries in the world.

PABLO: For those who can get work.

JOSEPH: Specialize at something and you'll find work.

PABLO: How?

JOSEPH: That's *your* problem.

PABLO: You see? In this world nobody helps you.

JOSEPH: I'm not your brother! Go to the Police Headquarters if you need help.

PABLO: And there I'll find somebody like you. I'll be lucky if he doesn't beat me up.

JOSEPH: Have you ever gone to *my* Precinct?

PABLO: No.

JOSEPH: Try before criticizing.

PABLO: If they're all like you—

JOSEPH: We're different. On this side of the bridge—those who believe in Law and Order. On that side of the bridge—your kind, bums full of hostility.

Your suicide is the only contribution to Society. Happy landing, amigo! (*He points down; then he looks at his watch.*) It's getting late. I have an appointment . . .

PABLO: With the Ku Klux Klan, I bet!

JOSEPH: Not exactly. I'm going to the K.A.W.

PABLO: What's that?

JOSEPH: "Keep America White." You Latins—and the blacks, and the yellows, you're mongrelizing us. We must fight to survive. That's why no pure Aryan ever commits suicide.

PABLO: You're a Nazi.

JOSEPH: Do you know that's almost a compliment?

PABLO: I bet you've got a picture of Hitler hanging on the wall.

JOSEPH: No. He's in a drawer. It's a good picture, and I didn't want to throw it away.

PABLO (*incredulous*): I can't believe it. Are you serious?

JOSEPH: Of course I am. I've always admired Hitler. He believed in the superiority of the Aryan race. I am for the superiority of the Aryan race. He was for a New Order. I am a guardian of Order. And if I had something to say about it . . . it would be a New and Total Order, I assure you!

PABLO: You're a Fascist!

JOSEPH: That word is out. Commies like you have succeeded in making it sound like poison.

PABLO: I'm *not* a Commie!

JOSEPH: What else can a bum with five kids be?

PABLO: I'll sue you.

JOSEPH: Postmortem?

PABLO: I'm still alive.

JOSEPH: For how long?

PABLO: As long as I wish.

JOSEPH: You heathen! You even dare to take the place of Our Lord! (*ironically*) "As long as I wish." As long as *Our Lord* wishes! (*He looks up and crosses himself.*)

PABLO: *I*'m the judge of this day.

JOSEPH: And you've decided. Have a nice trip!

PABLO: I'll stay here as long as I want.

JOSEPH (*looking at his watch*): It's getting late.

PABLO: I'll see to it that you don't keep your appointment. People like you should be forbidden from meeting.

JOSEPH: Are you forgetting that this is a free country?

PABLO: I'll keep you here as long as I like.

JOSEPH: That's not fair. What I told you is confidential. . . . Please . . . (*He indicates he should jump.*)

PABLO: I'll stay as long as I like!

JOSEPH: You see? People like you can't be trusted! I was being friendly!

PABLO: "Friendly"? God help me!

JOSEPH: You can't trust anybody in this world!

PABLO: You're right.

JOSEPH: Especially half-breeds . . . (*He studies* PABLO.) You don't look like you'd have any Jewish blood. . . . Probably there's some Negro in you. . . . In Puerto Rico you're all half-Negro.

PABLO: Nazi!

JOSEPH: Why? Because I'm honest and tell you the truth? Let's stop pretending with each other. There's a superior race and inferior races. *We* have only two children. They're educated to lead. You boast about having five, six. There is no limit to how many. Then you commit suicide. Those children are left to us. Ignorant and defenseless. "An inferior race."

PABLO: People like you shouldn't exist.

JOSEPH: Let's face it. We not only exist. We rule. And there is never a suicide among us. (*looking again at his watch*) Please, amigo, it's getting late. . . . (*He looks below.*) And I'm beginning to feel dizzy. . . .

PABLO: It would be very funny if it were you who lost your balance and . . . (*points down*)

JOSEPH: Funny? (*He crosses his fingers.*) You have a morbid sense of humor! I've got a wife and two children!

PABLO: Do you really think your family is superior to mine?

JOSEPH: Can you even doubt it? We have genetic, intellectual, and moral superiority.

PABLO (*incredulous*): You must be joking!

JOSEPH: I'm definitively not joking! Now please . . . (*He points down.*) Bon voyage, amigo!

PABLO: You promised the Lieutenant to—

JOSEPH: Promises. I'm fickle like a sailor. I was in the Navy. What about you?

PABLO: Infantry.

JOSEPH: That figures.

PABLO: Your army was happy to get me.

JOSEPH: Who else would we send to the front line? You and the Negroes are ideal for that.

LIEUTENANT (*offstage, his voice coming from below*): Well, have you made up your mind? We're blocking traffic here!

JOSEPH (*shouting*): He's coming right down! We're discussing our glorious army! Our friend Pablo was in the Infantry!

LIEUTENANT (*offstage, from below; rhetorical*): Three cheers for the Infantry!

PABLO: You hypocrite!

JOSEPH: Whatever you want, but make up your mind. Did you notice how subtle I was? I said, "He's coming right down!" I didn't lie. You're going down either way.

PABLO: I've never met anyone like you. Never. You're inhuman.

JOSEPH: Me, inhuman? You must be joking. Look. I'll prove to you that I'm not only kind but a friend. If you get it over with quickly (*He points below.*), I'll make a deal with you.

PABLO: What deal?

JOSEPH: First of all, I won't tell a soul that you're a Red. That way your family—

PABLO: I'm *not* a Red! You bastard—

JOSEPH (*ignoring him*): —your family will get sympathy and help. There'll be more money for that mess of your wife and for the five brats. And . . . there's something else . . . (*He hesitates.*)

PABLO: What?

JOSEPH: You're so sensitive on this subject that I don't know how to put it . . . (*He hesitates.*)

PABLO: Go on.

JOSEPH: We're friends now, right?

PABLO: God help me!

JOSEPH: You must admit you've gotten to know me a little—

PABLO: Yes, I know you. I thought they took care of your kind for good.

JOSEPH: We? The Master Race, born to lead? You're wrong.

PABLO: No. I'm not wrong.

JOSEPH: Well, do you want to hear the second part of my deal? Yes or no?

PABLO: Go on, Superman.

JOSEPH: Better Superman than a Red bum and a suicide, too! This is what I propose. . . . If you jump now and let me get to my meeting (*He looks at his watch again.*) I promise you—my word of honor—that I'll take care of your daughter.

PABLO (*tense*): What do you mean by that?

JOSEPH: She has a charming little figure and sad, sad eyes. . . . Once she recovers from this shock (*He indicates the jump.*), I'll protect her.

PABLO: From whom?

JOSEPH: From the world. You know how things are. Would you rather have her fall into the hands of some pimp? Isn't it better with somebody you know?

PABLO (*with hatred*): Are you telling me . . . ?

JOSEPH: She'll have a better start with a respectable man like me.

PABLO: You're a worm.

JOSEPH: Let's be reasonable. Try to be calm and objective. Not a Latin father. . . .

PABLO: Bastard!

JOSEPH (*ignoring him*): She'll be better off with someone like me. At least you know me and . . . maybe admire me . . . (PABLO *spits.*)

JOSEPH: Did you see? It dissolved halfway down. You won't dissolve halfway down. Would you prefer that?

PABLO (*with determination*): I'll denounce you! You're a disgrace to the police, to America, to the white race! You're the most sadistic bastard alive! I'll tell them what you really are! (*He is now determined to have* JOSEPH *denounced; he has forgotten about his suicide and prepares to descend.*)

JOSEPH (*worried*): But I was being friendly . . . What I told you is very confidential. . . .

PABLO: As long as there are people like you around, no one is safe! It's true; only a coward gives up and escapes. We must defend ourselves with every weapon. And life—even my life—is a useful weapon.

(*He descends and disappears.* JOSEPH *is alone now. His face is relaxed and relieved. He has become "human" now. He takes out a small walkie-talkie.*)

JOSEPH (*into the walkie-talkie*): It's all right. He's on his way down. . . . He'll accuse me of everything in the book. Promise him that we'll have a confrontation. . . . tomorrow morning. . . . I'm too tired today. . . .

(*The* LIEUTENANT *reappears beside* JOSEPH. *He has the same type of walkie-talkie. Evidently, he has heard everything.*)

LIEUTENANT: You're great, Joe! You're the most valuable man I have! You save them all!

JOSEPH (*with sadness and frustration*): All?

LIEUTENANT (*ignoring*): Your performance was perfect. Precise and effective. You were in top form today. You'd have convinced a corpse.

JOSEPH: Did you hear everything?

LIEUTENANT: From beginning to end. (*indicates his walkie-talkie*)

JOSEPH: Did I seem sincere?

LIEUTENANT: Completely.

JOSEPH: On every point?

LIEUTENANT: On every point.

JOSEPH (*almost to himself*): It no longer sounds like an act.. . .

LIEUTENANT: Not at all!

JOSEPH (*bitterly*): When one lies professionally, one learns to lie well.

LIEUTENANT: By the way, what made you say "nine hundred thousand" Indonesians? I've heard that only three hundred thousand were killed.

JOSEPH: I read it in a British newspaper. They always tell the truth.

LIEUTENANT (*after a brief pause*): It's a delicate subject. I don't think you should have—

JOSEPH (*sarcastic*): Any other complaints?

LIEUTENANT: Oh no! The essential thing is to save a life. Saving nine lives out of ten is an impressive record. You're the only one in this city who can do it. I must admit your method is infallible.

JOSEPH: No method is infallible.

LIEUTENANT: Are you still thinking of that poor old Jew?

(JOSEPH *nods.*)

JOSEPH: I shouldn't have made him believe I was a Nazi. It was a tragic mistake. I can still see his eyes. . . . There was terror in them. . . . He saw a real Nazi in me.

LIEUTENANT: He was very old and very tired. Too many months in that concentration camp. It was hopeless. Nobody could have saved him.

JOSEPH (*bitterly*): Maybe I'm too convincing. If you preach hatred, it gets into your blood.

LIEUTENANT: But you save their lives! That's what counts!

JOSEPH: Do you think I'm really becoming a Nazi?

LIEUTENANT: Nonsense! It's ridiculous!

JOSEPH: They believe me. They hate me.

LIEUTENANT: You've learned your role well. That's all. And you've put your heart and soul into your work. That's why you've succeeded. You'll be getting another medal, your ninth. . . . (*He studies* JOSEPH.) And there'll be a tenth, too, I'm sure.

JOSEPH (*slowly, almost to himself*): I reminded him of his past . . . a terrifying past. . . . He was frightened. . . . (*to the* LIEUTENANT) Is it really the past? Behind us forever?

LIEUTENANT: Forever.

JOSEPH: Then why was he so terrified? Why did he kill himself?

LIEUTENANT: Forget it, Joe. Don't poison your life with the memory of an old man who was doomed anyway. Think of the young people you've saved. Nine lives! Think of those nine families that are grateful to you! . . . And now, let's go down.

(*a silence.* JOSEPH *is far away in his own thoughts.*)

Aren't you coming down?

JOSEPH: Just a few more minutes. . . . The air is so pure up here. . . .

LIEUTENANT: As you wish. (*He pats* JOSEPH's *knee with understanding.*)

(*The* LIEUTENANT *descends, disappears.* JOSEPH *remains alone. He closes his eyes and takes in the quiet and pure air of that height.*)

SLOW BLACKOUT

About Love

Love has many faces. Because the emotion is at once our most common and yet our most intense, love's many faces are often used as dramatic subject matter. Therefore, we have love comedies and love tragedies and numerous kinds of love plays which fall in between. Just as there are different kinds of love plays, there are different kinds of love: puppy love, parent love, brother love, married love, courtship love, love of nature, love of money, love of love. The combinations are endless and the subjects are unlimited.

Given all the possible combinations, it is impossible to define the "love theme." As a compromise, we have chosen four plays about one aspect of Love, dealt with in a similar tone—courtship in a light, humorous fashion.

When we experience it, courtship is a very serious thing. Yet, when we observe others courting, it seems humorous. Apparently, we are able to see ourselves in the courtship situation, and as a testament to our objectivity we are able to laugh. The situation never seems to lose its relevance, for we can all remember various aspects of our courting. More often than not, those aspects were humorous.

Pyramus and Thisbe has a sad ending; yet the courtship is funny because of the circumstances. Circumstances often affect courtship. In *Here We Are,* the couple is newly married, but are definitely still courting one another. This play is about the complications and results of a successful courtship. *The Golden Axe* concerns a courtship situation and how it is resolved through an unlikely kind of love—love of nature. *Sunday Costs Five Pesos* is about a triangle courtship in a foreign country. This kind of courtship may seem strange, but it is nonetheless humorous, for the triangle situation is familiar to us all.

Love, then, has many faces. This section shows you part of one of the faces. The face is smiling.

Here We Are

DOROTHY PARKER

Characters

HE

SHE

Reading Guides

1. In *Here We Are* the pauses are as significant as the dialogue. Much of the humor comes from what the two people are thinking, not from what they are saying.

2. Many of the lines in this play have double meanings. Be aware of them and you will enjoy the humor more fully.

SCENE: *A compartment in a Pullman car. He is storing the suitcases in the rack and hanging up coats. She is primping. He finishes disposing of the luggage and sits.*

HE: Well!

SHE: Well!

HE: Well, here we are.

SHE: Here we are, aren't we?

HE: Eeyop. I should say we are. Here we are.

SHE: Well!

HE: Well! Well! How does it feel to be an old married lady?

SHE: Oh, it's too soon to ask me that. At least—I mean. Well, I mean, goodness, we've only been married about three hours, haven't we?

HE: We have been married exactly two hours and twenty-six minutes.

SHE: My, it seems like longer.

HE: No, it isn't hardly half-past six yet.

SHE: It seems like later. I guess it's because it starts getting dark so early.

HE: It does, at that. The nights are going to be pretty long from now on. I mean. I mean—well, it starts getting dark early.

SHE: I didn't have any idea what time it was. Everything was so mixed up, I sort of don't know where I am, or what it's all about. Getting back from the church, and then all those people, and then changing all my clothes, and then everybody throwing things, and all. Goodness, I don't see how people do it every day.

HE: Do what?

SHE: Get married. When you think of all the people, all over the world, getting married just as if it was nothing. Chinese people and everybody. Just as if it wasn't anything.

HE: Well, let's not worry about people all over the world. Let's don't think about a lot of Chinese. We've got something better to think about. I mean. I mean—well, what do we care about them?

SHE: I know, but I just sort of got to thinking of them, all of them, all over everywhere, doing it all the time. At least, I mean—getting married, you know. And it's—well, it's sort of such a big thing to do, it makes you feel queer. You think of them, all of them, all doing it just like it wasn't anything. And how does anybody know what's going to happen next?

HE: Let them worry; we don't have to. We know darn well what's going to happen next. I mean—well, we know it's going to be great. Well, we know we're going to be happy. Don't we?

SHE: Oh, of course. Only you think of all the people, and you have to sort of keep thinking. It makes you feel funny. An awful lot of people that get married, it doesn't turn out so well. And I guess they all must have thought it was going to be great.

HE: Aw, come on, now, this is no way to start a honeymoon, with all this thinking going on. Look at us—all married and everything done. I mean. The wedding all done and all.

SHE: Ah, it was nice, wasn't it? Did you really like my veil?

HE: You looked great, just great.

SHE: Oh, I'm terribly glad. Ellie and Louise looked lovely, didn't they? I'm terribly glad they did finally decide on pink. They looked perfectly lovely.

HE: Listen, I want to tell you something. When I was standing up there in that old church waiting for you to come up, and I saw those two bridesmaids, I thought to myself, I thought, "Well, I never knew Louise could look like that!" I thought she'd have knocked anybody's eye out.

SHE: Oh, really? Funny. Of course, everybody thought her dress and hat were lovely, but a lot of people seemed to think she looked sort of tired. People have been saying that a lot, lately. I tell them I think it's awfully mean of them to go around saying that about her. I tell them they've got to remember that Louise isn't so terribly young any more, and they've got to expect her to look like that. Louise can say she's twenty-three all she wants to, but she's a good deal nearer twenty-seven.

HE: Well, she was certainly a knockout at the wedding. Boy!

SHE: I'm terribly glad you thought so. I'm glad someone did. How did you think Ellie looked?

HE: Why, I honestly didn't get a look at her.

SHE: Oh, really? Well, I certainly think that's too bad. I don't suppose I ought to say it about my own sister, but I never saw anybody look as beautiful as Ellie looked today. And always so sweet and unselfish, too. And you didn't even notice her. But you never pay attention to Ellie, anyway. Don't think I haven't noticed it. It makes me feel just terrible. It makes me feel just awful that you don't like my own sister.

HE: I do so like her! I'm crazy for Ellie. I think she's a great kid.

SHE: Don't think it makes any difference to Ellie! Ellie's got enough people crazy about her. It isn't anything to her whether you like her or not. Don't flatter yourself she cares! Only, the only thing is, it makes it awfully hard for me you don't like her, that's the only thing. I keep thinking, when we come back and get in the apartment and everything, it's going to be awfully hard for me that you won't want all my family around. I know how you feel about my family. Don't think I haven't seen it. Only, if you don't ever want to see them, that's your loss. Not theirs. Don't flatter yourself!

HE: Oh, now, come on! What's all this talk about not wanting your family around? Why, you know how I feel about your family. I think your old lady—I think your mother's swell. And Ellie. And your father. What's all this talk?

SHE: Well, I've seen it. Don't think I haven't. Lots of people they get married, and they think it's going to be great and everything, and then it all goes to pieces because people don't like people's families, or something like that. Don't tell me! I've seen it happen.

HE: Honey, what is all this? What are you getting all angry about? Hey, look, this is our honeymoon. What are you trying to start a fight for? Ah, I guess you're just feeling sort of nervous.

SHE: Me? What have I got to be nervous about? I mean. I mean, goodness, I'm not nervous.

HE: You know, lots of times, they say that girls get kind of nervous and yippy on account of thinking about—I mean. I mean—well, it's like you said, things are all so sort of mixed up and everything, right now. But afterwards, it'll be all right. I mean. I mean—well, look, honey, you don't look any too comfortable. Don't you want to take your hat off? And let's don't ever fight, ever. Will we?

SHE: Ah, I'm sorry I was cross. I guess I did feel a little bit funny. All mixed up, and then thinking of all those people all over everywhere, and then being sort of 'way off here, all alone with you. It's so sort of different. It's sort of such a big thing. You can't blame a person for thinking, can you? Yes, don't let's ever, ever fight. We won't be like a whole lot of them. We won't fight or be nasty or anything. Will we?

HE: You bet your life we won't.

SHE: I guess I will take this darned old hat off. It kind of presses. Just put it up on the rack, will you, dear? Do you like it, sweetheart?

HE: Looks good on you.

SHE: No, but I mean, do you really like it?

HE: Well, I'll tell you, I know this is the new style and everything like that, and it's probably great. I don't know anything about things like that. Only I like the kind of a hat like that blue hat you had. Gee, I like that hat.

SHE: Oh, really? Well, that's nice. That's lovely. The first thing you say to me, as soon as you get me off on a train away from my family and everything, is that you don't like my hat. The first thing you say to your wife is you think she has terrible taste in hats. That's nice, isn't it?

HE: Now, honey, I never said anything like that. I only said—

SHE: What you don't seem to realize is this hat cost twenty-two dollars. Twenty-two dollars. And that horrible old blue thing you think you're so crazy about, that cost three ninety-five.

HE: I don't give a darn what they cost. I only said—I said I liked that blue hat. I don't know anything about hats. I'll be crazy about this one as soon as

I get used to it. Only it's kind of not like your other hats. I don't know about the new styles. What do I know about women's hats?

SHE: It's too bad you didn't marry somebody that would get the kind of hats you'd like. Hats that cost three ninety-five. Why didn't you marry Louise? You always think she looks so beautiful. You'd love her taste in hats. Why didn't you marry her?

HE: Ah, now, honey, for heaven's sakes!

SHE: Why didn't you marry her? All you've done, ever since we got on this train, is talk about her. Here I've sat and sat, and just listened to you saying how wonderful Louise is. I suppose that's nice, getting me off here all alone with you, and then raving about Louise right in front of my face. Why didn't you ask her to marry you? I'm sure she would have jumped at the chance. There aren't so many people asking her to marry them. It's too bad you didn't marry her. I'm sure you'd have been much happier.

HE: Listen, baby, while you're talking about things like that, why didn't you marry Joe Brooks? I suppose he could have given you all the twenty-two-dollar hats you wanted, I suppose!

SHE: Well, I'm not so sure I'm not sorry I didn't. There! Joe Brooks wouldn't have waited until he got me all off alone and then sneered at my taste in clothes. Joe Brooks wouldn't ever hurt my feelings. Joe Brooks has always been fond of me.

HE: Yeah, he's fond of you. He was so fond of you he didn't even send a wedding present. That's how fond of you he was.

SHE: I happen to know for a fact that he was away on business, and as soon as he comes back he's going to give me anything I want for the apartment.

HE: Listen, I don't want anything he gives you in our apartment. Anything he gives you, I'll throw right out the window. That's what I think of your friend Joe Brooks. And how do you know where he is and what he's going to do, anyway? Has he been writing to you?

SHE: I suppose my friends can correspond with me. I didn't hear there was any law against that.

HE: Well, I suppose they can't! And what do you think of that? I'm not going to have my wife getting a lot of letters from cheap traveling salesmen!

SHE: Joe Brooks is not a cheap traveling salesman! He is not! He gets a wonderful salary.

HE: Oh yeah? Where did you hear that?

SHE: He told me so himself.

HE: Oh, he told you so himself. I see. He told you so himself.

SHE: You've got a lot of right to talk about Joe Brooks. You and your friend Louise. All you ever talk about is Louise.

HE: Oh, for heaven's sakes! What do I care about Louise? I just thought she was a friend of yours, that's all. That's why I ever noticed her.

SHE: Well, you certainly took an awful lot of notice of her today. On our wedding day! You said yourself when you were standing there in the church you just kept thinking of her. Right up at the altar. Oh, right in the presence of God! And all you thought about was Louise.

HE: Listen, honey, I never should have said that. How does anybody know what kind of crazy things come into their heads when they're standing there waiting to get married? I was just telling you that because it was so kind of crazy. I thought it would make you laugh.

SHE: I know, I've been all sort of mixed up today, too. I told you that. Everything so strange and everything. And me all the time thinking about all those people all over the world, and now us here all alone, and everything. I know you get all mixed up. Only I did think, when you kept talking about how beautiful Louise looked, you did it with malice and forethought.

HE: I never did anything with malice and forethought! I just told you that about Louise because I thought it would make you laugh.

SHE: Well, it didn't.

HE: No, I know it didn't. It certainly did not. Ah, baby, and we ought to be laughing, too. Hell, honey lamb, this is our honeymoon. What's the matter?

SHE: I don't know. We used to squabble a lot when we were going together and then engaged and everything, but I thought everything would be so different as soon as you were married. And now I feel so sort of strange and everything. I feel so sort of alone.

HE: Well, you see, sweetheart, we're not really married yet. I mean. I mean—well, things will be different afterwards. Oh, hell. I mean, we haven't been married very long.

SHE: No.

HE: Well, we haven't got much longer to wait now. I mean—well, we'll be in New York in about twenty minutes. Then we can have dinner, and sort of see what we feel like doing. Or, I mean—is there anything special you want to do tonight?

SHE: What?

HE: What I mean to say, would you like to go to a show or something?

SHE: Why, whatever you like. I sort of didn't think people went to theaters and things on their—I mean, I've got a couple of letters I simply must write. Don't let me forget.

HE: Oh, you're going to write letters tonight?

SHE: Well, you see, I've been perfectly terrible. What with all the excitement and everything. I never did thank poor old Mrs. Sprague for her berry spoon, and I never did a thing about those book ends the McMasters sent. It's just too awful of me. I've got to write them this very night.

HE: And when you've finished writing your letters, maybe I could get you a magazine or a bag of peanuts.

SHE: What?

HE: I mean, I wouldn't want you to be bored.

SHE: As if I could be bored with you! Silly! Aren't we married? Bored!

HE: What I thought, I thought when we got in, we could go right up to the Biltmore and anyway leave our bags, and maybe have a little dinner in the room, kind of quiet, and then do whatever we wanted. I mean. I mean—well, let's go right up there from the station.

SHE: Oh, yes, let's. I'm so glad we're going to the Biltmore. I just love it. The twice I've stayed in New York we've always stayed there, Papa and Mamma and Ellie and I, and I was crazy about it. I always sleep so well there. I go right off to sleep the minute I put my head on the pillow.

HE: Oh, you do?

SHE: At least, I mean, 'way up high it's so quiet.

HE: We might go to some show or other tomorrow night instead of tonight. Don't you think that would be better?

SHE: Yes, I think it might.

HE: Do you really have to write those letters tonight?

SHE: Well, I don't suppose they'd get there any quicker than if I wrote them tomorrow.

HE: And we won't ever fight any more, will we?

SHE: Oh, no. Not ever! I don't know what made me do like that. It all got so sort of funny, sort of like a nightmare, the way I got thinking of all those people getting married all the time; and so many of them, everything spoils on account of fighting and everything. I got all mixed up thinking about them. Oh, I don't want to be like them. But we won't be, will we?

HE: Sure we won't.

SHE: We won't go all to pieces. We won't fight. It'll all be different, now we're married. It'll all be lovely. Reach me down my hat, will you, sweetheart? It's time I was putting it on. Thanks. Ah, I'm sorry you don't like it.

HE: I do so like it!

SHE: You said you didn't. You said you thought it was perfectly terrible.

HE: I never said any such thing. You're crazy.

SHE: All right, I may be crazy. Thank you very much. But that's what you said. Not that it matters—it's just a little thing. But it makes you feel pretty funny to think you've gone and married somebody that says you have perfectly terrible taste in hats. And then goes and says you're crazy, besides.

HE: Now, listen here, nobody said any such thing. Why, I love that hat. The more I look at it the better I like it. I think it's great.

SHE: That isn't what you said before.

HE: Honey, stop it, will you? What do you want to start all this for? I love the damned hat. I mean, I love your hat. I love anything you wear. What more do you want me to say?

SHE: Well, I don't want you to say it like that.

HE: I said I think it's great. That's all I said.

SHE: Do you really? Do you honestly? Ah, I'm so glad. I'd hate you not to like my hat. It would be—I don't know, it would be sort of such a bad start.

HE: Well, I'm crazy for it. Now we've got that settled, for heaven's sakes. Ah, baby. Baby lamb. We're not going to have any bad starts. Look at us—we're on our honeymoon. Pretty soon we'll be regular old married people. I mean. I mean, in a few minutes we'll be getting in to New York, and then we'll be going to the hotel, and then everything will be all right. I mean—well, look at us! Here we are married! Here we are!

SHE: Yes, here we are, aren't we?

CURTAIN

Pyramus and Thisbe

WILLIAM SHAKESPEARE

Characters

THESEUS, *King of Athens*
HIPPOLYTA, *Queen of Athens*
COURTIER
QUINCE
PYRAMUS
THISBE
WALL
LION
MOONSHINE

Reading Guides

1. Don't be frightened by Shakespeare. He does, after all, write in English. Reading him, when you're not used to it, requires more concentration, but once you have passed that barrier, you will find delight in his words.

2. *Pyramus and Thisbe* is part of *A Midsummer Night's Dream.* It is a play within a play. In fact, it is a farce within a comedy. Quince, Bottom, Flute, Snout, Snug, and Starveling are characters in *A Midsummer Night's Dream* who perform the play *Pyramus and Thisbe* for Theseus and Hippolyta. They play the following roles: Quince, *a carpenter* (Prologue); Bottom, *a weaver* (Pyramus); Flute, *a bellowsmender* (Thisbe); Snout, *a tinker* (Wall); Snug, *a joiner* (Lion); and Starveling, *a tailor* (Moonshine).

3. If you read the prologue carefully (Quince's opening speech), you will find that he tells the whole story even before the play begins. From that point on you can enjoy the characters' bumbling, rough attempts at acting and speaking. Read the words carefully, for Shakespeare has great fun with these characters and their mistakes.

ATHENS. *The palace of* THESEUS. *A company of workmen (guild) are about to perform a play for* THESEUS, *King of Athens, and his new bride* HIPPOLYTA *as a celebration of their wedding. The workmen are not experienced actors. They are very clumsy and awkward with the dialogue and the actions, but they mean well. They are dressed in homespun clothes.*

THESEUS *and* HIPPOLYTA *enter and take their places. They are followed by the court retinue.*

COURTIER (*to* THESEUS): So please your Grace, the Prologue is address'd.
THESEUS: Let him approach.

(*trumpet flourish*)
(QUINCE *enters to deliver the prologue to the play.*)

QUINCE: If we offend, it is with our goodwill
That you should think, we come not to offend,
But with goodwill. To show our simple skill
That is the true beginning of our end.
Consider then we come but in despite.
We do not come as minding to content you,
Our true intent is. All for your delight
We are not here. That you should here repent you,
The actors are at hand, and by their show
You shall know all that you are like to know.

(*Trumpet flourish.* PYRAMUS, THISBE, WALL, MOONSHINE, *and* LION *enter. These parts are all played by men.* QUINCE *introduces them.*)

QUINCE: Gentles, perchance you wonder at this show;
But wonder on till truth make all things plain.
This man is Pyramus, if you would know;
This beauteous lady Thisby is certain.
This man, with lime and roughcast, does present
Wall, that vile Wall which did these lovers sunder;
And through Wall's chink, poor souls, they are content
To whisper. At which let no man wonder.
This man, with lantern, dog, and bush of thorn,
Presenteth Moonshine; for, if you will know,
By moonshine did these lovers think no scorn
To meet at Ninus' tomb, there, there to woo.

This grisly beast, which Lion hight by name,
The trusty Thisby, coming first by night,
Did scare away, or rather did afright;
And, as she fled, her mantle she did fall,
Which Lion vile with bloody mouth did stain.
Anon comes Pyramus, sweet youth and tall
And finds his trusty Thisby's mantle slain;
Whereat, with blade, with bloody blameful blade,
He bravely broach'd his boiling bloody breast;
And Thisby, tarrying in mulberry shade,
His dagger drew and died. For all the rest,
Let Lion, Moonshine, Wall, and lovers twain
At large discourse, while here they do remain.

(*They all exit except for* WALL.)

WALL (*He stands in the middle of the stage holding out two fingers spread apart like scissors.*): In this same
interlude it doth befall
That I, one Snout by name, present a wall;
And such a wall, as I would have you think,
That had in it a crannied hole or chink,
Through which the lovers, Pyramus and Thisby,
Did whisper often very secretly.
This loam, this roughcast, and this stone doth show
That I am that same wall; the truth is so;
And this the cranny is, right and sinister,
Through which the fearful lovers are to whisper.

(PYRAMUS *enters and goes to* WALL.)

PYRAMUS: O grim-looked night! O night with hue so black
O night, which ever art when day is not
O night, O night! Alack, alack, alack,
I fear my Thisby's promise is forgot
And thou, O Wall, O sweet, O lovely Wall,
That stand'st between her father's ground and mine!
Thou Wall, O Wall, O sweet and lovely Wall,
Show me thy chink, to blink through with mine eyne!

(WALL *holds up his fingers and* PYRAMUS *looks through.*)

Thanks, courteous Wall; Jove shield thee well for this!
But what see I? No Thisby do I see.
O wicked Wall, through whom I see no bliss!
Curs'd be thy stones for thus deceiving me!

(THISBE *enters and goes to* WALL.)

THISBE: O Wall, full often has thou heard my moans,
For parting my fair Pyramus and me!
My cherry lips have often kiss'd thy stones,
Thy stones with lime and hair knit up in thee.
PYRAMUS: I see a voice! Now will I go to the chink,
To spy and I can hear my Thisby's face.

(*He looks through* WALL'S *fingers again.*)

Thisby!
THISBE (*looking through* WALL'S *fingers from the other side*): My love, thou art my love, I think.
PYRAMUS: Think what thou wilt, I am thy lover's grace;
And, like Limander, am I trusty still.
THISBE: And I like Helen, till the Fates me kill.
PYRAMUS: Not Shafalus to Procrus was so true.
THISBE: As Shafalus to Procrus, I to you.
PYRAMUS: O, kiss me through the hole of this vile wall!
THISBE: I kiss the wall's hole, not your lips at all.
PYRAMUS: Wilt thou at Ninny's tomb meet me straightway?
THISBE: 'Tide life, 'tide death, I come without delay.

(PYRAMUS *and* THISBE *exit in different directions.*)

WALL: Thus have I, Wall, my part discharged so;
And, being done, thus Wall away doth go.

(WALL *exits.*)
(LION *and* MOONSHINE *enter.*)

LION (*to the audience*): You, ladies, you, whose gentle hearts do fear
The smallest monstrous mouse that creeps on floor,
May now perchance both quake and tremble here,
When Lion rough in wildest rage doth roar.

Then know that I, as Snug the joiner, am
A lion fell, nor else no lion's dam;
For, if I should as Lion come in strife
Into this place, 'twere pity on my life.

MOONSHINE (*stepping forward to speak to the audience. He is carrying a lantern and a thornbush, and is leading a dog.*): This
lantern doth the horned moon present;
Myself the man i' th' moon do seem to be.

(MOONSHINE *pauses, as if he has forgotten what he is supposed to say.*)

All that I have to say, is, to tell you that the lantern is the moon; I, the man i' th' moon; this thornbush, my thornbush, and this dog, my dog.

(THISBE *enters.*)

THISBE: This is old Ninny's tomb. Where is my love?
LION (roaring): G-R-R-R-R-R-R-R-R-R.

(THISBE, *frightened, runs off, but in the process she drops her mantle.* LION *grabs the mantle in his mouth and shakes it.* LION *drops the mantle and exits.*)
(PYRAMUS *enters.*)

PYRAMUS: Sweet Moon, I thank thee for thy sunny beams;
I thank thee, Moon, for shining now so bright;
For, by thy gracious, golden, glittering gleams,
I trust to take of truest Thisby's sight.

(*He sees* THISBE'*s mantle.*)

But stay, O spite!
But mark, poor knight,
What dreadful dole is here!
Eyes, do you see?
How can it be?
O dainty duck! O dear!
Thy mantle good,
What, stain'd with blood!
Approach, ye Furies fell!

O Fates, come, come,
Cut thread and thrum;
Quail, crush, conclude, and quell!
O wherefore, Nature, didst thou lions frame?
Since Lion vile hath here deflow'r'd my dear;
Which is—no, no—which was the fairest dame
That liv'd, that lov'd, that lik'd, that look'd with cheer.
Come, tears, confound
Out, sword, and wound
The pap of Pyramus;
Ay, that left pap,
Where heart doth hop.

(*He draws his sword and stabs himself.*)

Thus die I, thus, thus, thus.
Now am I dead,
Now am I fled;
My soul is in the sky
Tongue, lose thy light;
Moon, take thy flight.

(MOONSHINE *exits.*)

Now, die, die, die, die, die.

(PYRAMUS *dies.*)
(THISBE *enters and sees* PYRAMUS *on the ground.*)

THISBE: Asleep, my love?
What, dead, my dove?
O Pyramus, arise!
Speak, speak! Quite dumb?
Dead, dead? A tomb
Must cover thy sweet eyes.
These lily lips,
This cherry nose,
These yellow cowslip cheeks,
Are gone, are gone!
Lovers, make moan.
His eyes were green as leeks.
O Sisters Three,

Come, come to me,
With hands as pale as milk;
Lay them in gore,
Since you have shore
With shears his thread of silk.
Tongue, not a word!
Come, trusty sword;
Come, blade, my breast imbrue

(*She takes* PYRAMUS' *sword and stabs herself.*)

And farewell, friends;
Thus, Thisby ends
Adieu, adieu, adieu.

(THISBE *dies.*)

THESEUS (*Seeing that it is the end of the play, stands to dismiss the company.*): The iron tongue of midnight hath told twelve.
Lovers, to bed; 'tis almost fairy time.
I fear we shall outsleep the coming morn
As much as we this night have overwatch'd.
This palpable-gross play hath well beguil'd
The heavy gait of night. Sweet friends, to bed.
A fortnight hold we this solemnity
In nightly revels and new jollity.

(*They all exit as the* CURTAIN *falls.*)

The Golden Axe

RALPH SCHOLL

Characters

JEB WILLIKER
SHERIFF HENRY THOMPSON
YOUNG WIDOW EVANS

Reading Guides

1. The major character in *The Golden Axe* speaks the least. Therefore, it is necessary to imagine his reactions to the other characters in order to get the humor from the play.

2. Since this play concerns natural beauty, your conception of the scene is important. In order to share (identify with) Jeb's conflict, you have to be able to imagine a scene as beautiful as the one he describes.

The Golden Axe

IT IS LATE ON A SUMMER AFTERNOON, *in an old-fashioned farmhouse kitchen in the Missouri Ozarks. It has that "bachelor lives here" quality. Up right is a cookstove. Up center is an old-fashioned sink upon which sits a bucket of drinking water and a dipper. Above the sink is a cracked mirror hanging on the wall. A door at the right of the stage leads to the outside of the house. Near the door that opens to the outside is a large window. In the center of the room, and to the left, is a large old-fashioned table. Around it are three chairs. A fourth chair is down right center. To the left of the room is another door which is closed.*

When the curtain opens, we see JEB *sitting in the chair that is down right center. He is Lincolnesque, and moves his long gangly body rather lazily. He wears bib overalls, a blue shirt, and clodhopper shoes. He is one of those farmers who chew tobacco constantly, yet, miraculously, never spit. Right now, his face serious, he is bending over a double-bitted axe while he sharpens it to a fine edge with a whetstone. The* SHERIFF *is striding back and forth in front of* JEB. *The* SHERIFF *is short and paunchy. Ordinarily, his jowled face is good-humored, jovial, and friendly; but right now he is upset and wears a worried expression. He is one of those short, fat men who are constantly moving about, never at rest, and consequently always puffing. Like* JEB, *the* SHERIFF *wears bib overalls, but owing to the dignity of his position in life (that of Sheriff of Saline Creek County) he wears a white shirt, a large red tie, and a double-breasted suit coat. Pinned proudly and conspicuously to the front of this coat is a large silver star which says simply "Sheriff." On his hip he wears an old Colt revolver. Suddenly the* SHERIFF *stops striding back and forth in front of* JEB, *and brings his fist down on the table.*

SHERIFF (*desperately*): Don't do it, Jeb, don't do it!

JEB (*with quiet determination, still sharpening the axe*): Got to, Henry.

SHERIFF (*after a thoughtful pause, regretfully*): If you go ahead and use that axe, you know what that means, Jeb.

JEB: Yep, I know.

SHERIFF (*exasperated*): Then why do it?

JEB: Got to.

SHERIFF: But why?

JEB: Cain't stop meself.

SHERIFF: Well, why don't you *try?*

JEB (*rubbing whetstone on the axe*): Wouldn't like meself.

SHERIFF: But the *law,* Jeb?

JEB (*disgustedly*): Humph!

SHERIFF (*suddenly brisk and efficient, taking command of the situation*): Jeb, as Sheriff of this here county, I got to take action. God knows what they'll do to you! So I just ain't a-gonna let you do it!

JEB: No?

SHERIFF: No! I'll put you in jail first—for your own good.

JEB (*calmly, still whetting the axe*): Cain't.

SHERIFF: Cain't what?

JEB: Cain't put me in jail. Ain't done nothin'. You got to wait 'til I done somethin' 'fore you kin put me in jail. (*looking up from the axe to the* SHERIFF) And I ain't done nothin', so you cain't put me in jail yet.

SHERIFF (*moving away, reflectively rubbing his hand on his chin*): Yeah, I guess that's so, Jeb. (*shrewdly*) Well, I guess I cain't stop you, all right. . . . (*in a casual, offhand manner*) When you figure on doin' it, Jeb?

JEB (*testing the edge of the axe with his thumb*): Soon's this here axe is sharp 'nough—and you ain't around.

SHERIFF (*triumphantly, sitting down*): Then, by Grabees, I'm goin' to just set here and watch you! And just as you go to do it, I'm goin' to stop you and put you in jail for disturbin' the peace!

JEB: Cain't do that, Henry.

SHERIFF: Now why the hell cain't I?

JEB: 'Cause I kin outset you. I been settin' here a year and not doin' it, so I guess I kin set a little longer. (*continuing to whet the axe*) 'Sides, you got to go vote gettin' tonight. You know well as I do that sooner or later I'm goin' to do it. So you might jist as well traipse off 'fore it gits dark and git your votes, and let me do what I got to do now and git it over with.

(*The* SHERIFF *puts his hand on* JEB*'s shoulder.*)

SHERIFF (*sentimentally*): Jeb, me and you has always been friends, ain't we?

JEB: Yep. We always been friends. We're still friends.

SHERIFF: That's right. (*speaking warmly and affectionately*) Now look here, Jeb . . . (*The* SHERIFF *takes off his badge.*) I'm a-layin' down my badge on the table here . . . (*he lays down the badge, takes his gun out and lays it on the table.*) And I'm a-layin' down my gun, too. . . . Now don't think of me as Sheriff no more. Think of me as a friend. We've had good times as friends, ain't we?

JEB: Sure have.

SHERIFF: How long've we knowed each other? How long've we been friends, Jeb?

JEB: Ever since we been born.

SHERIFF: You damn right! We been friends ever since both of us was born. Why, we growed up together. We played together as kids. We chased the gals together. Hell, we even both courted Sally. And when she chose me, who was the best man at my weddin' ten year ago?

JEB: Me.

SHERIFF: You damn tootin', you was! That's the kind of friends we was! And it's the kind of friends we still are now.

JEB: Sure are.

SHERIFF: Why, even now when you're a-sparkin' the young Widder Evans, and I come right out and say what I think of her, and she comes right out and tells you what she thinks of me—it don't make no difference. 'Cause me and you are still the same old friends, ain't we?

JEB: Yep, and we'll still be friends even if'n I get the young Widder to marry me—which ain't likely.

SHERIFF (*getting emotional and oratorical*): Damn right we'll be friends! Why, we been friends through good times and bad times, when the Democrats was in and when the Democrats was out. But no matter what the times, we've been friends through it all. Ain't that so?

JEB: Yep.

SHERIFF: Then as a friend, Jeb, I'm askin' you from the bottom of my heart: will you put that damned axe down before somethin' terrible happens? (*gently, softly*) Will you, Jeb, for a friend?

(*While the* SHERIFF *leans toward him, tensed and waiting for an answer to his question,* JEB *puts down the axe, slowly and thoughtfully uncrosses his legs, takes out of his pocket a plug of tobacco, then a pocketknife, and carves a piece off the plug into his mouth. He returns the knife to his pocket, absently puts the tobacco on the table, and very slowly recrosses his legs. Then he speaks to the waiting* SHERIFF.)

JEB: Nope.

SHERIFF (*sighing*): I guess it jist ain't no use.

JEB: I told you it weren't.

SHERIFF: But why, Jeb? *Why?*

JEB: Come here, Henry. (JEB *goes to the open door that leads to the yard outside the house. The* SHERIFF *follows him. They stand there, looking out.*) Look out there, Henry. Acrost that new highway in front of my door is the hills. And behind the hills is the settin' sun. You know, some folks like sunup, but me, I like my sundown best.

SHERIFF: Never could figure out why some folks like one better'n t'other. Why do you like sunset best, Jeb?

JEB: I'm awake more.

SHERIFF (*thoughtfully*): Hmmm. . . . I ain't never thought of it that-a-way.

JEB: You know, Henry, I ain't never seen nothin' prettier happen in God's whole world than what I seen right here, standin' at my own door or settin' out there on the porch.

SHERIFF: I know just what you mean.

JEB: Why, I seen them hills out there look like God had all of a sudden busted a great big gold egg plop smack dab on top of 'em—and I've watched while the gold all run down, catchin' on the tops of the trees and stumps and rocks, makin' the tree tops look all stickery with gold, like the hairs on the leg of a bee in the sun.

SHERIFF: Purty, all right.

JEB: Yep, I've set and watched while the evenin' run in like blue water, fillin' up all the hollers and then floodin' over the tops of the trees.

SHERIFF (*sadness in his voice*): Yeah, Jeb, I seen it before like that myself.

JEB: But do you see it now, Henry?

SHERIFF: No.

JEB (*angrily*): You damned right you don't! And neither do I! And why? Because they put that God-damned signboard up on the edge of the highway, and that signboard's as big as a barn. A body cain't stand here nor set out there on the porch and see the sunset on them hills no more. Everthin's all hid behind that sign! All you kin see is that great skinny woman on that signboard.

SHERIFF (*sadly, but trying to calm* JEB *down*): Well, I admit you cain't see the sunset no more, Jeb, and that gal is purty skinny—bet she's near a hundred foot tall—and she ain't actin' ladylike neither, come to think of it. But still, you oughtn't to go out there and chop that signboard down, Jeb.

(JEB *goes back to his chair, still carrying his axe, and sits down. His shoulders sag, but he speaks with determination.*)

JEB: Henry, that sign's been up there almost a year, now. I caint' fight it no more. I got to cut 'er down.

SHERIFF: You do that and you'll have to go to jail, Jeb. And you cain't scrape up enough money to hire a lawyer, or even bail yourself out. I don't know what'll happen to you. Why, they'll prob'ly take you out of my jail and put you in some dirty old big city prison. And then you'll *never* git to see the sunset!

JEB: Some things a man has got to do, Henry.

SHERIFF: But Jeb, you ain't got no legal right to chop down that sign.

JEB: I got a right to see the sunset, Henry. That's my right.

SHERIFF: Maybe so, but that won't stand up in court.

(JEB *gets up and goes to the cracked mirror over the sink. He carefully selects a hair, pulls it out of his head, and, holding it between the thumb and forefinger of his left hand, cuts it with the axe.*)

JEB: Well, she's sharp 'nough.

SHERIFF: Say, Jeb, how come you look in the mirror to pull out a hair?

JEB: So's I git the gray ones while I'm at it. A young Widder don't like no gray-headed bachelor.

SHERIFF: You know, sometimes when I think about you and the Widder I git to worryin' a little. I'm afeerd you'll marry her and then she'll boss you to death. You'll do nothin' but *work* from sunup to sundown.

JEB: Well, Henry, I used to worry a little 'bout that, too. But I don't worry much no more.

SHERIFF: How come?

JEB: Well, I been sparkin' the Widder for two year now. And she still holds off. Somehow she don't seem eager to git married.

SHERIFF: Hell, she'll marry you, Jeb. The Widder's young, and the Widder's good lookin', but you don't have too much competition. 'Cause she's got one little thing against her that scares off all the rest of the single bucks in the county.

JEB: Maybe so, but she still don't seem eager.

SHERIFF: You're a brave man, Jeb. All the other bachelors 'round here would spark the Widder, but they're 'fraid to, seein' as how she buried two husbands in ten year.

JEB: Hell, her husbands jist got sick like everybody else does once't in awhile. Only they died, 'stead of gittin' well.

SHERIFF: They died 'cause they was all wore out from workin' too hard. The Widder just managed them to death. Only you don't want to admit it, even to yourself. (*after a pause*) Maybe she's been holdin' off 'cause you ain't rich enough . . .

JEB: 'Tain't that. Why, I paid seven hundred dollar for this here farm. 'Course it ain't nothin' but red dirt, and rocks and scrub oak—but that seven hundred dollar was my life's work. And the farm's all mine, so I ain't so poor.

SHERIFF: Hell, the Widder's jist playin' hard to git.

JEB: Think so?

SHERIFF: Sure. Why, I seen her sell an old wore-out horse collar to John Hanks once't. And the way she acted you'd've thought it was the best horse collar in the county—even if the stuffin' was all comin' out of it. She acted like it plumb broke her heart to have to part with it. Why, poor old John was a-beggin' her to sell it to him for four dollar 'fore it was all over. And it weren't worth two bits. But you know how it is, when a thing is hard to git, people wants it more. And the Widder knows that. . . . Excuse me for comparin' the woman you love to a wore-out horse collar, Jeb. Didn't mean it the way it sounded.

JEB: That's all right, Henry. Lots of folks in this county think the Widder is a little greedy when it comes to money.

SHERIFF: You know, Jeb, the Widder is a law abidin' woman. If you go ahead with that there axe, I kin tell you somethin' for sure: she ain't never goin' to have nothin' to do with you agin.

JEB (*sadly*): That so? (*with a touch of rancor*) Well, to tell the truth, I'm kind of mad at her now, anyways.

SHERIFF: How come?

JEB: Well, she come over here to borry some 'taters this mornin'.

SHERIFF: Hell, jist 'cause a body borries 'taters once't in awhile ain't no call to git mad at 'em—unless they don't pay 'em back.

JEB: But her borryin' them 'taters was jist an excuse so's she could torment me to tell her what I was goin' to do 'bout that sign—and then to run to town and git you to stop me.

SHERIFF: Jist doin' my duty, Jeb.

JEB: I know, Henry, and I forgive you for it.

(*The men are silent for a moment. The* SHERIFF *is thinking. Then he speaks.*)

SHERIFF: Look here, Jeb: be reasonable. Why, the Widder told me the sign company pays the county ninety dollar a year for that land. County got it for back taxes from John Hanks five year ago, you know. Now ain't they got a right to that money?

JEB: Henry, I ain't sayin' it's wrong for the county to own a piece of ground. But does any man own the air?

SHERIFF: No, I guess no man owns the air, Jeb.

JEB: Damn right they don't. If they did, they'd charge you for breathin'. Ain't that so?

SHERIFF (*thoughtfully*): Well—bein' a legal man—(*stopping and pondering for a moment*) my opinion is this: Yes. If somebody owned the air, they would charge you for usin' it. Besides, if somebody owned the air the government would tax 'em for it. . . . So I guess nobody owns the air. (*The* SHERIFF *and* JEB *are silent and thoughtful for a moment. Then the* SHERIFF *speaks.*) Sure I cain't change your mind, Jeb?

JEB: Yep, I'm sure.

SHERIFF: Well, I done said my piece, and it's time to be off politickin' if I don't want to lose no votes. (*The* SHERIFF *goes toward the door.* JEB *gets up and follows him. The* SHERIFF, *looking out the door, sees something that catches his interest. He cranes his neck, looking to his right.*) Hey, Jeb, here comes the Widder! She's runnin' lickety split down the highway toward us. Bet she's comin' here.

JEB (*a little exasperated*): Damn it, a man cain't seem to get a thing done 'round here with all this visitin' goin' on.

(*The* SHERIFF, *at the door, turns around.*)

SHERIFF: But I think you're makin' a mountain out of a molehill, Jeb. And that s'prises me—never knowed anythin' to rile *you* up afore. You was always so calm.

JEB: Henry, did you ever look out of your winder and see a woman taller 'n a barn? No matter if you look forty times a day, there she is, grinnin' down at you.

SHERIFF: Yeah, I guess it's been purty bad for you, Jeb. But you know, what they'll do to you after you chop 'er down is goin' to be a whole lot worse than what you got now.

JEB (*paying no attention to the* SHERIFF): Maybe I wouldn't mind so much if the signboard woman was sellin' somethin' I could use. Like if she was holdin' a big new shiny tractor in one hand and a manure spreader in th' other, maybe it wouldn't be so bad. (*talking like an obsessed man*) And she's skinny, too. She's so tall and she's all hollow cheeked, and one lip is all crooked where the paper was put on wrong, and she's flat chested, and . . . (*trying to get himself under control*) I tell you, Henry, that havin' a ninety-foot tall woman standin' over him all day *does* somethin' to a man!

(*The* SHERIFF *goes part way out the door.*)

SHERIFF: Well, I sure hope there ain't no hard feelin's on your part when I have to put you in jail for choppin' 'er down, Jeb.

JEB: There won't be, Henry.

SHERIFF: Fine. And say, be sure and fell 'er off the highway, won't you, Jeb?

JEB: Henry, did you ever know me to have a tree jump out of line?

SHERIFF: No, but this ain't quite like no tree! (*after a slight pause*) Well, 'night, Jeb. See you in jail.

JEB: 'Night, Henry.

(*The* SHERIFF *exits.* JEB *goes to the table. We hear the* SHERIFF *speaking to someone outside.*)

SHERIFF (*from off stage*): Evenin', Widder. Nice summer evenin', ain't it?

WIDOW (*from off stage, breathless from running*): Evenin', Sheriff. . . . I s'pose.

(JEB *picks up a plug of tobacco and turns toward the door. The* WIDOW EVANS *is standing in the open doorway. She is a busty, hippy woman. There is a shrewd, calculating look about her eyes and mouth, not in keeping with her flirtatious walk, or, at times, her glances. She is dressed in a neat print dress [made by herself from the flowered cotton prints that come on feed sacks] and in the pocket of her blouse she carries an account book and a pencil. Her breasts heave from the effort of running. She knocks on the doorjamb.* JEB *sighs, goes to the door with the axe still in his hand.*)

JEB (*sighing*): Might's well come on in, Widder.

WIDOW (*out of breath*): Jeb, I run all the way over here.

JEB (*calmly*): Runnin's bad for the heart, Widder. (JEB *and the* WIDOW *cross to the table.* JEB *gives the* WIDOW *a chair.*) Here, set down.

(*The* WIDOW *sits down.* JEB *remains standing.*)

WIDOW: Ever since this mornin' when you told me what you was goin' to do, I been thinkin' about it. And a little while ago I made up my mind. I got to stop you. (*looking up at him meaningfully*) And that means I got to tell you somethin' . . .

JEB: Now you jist set there a minute, Widder, and rest a mite. I'll be right back.

(JEB *moves toward the door with his axe in hand.*)

WIDOW (*standing up*): I run and I run and I run, and I kept sayin', "I hope he ain't done it yet. I got to tell him afore it's too late."

(JEB *turns around at the door, and faces her.*)

JEB: 'Scuse me, Widder. . . . Be back afore you kin ketch your breath.

(*The* WIDOW *runs toward him.*)

WIDOW: Jeb, wait!

JEB: Cain't wait.

WIDOW: But will you do me one last little favor 'fore you do it, Jeb?

JEB: What is it?

WIDOW: Set and talk with me for just a minute. I won't argue none. I jist want to talk. For jist one minute, Jeb.

(*The* WIDOW *grabs* JEB's *free hand.* JEB *allows himself to be led back to the table.*)

JEB: Might's well, I guess. Already been waitin' a year. But I got to do it 'fore it gits dark outside. . . . So I kin only listen for a minute.

(JEB *and the* WIDOW *go to the table and sit down.*)

WIDOW: Sure, Jeb. (*after a pause*) You know, Jeb, if I don't want to see somethin', I just close my eyes.

JEB: *Why* do you think God made sunsets, Widder?

WIDOW: Don't know. Never thought about it.

JEB: Well, I have—'specially for the last year. (*continuing, after a pause, to gather his ideas together*) Now you take a man—any man. Day in, day out, he's a-workin' and a-fightin' and a-pushin' and a-shovin' like a hog in a trough, jist to git by. And when the day's over, and comes time to quit, he's bone tired. So he comes out on his porch and watches the sunset. . . . Pretty soon he ain't tired no more.

WIDOW: 'Course he ain't. He's rested up some.

JEB: Nope, that ain't it, though I guess it helps out. It's 'cause he gits to thinkin' that sunsets and all the pretty things in the world are signs.

WIDOW (*eagerly*): Once't I seen a real purty sign. Showed a real good picture of a fur coat that was . . .

JEB (*interrupting*): I mean Nature's signs: God's way of lookin' down and talkin' to us.

WIDOW (*suddenly deflated*): Oh.

JEB: Yep, it's like He's sayin', "Hello, man, I ain't forgot you. Jist been a little busy, that's all. I know you're down there, and someday maybe me and you kin make this old world a purty good place to live in. But 'til I kin git to it, I just thought I'd put a few purty things like sunsets and rainbows and stuff like that in the sky for you to look up at—to sort of help you want to git your head out of the trough. (*slightest of pauses, then looking directly at the widow*) And you know, Widder, that's jist what them things does.

WIDOW (*after a pause*): Well, maybe so, Jeb. . . . But I say that if you destroy other men's *property,* that ain't Christian.

JEB: Widder, God made things like sunsets for everybody. And a few men ain't got no right to go around uglifying 'em up, even if they does make money by doin' it. (*continuing, after a thoughtful pause, almost to himself*) Signboard's bad 'nough by itself, but to have a woman holdin' . . . (*catching himself, embarrassed*) holdin' . . .

WIDOW (*impatiently*): holdin' what, Jeb?

JEB: Ain't you *seen?*

WIDOW: No. Never looked.

JEB: Well, I'll be damned! (*continuing, after a pause*) Well, she's—she's holdin' —holdin' . . . (*embarrassed, unable to bring himself to say it*) Well, maybe you better go look.

WIDOW: Well, maybe I better. (*The* WIDOW *gets up from the chair, crosses to the doorway and looks out. At first she is shocked, then insulted and angry. She turns back, returns to the table, sits down in her chair with an angry thump.*) Well, I never! It's hussies like her that makes it hard for us nice girls to git along.

(JEB *and the* WIDOW *are silent for a moment, then* JEB *stands up and speaks.*)

JEB: Well, I guess I better be gittin' along. Goin' to be dark purty soon.

(*The* WIDOW *stands, comes up close to* JEB, *who, a little frightened, keeps the axe between them.*)

WIDOW: Jeb, I know you're a-goin' to do it. But afore you do it, I got to tell you somethin'.

JEB: Ma'am?

WIDOW (*kittenishly*): Jeb, if I was to tell you somethin'—somethin' a lady never tells a gentleman—you wouldn't think bad of me, would you?

JEB: Guess not. (*curious*) What don't ladies tell gentlemen?

WIDOW (*pretending shyness*): Well—you know what I come over here for, don't you, Jeb?

JEB: Hell, yes! Like ever'body else in the county you're tryin' to talk me out of choppin' down that damned signboard. (JEB *turns toward the door.*) And that's just a waste of time. I got to go now.

WIDOW (*her hand on his arm, detaining him*): But, Jeb, don't you know there's another reason why I come over? 'Course I come over to stop you. I admit that. You're too smart for me to try and fool you by lyin' about it, so I ain't even tried. But there's another reason why I come over, Jeb. (*insinuatingly*) Don't you know the other reason?

JEB: Well, no. This mornin' you come over to borry some 'taters. (*straight-faced, kidding the* WIDOW *without her knowing it*) Need any more 'taters?

WIDOW: No, Jeb. That ain't why I come over. I *got* 'taters now. But why would a lady come over to visit a gentleman, Jeb?

JEB: Same reason a gentleman comes over to visit a lady, I guess.

WIDOW (*suggestively*): And why is that, Jeb?

JEB: You mean why does ladies and gentlemen visit each other?

WIDOW: Yes.

JEB: To see each other, I guess. (JEB *moves abruptly to go. The* WIDOW *tries desperately to detain him.*) 'Scuse me, Widder. I got to go now.

WIDOW (*frantically trying to detain him*): But Jeb, why should I run clear over here to stop you from goin' to prison if I didn't . . . (*pretending embarrassment*) if I didn't care for you?

JEB (*unbelievingly*): Widder!

WIDOW (*coyly*): Now what would you say, Jeb, if a lady told you . . . Now mind you, I'm only sayin' "If"; I'm a self-respectable woman—but what would you say if a lady told you that she'd like to spend out the rest of her years with you in holy wedlock?

JEB: Oh, Widder! (JEB *puts down the axe and draws her toward him, though not quite hugging her.*) Oh, Widder, I sure do thank you for askin' me to marry you!

(*The* WIDOW *stands away from him suddenly and haughtily.*)

WIDOW: I never asked you to marry me, Jeb!

JEB (*at a loss, not understanding*): You didn't?

WIDOW: I only said what "if" . . . I didn't say I would. A woman cain't.

JEB (*relieved*): Oh, well, how ever you want to git around it . . . (*continuing, as though making a formal speech*) Widder Evans, will you marry me?

WIDOW (*shyly*): 'Course. If you'll have me.

JEB: Oh, Widder, I'll have you! Don't worry none about *that!*

WIDOW (*hesitatingly*): Would you marry me, Jeb, even if you found out somethin' about me that you never knowed afore?

JEB: S'pose. People's all the time findin' out things they didn't know—after the knot's tied.

WIDOW: Well, there's somethin' you don't know. Somethin' about me . . . You see, Jeb, there's somethin' I been keepin' from you, and from the other people in Saline Crik County, too.

JEB: You ain't done nothin' illegal?

WIDOW: Oh, no! Ain't that! It's just that I, I . . . (*decisively*) Well, I jist got to tell you. I own that there land the signboard's on. Bought it from the county over a year ago.

JEB: Oh, Widder, why do you have to go and tell me that?

WIDOW: 'Cause someday you'd find out my secret. 'Sides, that signboard company pays me ninety dollar a year for that patch of ground. I won't git it, you know, if you cut their sign down, Jeb. (*coming close to him*) Jeb, for the love of me—for our future happiness in holy wedlock, will you *not* cut down that sign? Please?

JEB (*suddenly a broken man*): Why do you ask that, Widder? The one thing I cain't do. (JEB, *his shoulders drooping, stoops and picks up his axe, as he speaks brokenly.*) 'Bye, Widder!

(JEB *runs out the door with his axe. The* WIDOW *stands shocked and still for a moment, then runs to the door, calling out.*)

WIDOW: Jeb! Wait! Stop! *Please* stop, Jeb! (*The* WIDOW *stands looking out the door, horrified and unable to move.*) Oh, no. Oh, no. Jeb, oh no! Don't chop! Don't!

(*As the* WIDOW *stands there, we hear the furious chopping of wood. The* WIDOW'S *body jerks as if in pain, with each stroke of the axe. The stage lights begin to dim. Just before the stage is in total darkness, we hear* JEB'S *voice.*)

JEB (*calling out*): There she goes!

(*There is a tremendous crash. The stage is now totally dark, and remains so for a short period, to indicate the passing of time. Then a faint light shows on* JEB'S *axe, which is leaning against the table. The light makes the axe appear to be gold, and it is for a moment the only thing to be seen on the completely dark stage. Then the stage becomes visible, and then, fully lit. We see the* WIDOW *sitting in* JEB'S *kitchen, in a chair facing the open doorway. The* SHERIFF *is standing looking out the window, craning his neck to the right. On the table are a stack of opened letters, neat stacks of bills and rolls of silver, the* WIDOW'S *account book, her purse* [*a scalloped leather affair in keeping with her taste*]*, and a large cardboard box. The* WIDOW *is slowly and painstakingly writing something on a large tablet, her lips moving slowly as she wets her pencil and writes.*)

SHERIFF: Sure wish't he'd git here.

WIDOW (*looking up from the tablet*): Think he'll bring the mail out from town with him? Noon train prob'ly brought lots to the post office.

SHERIFF: Don't know. (*with a gesture of impatience*) I just wish't he'd *git* here! You know, I ought to've gone into town special to git him.

WIDOW: Body cain't be in two places at once't, Sheriff. (*gesturing toward the money*) You sure cain't leave here with all *this* around!

SHERIFF: I know, but jist the same, it don't seem right. When your best friend gits bailed out of jail, you ought to at least be there to greet him.

WIDOW: Maybe he got helt up with his fancy new lawyer. You know how them people talk.

SHERIFF: No, t'ain't that. I'll bet a dollar that John Hankses' old car broke down on the way out of town and he's havin' to walk home.

WIDOW: How's Jeb lookin', Sheriff—poorly?

SHERIFF: Hell, no! Looks better'n he ever did. Ought to. Ate 'nough of Sally's good cookin'. Never seen a man eat so much and stay so skinny. (*continu-*

ing, after a pause) He ate all his meals over home, you know. Easier to take him to the house than bring all that food over to the jail. (*another pause*) In all that time, how come you didn't visit him? (*sarcastically*) Visitin's allowed, y'know.

WIDOW: You don't think he'll hold it agin me, do you?

SHERIFF: Don't know. (*looking out the window*) Sun'll be down in a little while. Hope he don't miss his very first sunset at home. You know how he is about sunsets.

(*The* SHERIFF *turns away from the window, goes to the table and starts to lift up the top flap of the box just as the* WIDOW *looks up from her writing tablet. Like a flash, her arm goes out and she slaps the top of the box down. The* SHERIFF *looks a little hurt, a little guilty.*)

WIDOW: For the last time, Sheriff, I'm tellin' you not to peek into that box! It's a s'prise for Jeb. And if I kin stand not lookin', so kin you.

SHERIFF: But *you* know what's in it, and I don't.

WIDOW: Don't make no difference.

SHERIFF (*very inquisitive*): Is it somethin' you bought out of the catalogue?

WIDOW: No, I had it made up and sent here to Headquarters. Now you go on and watch out the winder for Jeb! Maybe he'll bring us some letters from places we ain't even heard of yit. (*The* WIDOW *selects an envelope from the stack on the table in front of her.*) Did you see this one? Come in jist yestiday. (*reading, by syllables*) It's from Henry Hamson, Esq., from Barnstaples, Somersetshire, England, to Jeb Wiliker, Esq. (*looking up at the* SHERIFF) And he sent ten dollar, too! Seems like the whole world knows about Jeb now. And everbody's tryin' to help him out.

SHERIFF: Funny how people is that way.

WIDOW: Yeah, ever'body tryin' to help him fight it out in court—and emergency citizens' committees formin' themselves. Why, I tell you, Sheriff, it's really somethin'!

SHERIFF: Yep, I ain't never seen nothin' like it in Saline Crik County before.

WIDOW: Did you hear the latest the newspapers was sayin' about me and you?

SHERIFF: No, don't read what they say. They don't seem to like Jeb none, and I git mad when they say mean things about him.

WIDOW: They say you're his best friend. They say I'm his manager—(*with a simper*) and his love life.

SHERIFF: Are you Jeb's manager, Widder?

WIDOW: Sure. Now he's been bailed out of jail and has got a fancy lawyer and people has sent in all that money, we're goin' to make us a national campaign.

SHERIFF: A what what?

WIDOW (*very excited*): Tell you all about it later. But it's really goin' to be somethin'! Oh, I tell you, Sheriff, I'm so excited about it all, I cain't hardly set still.

SHERIFF (*calmly*): Uh, huh. . . . How much money've people sent in so far?

WIDOW (*reaching across the table for her account book, and reading it*): Well, let me see. Just three week ago this afternoon Jeb chopped 'er down. (*looking up at the* SHERIFF) We didn't git nothin' the first week hardly, 'til the people heard about it in the papers. (*looking down at the account book*) And we got seventy-two dollar and twenty cents today. That makes . . .

(*The* SHERIFF, *who has just glanced out the window again, sees something slightly to his left. He interrupts the* WIDOW *before she can finish her sentence.*)

SHERIFF (*joyfully*): Here he comes! And he's walkin'! He's comin' right acrost the new highway to'ards us!

WIDOW: Oh, Sheriff, my heart's jist a-goin' pitter-patter.

SHERIFF: By Grabees, I bet John Hankses' old car broke down, and Jeb's taken the short cut over the ridge. And all the time I was lookin' for him to come down the highway.

WIDOW: Has he got any mail?

SHERIFF: Don't see any. (*abstracted*) Dang it, a man oughtn't to cross a highway lookin' back over his shoulder at the sunset, like that! (*moving quickly to the door*) 'Scuse me, Widder.

(*The* SHERIFF *goes out the door. The* WIDOW *primps furiously. From her purse, she whips out a mirror, checks her make up, adds some lipstick, then pats at her hair. She stands up, facing the door, and twists, turns, pulls and straightens her girdle. We hear steps on the porch outside, the* SHERIFF'*s laugh,* JEB'*s chuckle, and then the* SHERIFF *and* JEB *enter.* JEB *carries an ancient and battered suitcase. He walks toward the sink as the* WIDOW *speaks.*)

WIDOW (*her words coming out in a rush*): Oh, Jeb, I'm *so* glad to see you! I missed you so. And I wanted real bad to visit you in jail, but . . . (*a little embarrassed*) you know how people talks about a woman what hangs around jails.

(JEB *puts the suitcase down on the sink.*)

SHERIFF (*to* JEB): I was tellin' the Widder that John Hankses' old car broke down on the way out from town, and you had to walk, so you took a short cut over the ridge. Bet I was right, wasn't I, Jeb?

JEB (*turning around, to the* SHERIFF): Sure was.

WIDOW (*with a rush of words*): Oh, Jeb, I got so much to tell you and show you. Oh, I got so many wonderful plans, I jist don't know where to begin!

JEB: I got somethin' to tell you too, Widder . . .

WIDOW (*interrupting*): Say, Jeb, did you git things all fixed up with your fancy new lawyer? (JEB *nods, and opens his mouth to speak. The* WIDOW *again cuts him off. She speaks softly, affectionately.*) Bet he near talked your arm off, didn't he?

JEB (*sighing, shaking head like a man who has suffered*): Sure did. But Widder, I . . .

WIDOW (*interrupting*): Oh, Jeb, I know how you must have suffered in jail and all. No, you don't need to say you ain't. I know how it must've been. Jeb, I want you to know I forgive you for everthin'. Everthin'! I forgive you and make up with you. (JEB *tries to speak; the* WIDOW *holds up her hand.*) No, don't say anythin', Jeb! We'll jist forgit it all. You don't need to say a thing, 'cause it's all forgot. (*moving quickly, picking up the account book*) Now, Jeb, first off I want to show you this! Nine hundred and eighty-six dollar and seventy-four cents! That's how much people sent in since you chopped 'er down. Just three weeks ago this afternoon, and we already got near a thousand dollar!

(JEB *whistles a long, low whistle.*)

SHERIFF: Makes you feel real good when people are so nice they send money to bail you out of jail, don't it, Jeb?

JEB (*to the* SHERIFF): Sure does. (*to the* WIDOW) But I . . .

WIDOW (*interrupting*): Oh, we're jist beginnin', Jeb! Now you're out of jail, we kin really git our national campaign started. I tell you it's really goin' to be somethin', too.

SHERIFF: What's a national campaign?

WIDOW: You know—what you have when you have a national organization. When you have a national organization, you have a national campaign. Ain't you never heerd of them?

SHERIFF: No.

WIDOW: Well, this is the way it works. (*to* JEB) You go around different places, Jeb. You go all over the country. And everwhere you go you make speeches . . . (JEB *opens his mouth to say something, but before he can speak the* WIDOW *cuts him off, pointing to the tablet on the table.*) Like the one I'm writin' now. And after you make your speech, people gives money so's they can join up in the organization.

SHERIFF: What organization?

WIDOW (*proudly*): We call it the organization of the Golden Axe! (*The* SHERIFF *and* JEB *look blank.*) People has always hated signboards, but 'til Jeb here done it, they was always afeerd to cut 'em down. So now we form committees—organizations always does that—and the people goes out at night in secret and chops 'em down. (*The* WIDOW *reaches into the cardboard box.*) And whenever they chops down a signboard, they gits a little golden axe (*taking out a tiny gold pin and holding it up*) like this! (*The* SHERIFF *takes the pin from the* WIDOW *and inspects it closely. He is impressed. While the* SHERIFF *and* WIDOW *talk,* JEB *drifts inconspicuously toward the door, where he leans against the doorjamb, looking out at the sunset. The* WIDOW *continues talking to the* SHERIFF.) They jist come in this mornin'. Ain't they somethin'? (*pretending modesty*) 'Course they ain't *real* gold. But they *look* like it.

SHERIFF: But what happens when people gits caught choppin' down the signboards?

WIDOW: We use some of our money we collected to git 'em out of jail and hire a fancy lawyer. Oh, I tell you, Sheriff, it's really goin' to be somethin'! And Jeb will make a real good president for the organization.

SHERIFF: I see. And what did you say you'd be, Widder?

WIDOW: Jeb's manager. That's all I want. . . . No, sir, no limelight for me! If I kin help out a little, that's all *I* want. (*seeing* JEB *start out the door*) Where you goin', Jeb?

JEB: Out on the porch.

WIDOW: But you won't be able to hear me out there, Jeb.

JEB: I kin hear you real good, Widder.

(JEB *goes out the door.*)

WIDOW (*to the* SHERIFF): Wish't he'd stay and set in the house, stid of out there on the porch watchin' the sun go down. Ain't civilized to set out there like that.

SHERIFF: You know, I ain't never seen a man about sunsets the way Jeb is. He waits for sunsets like a cat waits for milkin' time.

(*The* WIDOW *reaches for the writing tablet.*)

WIDOW: 'Scuse me for jist a minute, Sheriff. Got to finish my speech—jist a couple a words and then you kin hear me read it. (*The* WIDOW *begins to read what she has written on the pad, her lips moving slightly. Once she wets her pencil and makes a slight change. The* SHERIFF *gets up, takes a bag from his pocket, and puts the money from the table into it.*) You goin', Sheriff?

SHERIFF: Yep, cain't stay, Widder, though I'd like to. But I got to take keer of this, seein' as how it's my official responsibility. Then I'd best be gittin' on home, I guess. (*The* SHERIFF *goes to the door, looks out, and speaks to* JEB.) Say, Jeb, that's a real purty one this evenin'. And you can really see it, too, now that the sign's down.

WIDOW (*looking up*): Ain't you goin' to stay and listen to the speech I writ for Jeb, Sheriff?

SHERIFF: No, thank you jist the same. But I got to take this to town and put it in the safe—then I'd best be gittin' on.

WIDOW: Why don't you stay for jist a minute, Sheriff? (*gesturing toward the tablet*) It's a real good speech. I'd like to have you hear it.

SHERIFF: No, don't guess I'd better stay, Widder. One time I stayed too long where they was havin' a fire and I got all my hair burnt off. So I guess I'd better be goin'.

WIDOW (*miffed*): Oh, all right. Evenin' to you, then.

SHERIFF: 'Bye, Widder. (*The* SHERIFF *exits, then speaks from off stage.*) See you later, Jeb.

JEB (*off stage*): You bet, Henry. And thanks again to you and Sally for makin' everthin' so nice for me while I was in your jail.

WIDOW (*puzzled, speaking to herself*): Now I wonder what he meant by that business about a fire? (*She shrugs her shoulders, turns toward the door, and yells out to* JEB, *commandingly.*) Jeb, you git in here and hear my speech! Right now, 'fore I git mad agin and decide to change my mind about makin' up with you! (JEB *enters lazily. He leans against the doorjamb and looks outside.*) Jeb, I got you a real good speech writ. It's the kind that gits people all worked up so they start puttin' out the money. With you president, and me manager, we ought to do real well. But I'll tell you all about that later. Right now I want to read you my speech. (*The* WIDOW *does not notice* JEB'*s posture at the door, his back to her. She continues oratorically, with flourishes.*) Dear Friends! (*to* JEB, *who still has his back turned*) They always start out speeches that way. . . . Dear Friends! Makes a nice friendly touch, don't it? Dear Friends, what do you think of when you think of an axe? Why, you think of George Washington, that's what you think of! 'Course he didn't use an axe, properly speakin'; he used a hatchet, but that was only 'cause he was a boy. If he'd've been a man, he'd've used an axe. And Dear Friends, what do you think of when you think of George Washington? Why, you think of honesty, and presidents, and great national heroes. Don't you, Friends? Oh, I know, lots of you right now are sayin', "Humph! George Washington, he was a great national hero, all right, but that was a long time ago. And he's dead now." (*waving her arms and pounding the table*) But I'll tell you all somethin' you didn't know! GEORGE WASHINGTON AIN'T DEAD! No, he's alive, right here in this very room—in this very auditorium—in this big city that seats thousands. . . . (*interpolating to* JEB, *who still has his back to her*) I say that, you see, 'cause that's where you'll be givin' the speech, Jeb. (*continuing in speech-making tone*) No, sir, Friends! GEORGE WASHINGTON AIN'T DEAD; HE'S RIGHT HERE IN THIS AUDITORIUM! No, don't turn your heads! You cain't see him. 'Cause he ain't here in the flesh, Friends. IT'S HIS SPIRIT THAT'S HERE! George Washington's spirit's right here in this room! And his spirit is carryin' an axe! And his spirit's in the heart of us all! How do I know this? I FEEL IT! I FEEL THE SPIRIT OF GEORGE WASHINGTON IN ME! I FEEL HIS STRENGTH *NOW!* POURIN' INTO MY ARMS, MAKIN' THEM WANT TO CHOP DOWN MORE SIGNS, AND MORE SIGNS AND MORE AND MORE AND MORE SIGNS . . . (*interpolating again,* JEB *still with his back to her*) Now how's *that* for a beginnin'? Oh, but that's just a beginnin'! (*Suddenly aware of* JEB's *back being turned, she interrupts herself.*) Why, Jeb, you ain't listenin'! Don't you like my speech?

JEB: *Nice* speech.

WIDOW: Do you think you kin make a speech like this, Jeb?

JEB: Nope.

WIDOW: Why not? (*offhandedly, trying to build his confidence*) Oh, jist 'cause you're a little afeerd is okay. Everbody's a little afeerd to make a speech in front of a lot of strangers, the first couple times.

JEB: Sorry, Widder, cain't make no speech.

WIDOW (*regretfully*): Well, I guess we *could* git around it somehow. Maybe I could make it, and tell them you was too modest. But you'll have to *be* there, seein' as how you're goin' to be president.

JEB: Cain't be no president, neither.

WIDOW (*surprised*): Cain't be president? (*her confidence a little shaken*) Oh, I'll bet you'll change your mind after awhile—when you see there ain't nothin' to it. Why, I'll do all the work, if that's what's botherin' you. You kin kind of lean on me at first. (*shyly*) 'Course, that'll be easy, 'cause we'll be married pretty soon now. Have to be. People talks about single ladies what travels around with single gentlemen, you know.

JEB: Sorry, Widder, cain't marry you, neither.

WIDOW (*astonished*): What? You cain't *marry* me?

(JEB *turns away from the door and faces her.*)

JEB: Widder, I spent three weeks in jail, and that gives a man time to think. For the last two year I been sparkin' you, and all that time I been tryin' not to see some things. But now I cain't help seein' 'em. Not no more! You're the greediest, skinflintinest, crabbiest, jabberinest, lieinest, managinest, bossyinest, uglyfyinest woman in the whole county!

WIDOW (*with outraged dignity*): Why, I never . . .

JEB: So now git on out of here.

WIDOW: Well!

JEB: Widder, all of a sudden after I chopped down that there sign, you found out you was in business. So you tell me you forgive me, and you're goin' to make me president of a national organization, and sich stuff as that. And all the time you figure on gittin' rich!

WIDOW: I'm jist a poor helpless Widder, Jeb. Try to understand!

JEB: Git out of here, woman!

WIDOW (*turning to tears*): Oh, Jeb, please give me a chance't!

JEB: I said *git!*

(JEB *picks up the axe from where it leans against the table and slowly advances on the* WIDOW. *She retreats before him, backing to the door leading outside.*)

WIDOW (*desperately pleading*): Oh, Jeb, I'm all alone! I ain't got nobody to lean on. I'm jist a lonely widder, Jeb. That's what I am, a poor, weak, lonely widder.

(JEB *continues advancing.*)

JEB: No, you ain't! You're an uglyfyer! That's what you are!

WIDOW (*frantic*): Please, Jeb! Think of the national organization! All them people needs strength to use their axes! They needs leadership!

JEB (*still advancing*): Ever' man has got to chop down his own sign sooner or later. And he's got to do it all by himself. Now *git!*

WIDOW (*threatening*): I'll tell ever'body you're a bad man, Jeb!

(JEB *raises the axe menacingly.*)

JEB: Woman, I feel the spirit of George Washington in me—COMIN' INTO MY ARMS! (*The* WIDOW *breaks, turns, and runs out the door.* JEB *chuckles and puts the axe down against the doorjamb. For a moment, he stands there looking out the open door, watching the sunset sift slowly through the trees. He speaks quietly to himself.*) Sure is a purty sunset.

CURTAIN

Sunday Costs Five Pesos

JOSEPHINA NIGGLI

Characters

FIDEL, *who is in love with Berta*
BERTA
SALOMÉ, *Berta's friend*
TONIA, *Berta's friend*
CELESTINA, *Berta's rival*

Reading Guides

1. The mode of expression in *Sunday Costs Five Pesos* is quite different from most of the other plays because the characters are Mexican. Their language is emotional and colorful. Read carefully to get the full flavor.
2. It is important to differentiate among the four girls in order to understand fully the quadrangle conflict. Also, you should take the insults with good humor, for they are intended that way.

Sunday Costs Five Pesos

A HOUSED-IN SQUARE *in the town called the Four Cornstalks in the northern part of Mexico. On the left of the square is the house of* TONIA *with a door and a stoop. At the back is a wall cut neatly in half. The left side is the house of* BERTA, *and boasts not only a door but a barred window. On the right is a square arch from which dangles an iron lantern. This is the only exit to the rest of the town, for on the right side proper is the house of* SALOMÉ. TONIA'S *house is pink, and* SALOMÉ'S *is blue, while* BERTA'S *is content with being a sort of disappointed yellow. All three houses get their water from the well that is down center left.*

It is early afternoon on Sunday, and all sensible people are sleeping, but through the arch comes FIDEL DURÁN. *His straw hat in his hand, his hair plastered to his head with water, he thinks he is a very handsome sight indeed as he pauses, takes a small mirror from his pocket, fixes his neck bandanna . . . a beautiful purple one with orange spots, and shyly knocks, then turns around with a broad grin on his face.*

BERTA *opens the door.* BERTA *is very pretty, but unfortunately she has a very high temper, possibly the result of her red hair. She wears a neat cotton dress and tennis shoes, blue ones. Her hands fastened on her hips, she stands and glares at* FIDEL.

BERTA: Oh, so it is you!

FIDEL (*beaming on her*): A good afternoon to you, Berta.

BERTA (*sniffing*): A good afternoon indeed, and I bothered by fools at this hour of the day.

FIDEL (*in amazement*): Why, Berta, are you angry with me?

BERTA (*questioning Heaven*): He asks me if I am angry with him. Saints in Heaven has he no memory?

FIDEL (*puzzled*): What have I done, Berta?

BERTA (*sarcastically*): Nothing, Fidel, nothing. That is the trouble. But if you come to this house again I will show you the palm of my hand, as I'm showing it to you now. (*She slaps him, steps inside the door, and slams it shut.*)

FIDEL (*pounding on the door*): Open the door, Berta. Open the door! I must speak to you.

(*The door of* SALOMÉ'S *house opens, and* SALOMÉ, *herself, comes out with a small pitcher and begins drawing water from the well. She is twenty-eight, and so many years of hunting a husband have left her with an acid tongue.*)

SALOMÉ: And this is supposed to be a quiet street.

FIDEL (*who dislikes her*): You tend to your affairs, Salomé, and I will tend to mine. (*He starts pounding again. He bleats like a young goat hunting for its mother.*) Berta, Berta.

BERTA (*opens the door again*): I will not have such noises. Do you not realize that this is Sunday afternoon? Have you no thoughts for decent people who are trying to sleep?

FIDEL: Have you no thoughts for me?

BERTA: More than one. And none of them nice.

SALOMÉ: I would call this a lovers' quarrel.

BERTA: Would you indeed! (*glares at* FIDEL) I would call it the impertinence of a wicked man!

FIDEL (*helplessly*): But what have I done?

SALOMÉ: She loved him yesterday, and she will love him tomorrow.

BERTA (*runs down to* SALOMÉ): If I love him tomorrow, may I lose the use of my tongue, yes, and my eyes and ears, too.

FIDEL (*swinging* BERTA *to one side*): Is it fair, I ask you, for a woman to smile at a man one day, and slap his face the next? Is this the manner in which a promised bride should treat her future husband?

SALOMÉ (*grins and winks at him*): You could find yourself another bride.

BERTA (*angrily*): We do not need your advice, Salomé Molina. You and your long nose . . . sticking it in everyone's business.

SALOMÉ (*her eyes flashing*): Is this an insult to me? To me?

BERTA: And who are you to be above insults?

SALOMÉ: I will not stay and listen to such words!

BERTA: Did I ask you to leave the safety of your home?

SALOMÉ (*to* FIDEL): She has not even common politeness. I am going!

BERTA: We shall adore your absence.

SALOMÉ: If this were not Sunday, I would slap your face for you.

BERTA (*taunting*): The great Salomé Molina, afraid of a Sunday fine.

FIDEL (*wanting to be helpful*): You can fight each other tomorrow. There is no fine for weekdays.

SALOMÉ: You stay out of this argument, Fidel Durán.

FIDEL: If you do not leave us I will never find out why Berta is angry with me. (*jumps toward her*) Go away!

SALOMÉ (*jumps back, then tosses her head*): Very well. But the day will come when you will be glad of my company. (*She goes indignantly into her house.*)

FIDEL (*turns to* BERTA): Now, Berta.

BERTA (*interrupting*): As for you, my fine rooster, go and play the bear to Celestina García. She will appreciate you more than I.

FIDEL (*with a guilty hand to his mouth*): So that is what it is.

BERTA (*on the stoop of her own house*): That is all of it, and enough of it. Two times you walked around the plaza with the Celestina last night, and I sitting there on a bench having to watch you. (*goes into the house*)

FIDEL (*speaking through the open door*): But it was a matter of business.

BERTA (*enters with a broom and begins to sweep off the stoop*): Hah! Give me no such phrases. And all of my friends thinking, "Poor Berta, with such a sweetheart." Do you think I have no pride?

FIDEL: But it is that you do not understand. . . .

BERTA: I understand enough to know that all is over between us.

FIDEL: Berta, do not say that. I love you.

BERTA: So you say. And yet you roll the eye at any passing chicken.

FIDEL: Celestina is the daughter of Don Nimfo García.

BERTA: She can be the daughter of the president for all of me. When you marry her, she will bring you a fine dowry, and there will be no more need of Fidel Durán trying to carve wooden doors.

FIDEL (*his pride wounded*): Trying? But I have carved them. Did I not do a new pair for the saloon?

BERTA: Aye, little doors . . . doors that amount to no more than that. . . . (*She snaps her fingers.*) Not for you the great doors of a church.

FIDEL: Why else do you think I was speaking with the Celestina?

BERTA (*stops sweeping*): What new manner of excuse is this?

FIDEL: That is why I came to speak with you. Sit down here on the step with me for a moment.

BERTA (*scandalized*): And have Salomé and Tonia say that I am a wicked, improper girl?

FIDEL (*measuring a tiny space between his fingers*): Just for one little moment. They will see nothing.

BERTA (*sitting down*): Let the words tumble out of your mouth, one, two, three.

FIDEL: Perhaps you do not know that the town of Topo Grande, not thirty kilometers from here, is building a new church.

BERTA (*sniffs*): All the world knows that.

FIDEL: But did you know that Don Nimfo is secretly giving the money for the building of that church?

BERTA: Why?

FIDEL: He offered the money to the Blessed Virgin of Topo Grande if his rooster won in the cockfight. It did win, so now he is building the church.

BERTA (*not yet convinced*): How did you find out about this? Or has Don Nimfo suddenly looked upon you as a son, and revealed all his secrets to you?

FIDEL: Last night on the plaza the Celestina happened to mention it. With a bit of flattery I soon gained the whole story from her.

BERTA: So that is what you were talking about as you walked around the plaza? (*stands*) It must have taken a great deal of flattery to gain so much knowledge from her.

FIDEL (*stands*): Do you not realize what it means? They will need someone to carve the new doors.

(*He strikes a pleased attitude, expecting her to say, "But how wonderful, Fidel."*)

BERTA (*knowing very well what* FIDEL *expects, promptly turns away from him, her hand hiding a smile, as she says with innocent curiosity*): I wonder whom Don Nimfo will get? (*with the delight of discovery*) Perhaps the Brothers Ochóa from Monterrey.

FIDEL (*crestfallen*): He might choose me.

BERTA: You? Hah!

FIDEL: And why not? Am I not the best wood carver in the valley?

BERTA: So you say.

FIDEL: It would take three years to carve those doors, and he would pay me every week. There would be enough to buy you a trousseau and enough left over for a house.

BERTA: Did you tell all that to the Celestina?

FIDEL: Of course not! Does a girl help a man buy a trousseau for another girl? That was why it had to appear as though I were rolling the eye at her. (*He is very much pleased with his brilliance.*)

BERTA: Your success was more than perfect. Today all the world knows that the Celestina has won Berta's man.

FIDEL: But all the world does not know that Fidel Durán, who is I, myself, will carve those doors so as to buy a trousseau and house for Berta, my queen.

BERTA: Precisely. All the world does not know this great thing. . . . (*flaring out at him*) And neither do I!

FIDEL: Do you doubt me, pearl of my life?

BERTA: Does the rabbit doubt the snake? Does the tree doubt the lightning? Do I doubt that you are a teller of tremendous lies? Speak not to me of cleverness. I know what my own eyes see, and I saw you flirting with the Celestina. Last night I saw you . . . and so did all the world!

FIDEL (*beginning to grow angry*): So that is how you trust me, your intended husband.

BERTA: I would rather trust a hungry fox.

FIDEL: Let me speak plainly, my little dove. Because we are to be married is no reason for me to enter a monastery.

BERTA: And who says that we are to be married?

FIDEL (*taken aback*): Why . . . I said it.

BERTA: Am I a dog to your heel that I must obey your every wish?

FIDEL (*firmly*): You are my future wife.

BERTA (*laughs loudly*): Am I indeed?

FIDEL: Your mother has consented, and my father has spoken. The banns have been read in the church! (*folds his arms with satisfaction*)

BERTA (*screaming*): Better to die without children than to be married to such as you.

FIDEL (*screaming above her*): We shall be married within the month.

BERTA: May this hand rot on my arm if I ever sign the marriage contract.

FIDEL: Are you saying that you will not marry me?

BERTA: With all my mouth I am saying it, and a good day to you. (*steps inside the house and slams the door; immediately opens it and sticks her head out*) Tell that good news to that four-nosed shrew of a Celestina. (*slams the door again*)

(FIDEL *puts on his hat and starts toward the archway, then runs down and pounds on* TONIA's *door, then runs across and pounds on* SALOMÉ's, *In a moment both girls come out.* TONIA *is younger and smaller in size than either* SALOMÉ *or* BERTA *and has a distressing habit of whining.*)

SALOMÉ: What is the meaning of this noise?

TONIA: Is something wrong?

FIDEL: I call you both to witness what I say. May I drop dead if I am ever seen in this street again!

(*He settles his hat more firmly on his head, and with as much dignity as he can muster, he strides out through the arch. The girls stare after him, then at* BERTA's *door, then at each other. Both shrug, then with one accord they run up and begin knocking on the door.*)

SALOMÉ: Berta!

TONIA: Berta, come out!

(BERTA *enters. She is obviously trying to keep from crying.*)

SALOMÉ: Has that fool of a sweetheart of yours lost his mind?

TONIA: What happened?

BERTA (*crying in earnest*): This day is blacker than a crow's wing. Oh, Salomé!

(*She flings both arms about the girl's neck and begins to wail loudly.* TONIA *and* SALOMÉ *stare at each other, and then* TONIA *pats* BERTA *on the shoulder.*)

TONIA: Did you quarrel with Fidel?

SALOMÉ: Of course she quarrelled with him. Any fool could see that.

BERTA: He will never come back to me. Never!

TONIA (*to* SALOMÉ): Did she say anything about the Celestina to him?

SALOMÉ (*to* BERTA): You should have kept your mouth shut on the outside of your teeth.

BERTA: A girl has her pride, and no Celestina is going to take any man of mine.

TONIA: But did she take him?

BERTA (*angrily to* TONIA): You take your face away from here!

SALOMÉ: The only thing you can do now is to ask him to come back to you.

TONIA (*starting toward the archway*): I will go and get him.

BERTA (*clutches at her*): I will wither on my legs before I ask him to come back. He would never let me forget that I had to beg him to marry me. (*wails again*) And now he will marry the Celestina. (TONIA *begins to cry with her.*)

TONIA: There are other men.

BERTA: My heart is with Fidel. My life is ruined.

SALOMÉ (*thoughtfully*): If we could bring him back without his knowing Berta had sent for him. . . . (*She sits on the edge of the well.*)

TONIA: Miracles only happen in the church.

SALOMÉ (*catches her knee and begins to rock back and forth*): What could we tell him? What could we tell him?

TONIA: You be careful, Salomé, or you will fall in the well. Then we will all have to go into mourning, and Berta cannot get married at all if she is in mourning.

SALOMÉ (*snaps her fingers*): You could fall down the well, Berta! That would bring him back.

BERTA (*firmly*): I will not fall down the well and drown for any man, not even Fidel.

TONIA: What good would bringing him back do if Berta were dead?

SALOMÉ: Now that is a difficulty. (*begins to pace up and down*) If you are dead, you cannot marry Fidel. If you are not dead, he will not come back. The only thing left for you is to die an old maid.

TONIA: That would be terrible.

BERTA (*wailing*): My life is ruined. Completely ruined.

SALOMÉ (*with sudden determination*): Why? Why should it be?

TONIA (*with awe*): Salomé has had a thought.

BERTA: You do not know what a terrible thing it is to lose the man you love.

SALOMÉ: I am fixing up your life, not mine. Suppose . . . suppose you did fall in the well.

BERTA: I tell you I will not do it.

SALOMÉ: Not really, but suppose he thought you did. What then?

BERTA: You mean . . . pretend? But that is a sin! The priest would give me ten days' penance at confessional.

SALOMÉ (*flinging out her hands*): Ten days' penance or a life without a husband. Which do you choose?

TONIA: I will tell you. She chooses the husband. What do we do, Salomé?

SALOMÉ: You run and find this carver of doors. Tell him that a great scandal has happened . . . that Berta has fallen in the well.

TONIA (*whose dramatic imagination has begun to work*): Because she could not live without him. . . .

BERTA: You tell him that and I will scratch out both your eyes!

TONIA: On Sunday?

BERTA (*sullenly*): On any day.

SALOMÉ: Tell him that Berta has fallen in the well, and that you think she is dying.

TONIA: Is that all?

BERTA: Is that not enough?

SALOMÉ (*entranced with the idea*): Oh, it will be a great scene, with Berta so pale in her bed, and Fidel kneeling in tears beside it.

BERTA: I want you to know that I am a modest girl.

SALOMÉ (*irritated*): You can lie down on the floor then. (*glaring at* TONIA) What are you standing there for? Run!

TONIA (*starts toward the archway, then comes back*): But . . . where will I go?

SALOMÉ: To the place where all men go with a broken heart . . . the saloon. Are you going to stand there all day?

(TONIA *gives a little gasp and runs out through the arch.*)

BERTA: I do not like this idea. If Fidel finds out it is a trick, he will be angrier than ever.

SALOMÉ: But if he does not find out the truth until after you are married . . . what difference will it make?

BERTA: He might beat me.

SALOMÉ: Leave that worry until after you are married. (*inspecting* BERTA) Now how will we make you look pale? Have you any flour? Corn meal might do.

BERTA: No! No! I will not do it.

SALOMÉ: Now, Berta, be reasonable.

BERTA: If I had really fallen down the well, it would be different. But I did not fall down it.

SALOMÉ: Do you not want Fidel to come back to you? Are you in love with him?

BERTA: Yes, I do love him. And I will play no tricks on him. If he loves the Celestina better than he does me . . . (*with great generosity*) he can marry her.

SALOMÉ (*pleading with such idiocy*): But Tonia has gone down to get him. If he comes back and finds you alive . . . he will be angrier than ever.

BERTA (*firmly*): This is your idea. You can get out of it the best way you can. But Fidel will not see me lying down on a bed, nor on a floor, nor any place else.

SALOMÉ: Then there is only one thing to do.

BERTA: What is that?

SALOMÉ: You will go into the house, and I will tell him that you are too sick to see him.

BERTA: That will be just as bad as the other.

SALOMÉ: How can it be? Then if he finds out it is a trick, he will blame me, and you can pretend you knew nothing of it. I do not care how angry he is. I do not want to marry him.

BERTA (*with pleased excitement*): Then he could not be angry with me, could he? I mean if he thought I had nothing to do with it? And I would not have to do penance either, would I?

SALOMÉ: Not one day of penance. Tonia should have found him by now. (*goes to the arch and peers through*) Here they come . . . and Fidel is running half a block in front of her.

BERTA (*joyously*): Then he does love me!

SALOMÉ: Into the house with you. You can watch through the window.

BERTA (*on stoop*): Now, remember, if he gets angry, this was your idea.

SALOMÉ (*claps her hands*): And what a beautiful idea it is!

(BERTA *disappears into the house.* SALOMÉ *looks about her, then dashes over to her own stoop, sits down, flings her shawl over her face, and begins to moan loudly, rocking back and forth. In a moment* FIDEL *dashes through the arch, and stops, out of breath, at seeing* SALOMÉ.)

FIDEL (*gasping*): Berta!

SALOMÉ (*whose moaning grows louder*): Poor darling, poor darling. She was so young.

FIDEL (*desperately*): She is . . . she is dead?

SALOMÉ (*wailing*): She will make such a beautiful corpse. Poor darling. Poor darling.

(TONIA, *exhausted and out of breath, has reached the arch.*)

TONIA (*looks about her in astonishment*): Why, where is Berta? Did she go into the house?

SALOMÉ (*in normal tones*): Of course she went into the house, you fool. Did she not jump down the well? (*remembering* FIDEL) Poor darling.

TONIA (*blankly*): Did she really jump down it? I thought she just fell in by accident.

SALOMÉ (*grimly*): Are you telling this story . . . or am I? (*wailing*) Now she can never go to the plaza again.

(FIDEL *looks helplessly from* TONIA, *who cannot quite get the details of the story straight, to* SALOMÉ *who is having a beautiful time mourning.*)

FIDEL: Where is she? I want to see her.

TONIA (*coming out of her trance*): She is right in here. Did you say she was on the bed or on the floor, Salomé?

SALOMÉ (*getting between them and* BERTA'S *door*): You don't want to see her, Fidel. You know how people look after they've been drowned.

TONIA: But he was supposed to see her. That was why you sen . . .

SALOMÉ (*glaring at her*): Tonia, dear, suppose that you let me tell the story. After all, I was here and you were not.

FIDEL (*exploding*): For the love of the saints, tell me! Is she dead?

SALOMÉ (*thinking this over*): Well . . . not exactly.

FIDEL: You mean . . . you mean there is hope?

SALOMÉ: I would say there was great hope.

FIDEL (*takes off his hat and mops his face*): What can I do? Oh, if I could only see her. . . .

SALOMÉ: If you would go to the church and light a candle to Our Blessed Lady and ask her to forgive you for getting angry with Berta . . . perhaps things will arrange themselves.

FIDEL: Do you think she will get well soon?

SALOMÉ: With a speed that will amaze you.

FIDEL: I will go down and light the candle right now.

(*As he turns to leave, who should come through the archway but* CELESTINA GARCÍA. *She can match temper for temper with* BERTA *any day, and right now she is on the warpath. Brushing past these three as though they did not exist, she goes up to* BERTA'S *door and pounds on it.*)

CELESTINA: I dare you to come out and call this Celestina García a four-nosed shrew to her face.

SALOMÉ (*trying to push* FIDEL *through the arch*): You had best run to the church.

FIDEL (*pushing past her and going up to* CELESTINA): How dare you speak like that to a poor drowned soul?

SALOMÉ (*to* CELESTINA): Why do you not go away? We never needed you so little.

CELESTINA: So she is pretending to be drowned, eh? Is that her coward's excuse?

BERTA (*through window*): Who dares to call Berta Cantú a coward?

CELESTINA: You know well enough who calls you, and I the daughter of Don Nimfo García.

TONIA: Ai, Salomé! And now Fidel will know that Berta was not drowned at all.

FIDEL (*who has been listening to this conversation with growing surprise and suspicion, now turns furiously toward* BERTA'S *house*): Not drowned, eh? So this was a trick to bring me back, eh? I am through with your tricks, you hear me? Through with them!

BERTA (*through window*): You stay right there until I come out. (*She disappears from view.*)

FIDEL (*turning to* SALOMÉ): I see your hand in this.

SALOMÉ: The more fool you to be taken in by a woman's tricks.

CELESTINA: What care I for tricks? No woman is going to call me names!

BERTA (*coming through the door*): You keep silence, Celestina García. I will deal with you in a minute. And as for you, Fidel Durán. . . .

FIDEL (*stormily*): As for me, I am finished with all women. The world will see me no more. I will enter a monastery and carve as many doors as I like. Do you hear me, Berta Cantú?

BERTA (*putting both hands over her ears*): What do I care for your quack, quack, quack!

FIDEL: Now she calls me a duck! Good afternoon to you! (*He stalks out with wounded dignity.*)

CELESTINA (*catching* BERTA *by the shoulder and swinging her around*): I ask you again; did you call me a four-nosed shrew?

BERTA: I did, and I will repeat it with the greatest of pleasure. You are a four-nosed shrew and a three-eyed frog!

CELESTINA: I have always looked on you as my friend . . . you pink-toed cat!

BERTA: And I have always trusted you . . . you sly robber of bridegrooms!

(*She raises her hand to slap* CELESTINA. SALOMÉ *catches it.*)

SALOMÉ: This is Sunday, Berta! And Sunday costs five pesos.

TONIA: If you had to pay a fine for starting a fight on top of losing Fidel. . . . Ay, that would be terrible.

(BERTA *and* CELESTINA *glare at each other, and then slowly begin to circle each other, spitting out their insults as they do so.*)

CELESTINA: It is my honor that is making me fight, or I would wait until tomorrow.

BERTA: If I had five pesos to throw away, I would pull out your dangling tongue . . . leaving only the flapping roots.

CELESTINA: Ha! I make a nose at your words.

BERTA: As for you . . . you eater of ugly smelling cheese. . . .

(*They jump at each other, but remember the penalty just in time and pull back. Again they begin to circle around, contenting themselves with making faces at each other.* SALOMÉ *suddenly clasps her hands.*)

SALOMÉ: You are both certain that you want to fight today?

CELESTINA: Why else do you think I came here?

BERTA: These insults have gone too far to stop now.

SALOMÉ: The only thing that stands in the way is the five pesos for the Sunday fine.

TONIA: And five pesos is a lot of money.

SALOMÉ: Then the only thing to do is to play the fingers.

CELESTINA: What?

BERTA: Eh?

SALOMÉ: Precisely. Whoever loses strikes the first blow and pays the fine. Then you can fight as much as you like.

TONIA (*with awed admiration*): Ay, Salomé, you have so many brains.

CELESTINA (*doubtfully*): It is a big risk.

BERTA (*shrugging*): Perhaps you are afraid of taking a risk.

CELESTINA: I am not afraid of anything. But Tonia will have to be the judge. Salomé is too clever.

BERTA: Very well. But Salomé has to stand behind you to see that you do not cheat. I would not trust you any more than I would a mouse near a piece of fresh bacon.

CELESTINA (*pulls back her clenched fist, then thinks better of it, and speaks with poor grace*): Very well.

(CELESTINA *and* BERTA *stand facing each other.* TONIA *stands between them up on the stoop.* SALOMÉ *stands behind* CELESTINA.)

TONIA (*feeling a little nervous over this great honor of judging*): Both arms behind your backs. (*The girls link their arms behind them.*) Now, when I drop my hand, Berta will guess first as Celestina brings her fingers forward. The first girl to guess correctly twice wins. Are you ready? (*All nod*) I am going to drop my arm.

SALOMÉ: Celestina, put out your fingers before Berta guesses. We will have no cheating.

CELESTINA (*sullenly*): Very well. (*She puts out two fingers behind her, and* SALOMÉ, *seeing this, raises up her arm with two fingers extended, opening and closing them scissors fashion.* BERTA *frowns a little as she looks up at the signal, and* CELESTINA, *seeing this, swings around and looks at* SALOMÉ, *who promptly grins warmly and pretends to be waving at* BERTA. CELESTINA *then looks at* TONIA.)

BERTA: Very well.

CELESTINA (*guessing as* BERTA *swings her arm forward*): Three.

(BERTA *triumphantly holds up one finger. Biting her lip,* CELESTINA *starts to swing forward her own arm.* SALOMÉ, *intent on signalling* BERTA, *holds up her own five fingers spread wide, and does not notice until too late that* CELESTINA *has swung around to watch her.*)

CELESTINA (*screaming*): So I cheat, eh? (*With that she gives* SALOMÉ *a resounding slap on the cheek. The next moment the two women are mixed up in a beautiful howling, grunting fight, while* TONIA *and* BERTA, *wide-eyed, cling together and give the two women as much space as possible. Let it be understood that this is only a fight of kicking, hair-pulling, and scratching. There is no man involved, nor a point of honor. Rather a matter of angry pride. So the two are not attempting to mutilate each other. They are simply gaining satisfaction. The grand finale comes when* CELESTINA *knocks* SALOMÉ *to the ground and sits on her.*)

CELESTINA (*breathing hard*): There! That was worth five pesos.

TONIA: You have to pay it. And Don Nimfo will be angry with you.

CELESTINA (*pulling herself to her feet*): I am too tired to fight any more now, but I will be back next Tuesday, Berta, and then I will beat you up.

BERTA (*sniffing*): If you can.

CELESTINA (*warningly*): And there is no fine on Tuesday.

BERTA: Come any day you like. I will be ready for you.

TONIA (*to* CELESTINA): You should be ashamed to fight.

CELESTINA: Who are you to talk to me? (*stamps her foot at* TONIA *who jumps behind* BERTA.) Good afternoon, my brave little rabbits!

(*She staggers out as straight as she can, but as she reaches the archway she feels a twinge of agony and is forced to limp. By this time* SALOMÉ *has gathered together what strength she has left, and she slowly stands up. Once erect, she looks at* BERTA *and* TONIA *as though she were considering boiling in oil too good for them.*)

SALOMÉ (*with repressed fury*): My friends. My very good friends.

TONIA (*frightened*): Now, Salomé. . . .

SALOMÉ (*screaming*): Do not speak to me! Either of you! (*She manages to get to the door of her house.*) When I need help, do you give me aid? No! But just you wait . . . both of you!

TONIA: What are you going to do?

SALOMÉ: I am going to wait for a weekday, and then I am going to beat up both of you at once. One (*she takes a deep breath*) with each hand! (*She nearly falls through the door of her house.*)

BERTA (*with false bravado*): Who is afraid of her?

TONIA: I am. Salomé is very strong. It is all your fault. If you had not gotten mad at Fidel, this would not have happened.

BERTA (*snapping at her*): You leave Fidel out of this.

TONIA (*beginning to cry*): When Salomé beats me up, that will be your fault too.

BERTA: Stop crying!

TONIA: I am not a good fighter, but I can tell Fidel the truth about how you would not jump down the well to win him back.

BERTA: You open your mouth to Fidel and I will push you in the well.

TONIA: You will not have strength enough to push a baby in the well when they get through with you.

BERTA: Get out! Get out of here! (*She stamps her foot at* TONIA *and the girl, frightened, gives a squeak and runs into her own house.* BERTA *looks after her, then, beginning to sniffle, she goes over and sits on the well. She acts like a child who has been told that it is not proper for little girls to cry, and she is very much in need of a handkerchief. Just then* FIDEL *sticks his head around the arch.*)

FIDEL (*once more the plaintive goat*): Berta.

(BERTA *half jumps, then pretends not to hear him.*)

FIDEL (*enters cautiously, not taking his eyes off of* BERTA'S *stiff back. He moves around at the back, skirts* TONIA'S *house, then works his way round to her*): Berta.

BERTA (*sniffing*): What is it?

FIDEL (*circling the back of the well*): Are you crying, Berta?

BERTA (*stubbornly*): No!

FIDEL (*sitting beside her*): Yes, you are. I can see you crying.

BERTA: If you can see, why do you ask, then?

FIDEL: I am sorry we quarrelled, Berta.

BERTA: Are you?

FIDEL: Are you sorry?

BERTA: No!

FIDEL: I was hoping you were, because . . . do you know whom I saw on the plaza?

BERTA: Grandfather Devil.

FIDEL: Don Nimfo himself.

BERTA: Perhaps you saw the Celestina, too.

FIDEL (*placatingly*): Now, Berta, you know I do not care if I never see the Celestina again. (*pulls out a handkerchief and extends it to her*) Here, wipe your face with this.

BERTA: I have a handkerchief of my own. (*Nevertheless she takes it, and wipes her eyes and then blows her nose.*)

FIDEL: Don Nimfo said I could carve the church doors for him. But he said I would have to move to Topo Grande to work on them. He said I had to leave right away.

BERTA (*perking up her interest*): You mean . . . move away from here?

FIDEL: And I was wondering if we could get married tomorrow. I know this is very sudden, Berta, but after all, think how long I have waited to carve a church door.

BERTA: Tomorrow. (*She looks toward* SALOMÉ'S *house.*) They would both be too sore to do anything by tomorrow.

FIDEL (*too concerned with his own plans to hear what she is saying*): Of course I know that you may not be able to forgive me. . . .

BERTA: Fidel, I want you to understand that if I do marry you tomorrow . . . that means we will leave here tomorrow, eh?

FIDEL: Ay, yes. I have to be in Topo Grande on Tuesday.

BERTA: I hope you will always understand what a great thing I have done for you. It is not every girl who would forgive so easily as I.

FIDEL (*humbly*): Indeed, I know that, Berta.

BERTA: Are you quite sure that we will leave here tomorrow?

FIDEL: Quite sure.

BERTA: Very well. I will marry you.

FIDEL (*joyfully*): Berta! (*Bends forward to kiss her. She jumps up.*)

BERTA: Just a moment. We are not married yet. Do you think that I am just any girl that you can kiss me . . . like that! (*She snaps her fingers.*)

FIDEL (*humbly*): I thought . . . just this once. . . .

BERTA (*gravely thoughtful*): Well, perhaps . . . just this once . . . you may kiss my hand.

As he kisses it

THE CURTAINS CLOSE

About Age

Age, like youth, is a condition, not a time. One can meet sixteen-year-old graybeards.

Age presupposes the qualities of maturity and even of wisdom. Yet, maturity is not necessarily the result of years alone. Rather, it is the result of knowledge gained through experience, and experience most often comes with years. Obviously, age presupposes a physical condition, but physical condition is not the thrust of the four plays in this section.

Age, like youth, has its own problems which, while not necessarily those of youth, are similar. Age has experienced the problems of youth, of alienation, of love, and of marriage and must face its particular problems: financial insecurity, philosophical disillusionment, bittersweet memories, growing loneliness, and impending death.

In this regard, it seems that there are two general approaches to age—that which looks back to the past and that which looks forward to the future, whatever it may be. It is here we find the difference between age and agedness. Both conditions are worthy of examination, and these plays examine a miniscule part of both.

Charlie, in *The Beer Can Tree,* looks forward, although he takes pride in his past accomplishments. In *Waiting for the Bus* the characters obviously look back, but they look back to nothing. In *Something Unspoken* emotional panic develops as a result of insecurity. In *The Governor's Lady* loneliness and guilt create a horrible nightmare.

You will find that in these four plays age is both terrifying and comfortable, which indicates that age is like the rest of life—complex.

The Beer Can Tree

R. DAVID COX

Characters

THE MAN
CHARLIE

Reading Guides

1. Like many other plays in this book, the scene in *The Beer Can Tree* is important. You must imagine Charlie's tree to be as magnificent as he thinks it is.

2. You should watch Charlie carefully. He does not necessarily say what he thinks. He appears confidently in control, but underneath he is panicked. Thus, he must reason and speak with care not to reveal his true feelings.

The Beer Can Tree

MOUNTAIN SHACK. Broken steps, falling porch, loose boards. In front of the shack, off to the left, is a large pine tree. Beer cans are hung on the tree. Some of them are old and have been affected by the weather; others are newer and some are new. They cover the tree like Christmas baubles, except for a space at the top. At the side of the shack there is a ladder. A hammer, a large nail, and some wire are on the porch.

At rise of curtain, a MAN *stands looking at the tree shaking his head uncomprehendingly. He is neatly dressed, businesslike in an outdoor way. He is taking notes.*

CHARLIE *appears, silently, from the right. He is well over sixty, is shabbily dressed, and carries a six-pack of beer. He sets the beer down on the porch and walks over behind the* MAN. *They both stare at the tree.*

CHARLIE: Big tree.
MAN (*startled*): What?
CHARLIE: Big tree.
MAN: Yes, Yes, of course. It is a big tree.
CHARLIE: Sure is a big tree.
MAN: Yes, it is. I was just noticing.
CHARLIE: Pine.
MAN: I know.
CHARLIE: Lodgepole.
MAN: What's that?
CHARLIE: Lodgepole.
MAN: I think it's a jack pine.
CHARLIE: Some say jack; some say lodgepole.
MAN: Oh?
CHARLIE: I say lodgepole.
MAN: I've always heard jack.
CHARLIE: Some say jack; some say lodgepole.
MAN (*above it all*): Well, I don't want to argue about it.
CHARLIE: Nope.
MAN: It's a second generation tree; you can see that.
CHARLIE: Lodgepole always is.
MAN: Yes, they grow up fast—after a natural disaster.
CHARLIE: Fire.
MAN: Fire's usually man-made—careless people. I don't necessarily call that natural. Diseased trees, usually.
CHARLIE: Sometimes yes, sometimes no.
MAN: But *usually* it's people who start fires.
CHARLIE: I know.
MAN: Oh. You live around here, then.

CHARLIE: Yep.
MAN: Pass by here often?
CHARLIE: Not many folks do.
MAN: More and more everyday, though.
CHARLIE: Ever since they put in that cut.
MAN: Cut?
CHARLIE: The cut out there.
MAN: Oh, you mean the road.
CHARLIE: Cut. Some people call it a road; some, a cut.
MAN (*small laugh*): Well, I guess in the mountains one would call it a cut.
CHARLIE: Yes.
MAN: Uh . . . you know the man who lives here?
CHARLIE: A little.
MAN: Is he around?
CHARLIE: Most of the time. Most people are, up here.
MAN: Yes, I know.
CHARLIE: Oh?
MAN: Yes. I mean, I've been up here before.
CHARLIE: You from around here?
MAN: No, I'm from . . .
CHARLIE: Where you from? Town?
MAN: Yes, I'm from town.
CHARLIE: I just been in town.
MAN: That's funny. I didn't hear you drive up.
CHARLIE: That's because I walked.
MAN: Walked?
CHARLIE: Yep. Walked.
MAN: But it's thirty miles to town, through the mountains. It must take you two days.
CHARLIE: Each way. Four all together.
MAN: And you just sleep in the mountains?
CHARLIE: Yep.
MAN: How about the winter?
CHARLIE: What about it?
MAN: Do you sleep out in the winter?
CHARLIE: Not so much anymore. Used to a lot, but I'm tireder now.
MAN (*genuinely impressed*): Well, that's really something. Why, you must be about sixty.
CHARLIE: I guess.
MAN: Where do you live?
CHARLIE: Here.
MAN: Here? Here!

CHARLIE: Forty years now, more or less.

MAN: Then, I was talking to your neighbors down the road—I mean cut—you're Snowbound Charlie.

CHARLIE: In the winter. And winter is most of the time.

MAN: And you've been here forty years?

CHARLIE: More or less.

MAN (*turning to the tree*): Then this is your tree.

CHARLIE (*pride*): Sure is. Fine lodgepole.

MAN: The finest I've seen.

CHARLIE (*turning to the beer*): I've seen better.

MAN: Well, it's hard to tell, with the cans.

CHARLIE: What's that?

MAN: You can't see the tree for the . . .

(*He sees* CHARLIE *with the beer.*)

CHARLIE (*opening the beer and beginning to drink*): You a tourist?

MAN: No, I'm . . . do you put the cans on the tree?

CHARLIE: Cans?

MAN: Tree.

CHARLIE: Lodgepole don't usually have branches like that at the bottom. Some do; most don't.

MAN: Oh?

CHARLIE: This one has, though. No sun problem. Most lodgepole have a sun problem; they grow too close together. That one don't have a sun problem.

MAN: But some of these lower branches are dying.

CHARLIE: Maybe so, maybe not. Can't tell. Lodgepole fools you sometimes that way.

MAN: Maybe it's the cans.

CHARLIE: Nope. You say you're a tourist?

MAN: No, I . . .

CHARLIE: You look like a tourist, though not many come this way.

MAN: The way a man looks isn't always the way he is.

CHARLIE: Sometimes yes, sometimes no.

MAN: That's true, I guess.

CHARLIE: Like trees.

MAN: Yes, I like trees, a great deal I like them.

CHARLIE: What I said was, sometimes a tree looks the way it is, sometimes no.

MAN (*sarcastic*): And you've been studying them for forty years, I guess.

CHARLIE: More or less.

MAN (*walking to the tree and playing with one of the cans*): What do you do?

CHARLIE: Do?
MAN: Work at.
CHARLIE: Nothing, now.
MAN: What did you do forty years ago?
CHARLIE: Used to mine for tungsten. Made a little money, then quit.
MAN: Why'd you quit?
CHARLIE: Tungsten quit first.
MAN: I see. And the cans?
CHARLIE: What did you say you do?
MAN: I didn't say.

(CHARLIE *finishes his beer. Picks up the hammer and nail. He puts holes through the bottom of the can and the side of the can. Then he takes a short length of wire and makes a loop through the two holes.*)

I'm from the Parks Department.

(CHARLIE *walks to the side of the house, gets the ladder, takes the ladder to the tree. Sets the ladder up.*)

From the Parks Department. The Department of Parks.

(CHARLIE *climbs the ladder almost to the top.*)

Eyesore section.

(CHARLIE *carefully fits the loop of wire around a branch and hangs the beer can. Climbs down. Walks back to the six-pack of beer, opens another one, takes a drink, sits, looks up at the can he has placed, admires it.*)

MAN: I don't think you heard what I said.
CHARLIE: Nope.

(CHARLIE *gets up, admires the can from another direction and angle.* MAN, *who has been looking at* CHARLIE, *now looks at the new can, then looks away.*)

MAN: I'm from the Department of Parks.
CHARLIE: This is a park.
MAN: Yes, I know.
CHARLIE: Got a ninety-nine-year lease on it. Fifty-nine years to go.
MAN: I know, but . . .

(*He can't tell* CHARLIE *what he's here for.*)

How long you been hanging the cans?

(MAN *laughs at himself and the absurdity of the question.*)

CHARLIE: What's that?

MAN (*irritated*): You only hear what you want to hear, don't you?

CHARLIE: Don't know. Ever since they had cans, I guess. I remember I tried bottles, but they hang too heavy. Ruin the branches.

MAN: It might help if you could remember.

CHARLIE: Help what?

MAN: Help me to understand why you put beer cans on such a beautiful tree.

CHARLIE: Sure is a beautiful tree.

MAN (*patience going*): But you hang cans all over it!

CHARLIE: Parks Department, huh? That something new?

MAN: Well, my division is. (*pride*) I'm the division, that is. I mean, it really isn't a division yet. With one man and all. It's just a temporary name.

CHARLIE: What name?

MAN: Eyesore. My idea, too, and I've got to make it work. I mean, I told them it was such a problem that it needed a whole division. They said go ahead with it; we'll give you a chance to prove to us that there is a need for a whole division.

CHARLIE: A division, huh?

MAN (*laughing a little*): Yes, I started in the planting division, but I got this idea; so they said go ahead. I just sort of started at the top. All it takes is an idea.

CHARLIE: And a park.

MAN: Well, sure, that's why there is a Parks Department. Parks are for people.

CHARLIE: Like a beer?

MAN: A beer? No. I couldn't take your beer. I mean, you walked miles for it.

CHARLIE: No problem. Been doing it for years.

MAN: You mean, you've always been walking down for beer?

CHARLIE: I'll go down again tomorrow. Two days down, two days back.

MAN: And you just get beer?

CHARLIE: Six.

MAN (*absolutely dazed*): And then you sit down and drink them.

CHARLIE: Sit down and drink them.

MAN: And hang the cans on the tree. (*sarcasm*) Why don't you get twelve as long as you're there? I mean, they're not much more trouble to carry, are they?

CHARLIE: No trouble to carry. Just when I drink twelve, it goes to my head, and I get dizzy on the ladder.

MAN: Good grief—I just don't understand.

CHARLIE: Why you so interested in trees? You writing one of those books?

MAN: I . . . what? Writing a book? Of course not. I'm not writing a book! I mean, after all this time, you don't know why I'm here?

CHARLIE: You come here to see me?

MAN: Yes, as a matter of fact, I did.

CHARLIE: Sure you don't want a beer?

MAN (*frustrated*): Now look here. I'm from the Parks Department, Eyesore Division.

CHARLIE: That's what you said. Got your own division, too. That's good for a young man. Start at the top.

MAN: I came here to see you about this tree. It's an eyesore.

CHARLIE: Lodgepole.

MAN: You're avoiding me. It's an eyesore.

CHARLIE (*taking a long swallow of beer*): OK.

MAN: I'm here to do something about it.

CHARLIE: Not many around like it.

MAN: No, no, no. You've got the wrong idea. It's a crime to have that there where everybody from the cut can see it. It's . . . it's . . . an eyesore.

(CHARLIE *finishes his beer, takes the hammer and nail, makes the hole, and attaches the wire.*)

MAN: Now look. I know you've lived here a long time, but you can't make this park a dump for your beer cans. I admire your long walk to get it, but why don't you just bury the cans, instead of hanging them on the tree? You said yourself it's an unusual lodgepole.

(CHARLIE *climbs the ladder and carefully places the can.*)

I mean, it looks to me like you're raising a monument to beer, or beer cans, or whatever it is. People just don't hang beer cans on government property!

(CHARLIE *climbs back down the ladder, steps back to admire the can. Gets another beer.*)

Now, I didn't mean to shout, but the long and the short of it is that the tree has got to come down. There are just too many cans on it. Couldn't possibly take them off. We'll have to cut it down.

(*This stops* CHARLIE *cold.*)

I'm sorry it has to be that way. You're obviously fond of the tree, but you seem to be consciously creating an eyesore and enjoying it. Now, it's just this sort of thing that I suggested we have a division for. For just this sort of eyesore. I mean, why do you do it?

CHARLIE: I don't know.

MAN: You don't know? You don't know? That's what's wrong with this country. Nobody knows. Nobody does anything constructive to parks—just destructive. You've lived in these mountains all your life; you should love them. They've sheltered you, protected you, given you a living. Now you hang beer cans all over them.

CHARLIE: I don't think it looks as bad as all that.

MAN: Look at these cans—all rusty, ugly.

CHARLIE: Those were the first ones. I didn't know how to hang them. I hung them with the open side up; then the water'd get in them and rust off the bottoms. But I learned to hang them upside down. Now the water don't get in them; now they don't rust out the bottoms.

MAN: Rusty, shiny, it doesn't make any difference. They're beer cans.

CHARLIE: After I finish the job, then I'll replace these old rusty ones. Except the first one, that is.

MAN: I'm afraid you won't have time to finish. We're going to have to cut the tree down. It's my division's job.

CHARLIE: Took me awhile to learn to hang them at an angle. When I hung them straight up, snow'd catch on them, and the limbs'd get too heavy and break. Then I started hanging them at an angle. Now the snow don't stay on them, and they don't break.

MAN: Well, it's all very interesting, but don't you agree that it's an eyesore, and there is no room for eyesores in public parks.

CHARLIE: Nope.

MAN: No? No? Look at this littered mess!

CHARLIE: Mr. Eyesore Division—did you ever build anything?

MAN (*momentarily stunned*): Listen, I don't have to be here to be insulted. I didn't even have to come up here, except to see the tree. All I have to do is order it cut down. It's an eyesore. That's it.

(*He starts to leave.*)

CHARLIE: Mr. Eyesore. . . .

MAN: I'm not going to stay here to be insulted.

CHARLIE: Come on back. Let's talk for a minute. Sorry I insulted you.

(MAN *reluctantly returns.*)

So you're going to cut down my tree?

MAN (*still bellicose*): It's not your tree; it's the Parks Department's.

CHARLIE: Chop it down, drag it away, and burn it.

MAN: It's an eyesore; that's what we have to do.

CHARLIE: But you can't do it. It's my tree. I have a lease on it. Ninety-nine years.

MAN (*compassionate, now*): You've just got to understand, Charlie. It is your tree and it isn't. You've got a lease on it, but we own it. You must understand my position. I don't want to cut down the tree. (*pause*) After all, it is a nice tree.

CHARLIE: The park would take my tree?

MAN: It's not the tree, Charlie. It's the cans. Cans on a tree are . . . is . . . an eyesore.

CHARLIE: Say that in your rule book?

MAN: Rule book?

CHARLIE: You have an eyesore rule book?

MAN: Why, no, of course not. That would be silly.

CHARLIE: How do you know what an eyesore is, then? If you don't have a rule book?

MAN: I . . . well, I can just tell, that's all.

CHARLIE: Maybe you ought to write one, then, so other people could tell.

MAN: No, I've got no talent for that sort of thing.

CHARLIE: Tell me what an eyesore is; then maybe I'll let you cut the tree down.

MAN: Oh, that's easy. An eyesore is anything that offends the public eye, is ugly, and should be removed.

CHARLIE: You gonna cut down my cabin!

MAN: Your cabin?

CHARLIE: Isn't it ugly?

MAN (*with a little laugh*): No, not exactly.

CHARLIE: Is it pretty?

MAN: No, not exactly. You know what it is? It's quaint.

CHARLIE: How about me?

MAN (*embarrassed*): You?

CHARLIE: Am I ugly, pretty, or quaint?

MAN: I can't say that. I mean, you're a person. Persons aren't eyesores.

CHARLIE (*relentless*): Who's uglier—tree, house, or me?

MAN (*outraged*): The tree has cans hanging on it!

CHARLIE: If my house had cans, would you have to tear it down?

MAN: Of course not. It's your home.

CHARLIE: If I hung cans on myself and went around clanking, would you have to throw me on the dump and burn me?

MAN: Now you're being silly.

CHARLIE (*in earnest*): You won't take my house, or me, but you'll take my tree. We're all eyesores.

MAN: Charlie, I don't quite know how to explain it to you. A tree is a natural thing, a thing for people to enjoy. To enjoy looking at when they drive through the cut. A miner sitting in front of his shack—cabin—home—is quaint for the city people. That's part of the atmosphere. And parks are for people.

CHARLIE: You do have a rule book, then.

MAN (*with a compassionate smile*): In a way, I guess we do. In the Parks Department, we think everything has its place. When things are in order, you have a park. That's what a park is, everything in order.

CHARLIE (*seemingly beaten*): So my tree has to go to the county dump. So things will fit.

MAN: That's right, Charlie. It's a hard thing, but that's the way it is.

CHARLIE: Sometimes yes, sometimes no.

MAN (*a little embarrassed*): I'm just doing my job. (*patronizingly*) And you know, Charlie, I have built something. Lots of things. Useful things. A table. Bookcase for my books. Other things, too. Useful things. It was hard work, too.

CHARLIE: Want to have that beer, now?

MAN: Beer? Yes, I guess I could have one now. One won't bother me driving down the canyon.

CHARLIE (*opens beer*): We can sit here on the stoop and look quaint.

MAN (*drinks quietly for a moment*): You know, Charlie, I have an admission to make—now that business is out of the way. I was thinking, before you came up, I sort of envy your life up here. Simple and quiet. Hear the wind in the trees and feel the cold, clean air. Never anything to worry about.

CHARLIE (*looking at him*): Nope.

MAN: You can walk through the woods and the mountains. Just roam. I guess that's why I like working with parks. Pleasant surroundings. Nice people. And to think you been here forty years. You're a lucky man.

(CHARLIE *finishes his beer. He makes the holes in the can, puts the wire through, but remains seated.*)

CHARLIE (MAN *doesn't seem to notice*): I didn't build nothing useful, though. I started out to get rich. After about ten years, it just didn't matter. Had enough money to buy can goods.

MAN: For some people, that's a good life. And if you've built a good life, it's useful.

CHARLIE: I built that tree over there.

MAN: It really is one of the finest lodgepole pines I've ever seen.

CHARLIE: I built it, but can't finish it now. I can't seem to get my legs together to climb the ladder. Doesn't seem much worth it now. Guess that's the way things are.

MAN: Sometimes yes, sometimes no. A man's got to finish what he starts—if it's useful enough to start, It's useful enough to finish. That's the way I feel about my division.

CHARLIE: I want to, but I just can't bring myself to do it, now that I know it's useless. Maybe you'd give me hand. Got a can all ready.

MAN: Me? Oh no, no. I couldn't do that.

CHARLIE: Why not. It's coming down anyway.

MAN (*nervous laugh*): Well, I guess one more can wouldn't make it any more of an eyesore.

(*He takes the can, climbs the ladder, finds a place for the can, hangs it, comes down. He stands back, looking at the tree. He gets his beer and drinks absent-mindedly.*)

Which one did I put up? I can't find it.

CHARLIE: I think it's the one to the left of the one I put up.

MAN: Which one is that?

CHARLIE: Strike a line straight up from the ladder, you'll find mine. To the left is yours.

MAN: Oh, yeah. There it is. (*He giggles.*) Funny, isn't it.

CHARLIE: Sure is.

MAN: Cans on a tree. (*He finishes his beer.*)

CHARLIE: You fix that one. I've got to go around back. Beer, you know.

MAN: Oh, sure.

(CHARLIE *exits in the direction of the* MAN'S *car.* MAN *takes the hammer and nail, starts to make the holes, then stops. He goes to the tree, checks a can to see where the holes are properly made, then goes back and makes the holes, attaches the wire. He is very precise, an artist.* CHARLIE *returns.*)

Here it is, all fixed.

CHARLIE: Say, you learned how to fix those fast. Took me a long time to figure the right way.

MAN: Go ahead, put it up.

CHARLIE: Still don't feel much like it. You fixed it; you put it up.

MAN (*a little hesitation*): Well . . . OK.

(*He does so. When he gets down from the ladder,* CHARLIE *hands him the beer he has opened while the* MAN *was climbing the ladder. The* MAN *is admiring the can on the tree.* CHARLIE *hands him the beer. He drinks automatically.*)

CHARLIE: That's a good place. Looks real good, up there. High, too.

MAN: Pretty close to the top.

CHARLIE: You gotta be careful when you hang the next one.

MAN: Why? We just go on to the top. Then it's finished. Gotta finish what you start.

CHARLIE: Well, you see, if you hang them too close together, they hit one another when the wind blows. Spoils the sound of the wind in the park.

MAN: You're right. Hadn't thought of that. Wind in the park. That's a name for you. Wind in the park.

CHARLIE: Good name.

MAN (*finishing off his beer*): I've almost finished this one.

CHARLIE: Good. Put it up. My legs's still kind of wobbly.

MAN: Maybe we can reach the top. Finish it.

CHARLIE: Not today, I don't think. Only one more left.

MAN (*concerned*): Only one more can!

CHARLIE: That's right. Be another four days at least.

MAN: Four days!

CHARLIE: Yep, that's the way building is.

MAN (*attempting to mitigate the circumstances*): I know what. I'll get my car, run down, and get another pack. Be back before dark. We can finish it then.

CHARLIE: OK. You do that.

MAN: While I'm gone, you can put those two on. Right next to mine. If you put one to the right and one just under and to the left of the one I just put up, it will balance. Got to have balance.

CHARLIE: All right, I'll try it.

MAN: See you shortly.

(*He exits to the car.* CHARLIE *just sits, smiling. The* MAN *reenters. He is carrying a jacket.*)

The car's dead.

CHARLIE: Dead, huh? Well, that's the way it is with cars.

MAN: Won't start. Must be in the wires.

CHARLIE: Won't finish today, then.

MAN: But we'll finish . . . before the cutters come.

CHARLIE: Take four days for me to walk. When they coming?

MAN: Well . . . uh . . . four days is a long time.

CHARLIE: It's hard work for an old man.
MAN: Of course. It's a long walk.
CHARLIE: A young man might do it in three.
MAN (*uneasy*): Why, yes, it could be done in three.
CHARLIE: I used to could do it in three.
MAN: I'll tell you what. I'll walk down for the beer. I'll take the cut; it'll be easy.
CHARLIE (*thoughtful*): Never thought of that. It would be easier on the cut.
MAN: I'll leave now. (*takes jacket*)
CHARLIE: Be careful, now. Remember to always walk east going; west, coming. If it gets too dark, stop. But you've got a good moon tonight.
MAN: Sure. I'll be back. (*second thought*) It won't snow, will it?
CHARLIE: Too early. Later on it'll snow.
MAN: Yes, later on it'll snow.

(*He exits.* CHARLIE *sits and smiles.* MAN *reenters, slowly.*)

Charlie. Then it'll be finished. Then I can cut it down.
CHARLIE: Yep. It's an eyesore.
MAN: It is an eyesore. It has to come down.
CHARLIE: When it's finished.
MAN: When it's finished. (*leaving*) I'm gone again.
CHARLIE (*calling*): Remember. Only six.
MAN (*off*): Yeah . . . only six.

(*There is silence for a moment.* CHARLIE, *with a smile, gets up, goes inside the cabin, and returns with a bag and a spade. He goes to the tree and begins to take off cans, very slowly. As he drops them into the bag, he counts.*)

CHARLIE: One. Two. Three. Four. Five. Six. (*with finality*) Seven.

(*There is a slow dim to black and* CURTAIN.)

Something Unspoken

TENNESSEE WILLIAMS

Characters

MISS CORNELIA SCOTT
MISS GRACE LANCASTER

Reading Guides

1. The exposition in *Something Unspoken* does not arrive until very near the end of the play. For this reason, you must attempt to understand the character relationships even though you do not know the reasons for the relationships.
2. Two major conflicts operate simultaneously in this play. Both are critical to an understanding of the major character, Cornelia.

MISS CORNELIA SCOTT, sixty, a wealthy Southern spinster, is seated at a small mahogany table which is set for two. The other place, not yet occupied, has a single rose in a crystal vase before it. CORNELIA's position at the table is flanked by a cradle phone, a silver tray of mail, and an ornate silver coffee urn. An imperial touch is given by purple velvet drapes directly behind her figure at the table. A console phonograph is at the edge of a lighted area.

At rise of the curtain, she is dialing a number on the phone.

CORNELIA: Is this Mrs. Horton Reid's residence? I am calling for Miss Cornelia Scott. Miss Scott is sorry that she will not be able to attend the meeting of the Confederate Daughters this afternoon as she woke up this morning with a sore throat and has to remain in bed, and will you kindly give her apologies to Mrs. Reid for not letting her know sooner. Thank you. Oh, wait a moment! I think Miss Scott has another message.

(GRACE LANCASTER *enters the lighted area.* CORNELIA *raises her hand in a warning gesture.*)

—What is it, Miss Scott? (*There is a brief pause.*) Oh, Miss Scott would like to leave word for Miss Esmeralda Hawkins to call her as soon as she arrives. Thank you. Good-bye. (*She hangs up.*) You see I am having to impersonate my secretary this morning!

GRACE: The light was so dim it didn't wake me up.

(GRACE *is forty or forty-five, faded but still pretty. Her blonde hair, graying slightly, her pale eyes, her thin figure, in a pink silk dressing gown, give her an insubstantial quality in sharp contrast to* CORNELIA's *Roman grandeur. There is between the two women a mysterious tension, an atmosphere of something unspoken.*)

CORNELIA: I've already opened the mail.

GRACE: Anything of interest?

CORNELIA: A card from Thelma Peterson at Mayo's.

GRACE: Oh, how is Thelma?

CORNELIA: She says she's "progressing nicely," whatever that indicates.

GRACE: Didn't she have something removed?

CORNELIA: Several things, I believe.

GRACE: Oh, here's the "Fortnightly Review of Current Letters"!

CORNELIA: Much to my astonishment. I thought I had canceled my subscription to that publication.

GRACE: Really, Cornelia?

CORNELIA: Surely you remember. I canceled my subscription immediately after the issue came out with that scurrilous attack on my cousin Cecil Tutwiler

Bates, the only dignified novelist the South has produced since Thomas Nelson Page.

GRACE: Oh, yes, I do remember. You wrote a furious letter of protest to the editor of the magazine and you received such a conciliatory reply from an associate editor named Caroline something-or-other that you were completely mollified and canceled the cancellation.

CORNELIA: I have never been mollified by conciliatory replies, never completely and never even partially, and if I wrote to the editor-in-chief and was answered by an associate editor, my reaction to that piece of impertinence would hardly be what you call "mollified."

GRACE (*changing the subject*): Oh, here's the new catalogue from the Gramophone Shoppe in Atlanta!

CORNELIA (*conceding a point*): Yes, there it is.

GRACE: I see you've checked several items.

CORNELIA: I think we ought to build up our collection of Lieder.

GRACE: You've checked a Sibelius that we already have.

CORNELIA: It's getting a little bit scratchy. (*She inhales deeply and sighs, her look fastened upon the silent phone.*) You'll also notice that I've checked a few operatic selections.

GRACE (*excitedly*): Where, which ones? I don't see them!

CORNELIA: Why are you so excited over the catalogue, dear?

GRACE: I adore phonograph records!

CORNELIA: I wish you adored them enough to put them back in their proper places in albums.

GRACE: Oh, here's the Vivaldi we wanted.

CORNELIA: Not "we," dear. Just you.

GRACE: Not *you,* Cornelia?

CORNELIA: I think Vivaldi's a very thin shadow of Bach.

GRACE: How strange that I should have the impression you . . . (*The phone rings.*) Shall I answer?

CORNELIA: If you will be so kind.

GRACE (*lifting the receiver*): Miss Scott's residence! (*This announcement is made in a tone of reverence, as though mentioning a seat of holiness.*) Oh, no, no, this is Grace, but Cornelia is right by my side. (*She passes the phone.*) Esmeralda Hawkins.

CORNELIA (*grimly*): I've been expecting her call. (*into the phone*) Hello, Esmeralda, my dear. I've been expecting your call. Now where are you calling me from? Of course I know that you're calling me from the meeting, *ca va sans dire, ma petite!* Ha ha! But from which phone in the house; there's two, you know, the one in the downstairs hall and the one in the chatelaine's boudoir where the ladies will probably be removing their wraps. Oh. You're on the downstairs', are you? Well, by this time I presume that practically all the Daughters have assembled. Now go upstairs and call me back from there so we can talk with a little more privacy, dear, as I want to make my position very clear before the meeting commences. Thank you, dear. (*She hangs up and looks grimly into space.*)

GRACE: The—Confederate Daughters?

CORNELIA: Yes! They're holding the Annual Election today.

GRACE: Oh, how exciting! Why aren't you at the meeting?

CORNELIA: I preferred not to go.

GRACE: You preferred *not* to go?

CORNELIA: Yes, I preferred not to *go* . . . (*She touches her chest, breathing heavily as if she had run upstairs.*)

GRACE: But it's the annual election of officers.

CORNELIA: Yes! I told you it was!

(GRACE *drops a spoon.* CORNELIA *cries out and jumps a little.*)

GRACE: I'm so sorry. (*She rings the bell for a servant.*)

CORNELIA: Intrigue, intrigue and duplicity revolt me so that I wouldn't be able to breathe in the same atmosphere. (GRACE *rings the bell louder.*) Why are you ringing that bell? You know Lucinda's not here!

GRACE: I'm so sorry. Where has Lucinda gone?

CORNELIA (*in a hoarse whisper, barely audible*): There's a big colored funeral in town. (*She clears her throat violently and repeats the statement.*)

GRACE: Oh, dear. You have that nervous laryngitis.

CORNELIA: No sleep, no sleep last night.

(*The phone screams at her elbow. She cries out and thrusts it from her as if it were on fire.*)

GRACE (*picking up the phone*): Miss Scott's residence. Oh. Just a moment, please.

CORNELIA (*snatching the phone*): Esmeralda, are you upstairs now?

GRACE (*in a loud whisper*): It isn't Esmeralda, it's Mrs. C. C. Bright!

CORNELIA: One moment, one moment, one moment! (*She thrusts the phone back at* GRACE *with a glare of fury.*) How dare you put me on the line with that woman!

GRACE: Cornelia, I didn't, I was just going to ask you if you . . .

CORNELIA: *Hush!* (*She springs back from the table, glaring across it.*) Now give me that phone. (*She takes it, and says coldly.*) What can I do for you, please? No. I'm afraid that my garden will not be open to the Pilgrims this spring. I think the cultivation of gardens is an esthetic hobby and not a competitive sport. Individual visitors will be welcome if they call in advance so that I can arrange for my gardener to show them around, but no bands of Pilgrims, not after the devastation my garden suffered last spring—

Pilgrims coming with dogs—picking flowers and . . . You're entirely welcome; yes, good-bye. (*She returns the phone to* GRACE.)

GRACE: I think the election would have been less of a strain if you'd gone to it, Cornelia.

CORNELIA: I don't know what you are talking about.

GRACE: Aren't you up for office?

CORNELIA: "Up for office?" What is "up for office"?

GRACE: Why, ha ha! *running* for—something.

CORNELIA: Have you ever known me to *"run"* for anything, Grace? Whenever I've held an office in a society or club it's been at the *insistence* of the members because I really have an *aversion* to holding office. But this is a different thing, a different thing altogether. It's a test of something. You see I have known for some time, now, that there is a little group, a *clique,* in the Daughters, which is hostile to me.

GRACE: Oh, Cornelia, I'm sure you must be mistaken.

CORNELIA: No. There is a movement against me.

GRACE: A movement? A movement against you?

CORNELIA: An organized movement to keep me out of any important office.

GRACE: But haven't you always held some important office in the Chapter?

CORNELIA: I have never been *Regent* of it.

GRACE: Oh, you want to be *Regent?*

CORNELIA: No. You misunderstand me. I don't *"want"* to be Regent.

GRACE: Oh?

CORNELIA: I don't "want" to be anything whatsoever. I simply want to break up this movement against me and for that purpose I have rallied my forces.

GRACE: Your forces? (*Her lips twitch slightly as if she had an hysterical impulse to smile.*)

CORNELIA: Yes. I still have some friends in the Chapter who have resisted the movement.

GRACE: Oh?

CORNELIA: I have the solid support of all the older Board members.

GRACE: Why, then, I should think you'd have nothing to worry about.

CORNELIA: The Chapter has expanded too rapidly lately. Women have been admitted that couldn't get into a front pew at the Second Baptist Church! And that's the disgraceful truth . . .

GRACE: But since it's really a patriotic society . . .

CORNELIA: My dear Grace, there are two chapters of the Confederate Daughters in the city of Meridian. There is the Forrest chapter, which is for social riffraff, and there is *this* chapter which was *supposed* to have a *little* bit of *distinction!* I'm not a snob. I'm nothing if not democratic. You know *that!* But . . .

(*The phone rings.* CORNELIA *reaches for it, then pushes it to* GRACE.)

GRACE: Miss Scott's residence! Oh, yes, yes, just a moment! (*She passes phone to* CORNELIA.) It's Esmeralda Hawkins.

CORNELIA (*into the phone*): Are you upstairs now, dear? Well, I wondered, it took you so long to call back. Oh, but I thought you said the luncheon was over. Well. I'm glad that you fortified yourself with a bite to eat. What did the buffet consist of? Chicken a la king! Wouldn't you know it! That is so characteristic of poor Amelia! With bits of pimiento and tiny mushrooms in it? What did the ladies counting their calories do? Nibbled around the edges? Oh, poor dears!—and afterwards I suppose there was lemon sherbet with lady-fingers? What, lime sherbet! And *no* lady-fingers? *What a departure!* What a *shocking* apostasy! I'm quite stunned! Ho ho ho . . . (*She reaches shakily for her cup.*) Now what's going on? Discussing the Civil Rights Program? Then they won't take the vote for at least half an hour! Now Esmeralda, I *do* hope that you understand my position clearly. I don't wish to hold any office in the chapter unless it's by acclamation. You know what that means, don't you? It's a parliamentary term. It means when someone is desired for an office so unanimously that no vote has to be taken. In other words, elected automatically, simply by nomination, unopposed. Yes, my dear, it's just as simple as that. I have served as Treasurer for three terms, twice as Secretary, once as Chaplain—and what a dreary office that was with those long-drawn prayers for the Confederate dead! Altogether I've served on the Board for, let's see, fourteen years! Well, now, my dear, the point is simply this. If Daughters feel that I have demonstrated my capabilities and loyalty strongly enough that I should simply be named as Regent without a vote being taken—by unanimous acclamation!—why, then, of course I would feel obliged to accept. (*Her voice trembles with emotion.*) But if, on the other hand, the—uh—*clique!*—and you know the ones I mean!—is bold enough to propose someone else for the office . . . Do you understand my position? In that eventuality, hard as it is to imagine, I prefer to bow out of the picture entirely! The moment another nomination is made and seconded, my own must be withdrawn, at once, unconditionally! Is that quite understood, Esmeralda? Then good! Go back downstairs to the meeting. Digest your chicken a la king, my dear, and call me again on the upstairs phone as soon as there's something to tell me.

(*She hangs up and stares grimly into space.* GRACE *lifts a section of grapefruit on a tiny silver fork.*)

GRACE: They haven't had it yet?

CORNELIA: Had what, dear?

GRACE: The election!

CORNELIA: No, not yet. It seems to be—imminent, though.

GRACE: Cornelia, why don't you think about something else until it's over?

CORNELIA: What makes you think that I am nervous about it?

GRACE: You're—you're *breathing* so fast.

CORNELIA: I didn't sleep well last night. You were prowling about the house with that stitch in your side.

GRACE: I *am* so sorry. You know it's nothing. A muscular contraction that comes from strain.

CORNELIA: What strain does it come from, Grace?

GRACE: What strain? (*She utters a faint, perplexed laugh.*) Why!—I don't know . . .

CORNELIA: The strain of *what?* Would you like *me* to tell you?

GRACE (*rising*): Excuse me, I . . .

CORNELIA (*sharply*): Where are you going?

GRACE: Upstairs for a moment! I just remembered I should have taken my drops of belladonna!

CORNELIA: It does no good *after* eating.

GRACE: I suppose that's right. It doesn't.

CORNELIA: But you want to escape?

GRACE: Of course not.

CORNELIA: Several times lately you've rushed away from me as if I'd suddenly threatened you with a knife.

GRACE: Cornelia! I've been—jumpy!

CORNELIA: It's always when something is almost—*spoken*—between us.

GRACE: I hate to see you so agitated over the outcome of a silly club-woman's election.

CORNELIA: I'm not talking about the Daughters. I'm not even thinking about them, I'm . . .

GRACE: I wish you'd dismiss it completely from your mind. Now would be a good time to play some records. Let me put a symphony on the machine!

CORNELIA: No.

GRACE: How about the Bach for Piano and Strings? The one we received for Christmas from Jessie and Gay?

CORNELIA: "No," I said; "No," I said. No!

GRACE: Something very light and quiet, then, the old French madrigals, maybe?

CORNELIA: Anything to avoid a talk between us? Anything to evade a conversation, especially when the servant is not in the house?

GRACE: Oh, here it is! This is just the thing! (*She has started the phonograph. Landowska is playing a harpsichord selection. The phonograph is at the edge of the lighted area or just outside it.* CORNELIA *stares grimly as* GRACE *resumes her seat with an affectation of enchantment, clasping her hands and closing her eyes.*

She speaks in an enchanted voice.) Oh, how it smooths things over, how sweet, and gentle, and—pure.

CORNELIA: Yes! And completely dishonest.

GRACE: Music? Dishonest?

CORNELIA: Completely. It "smooths things over" instead of—speaking them out.

GRACE: "Music hath charms to soothe the savage breast."

CORNELIA: Yes, oh, yes, if the savage breast permits it.

GRACE: Oh, sublime—sublime!

CORNELIA (*grudgingly*): Landowska is an artist of rare precision.

GRACE (*ecstatically*): And such a noble face, a profile as fine and strong as Edith Sitwell's. After this we'll play Edith Sitwell's *Facade.* "Jane, Jane, tall as a crane, the morning light creaks down again . . ."

CORNELIA: Dearest, isn't there something you've failed to notice?

GRACE: Where?

CORNELIA: Right under your nose.

GRACE: Oh! You mean my flower?

CORNELIA: Yes! I mean your rose.

GRACE: Of course I noticed my rose; the moment I came in the room I saw it here.

CORNELIA: You made no allusion to it.

GRACE: I would have, but you were so concerned over the meeting.

CORNELIA: I'm not concerned over the meeting.

GRACE: Whom do I have to thank for this lovely rose? My gracious employer?

CORNELIA: You will find fourteen others on your desk in the library when you go in to take care of the correspondence.

GRACE: Fourteen other roses?

CORNELIA: A total of fifteen!

GRACE: How wonderful! Why fifteen?

CORNELIA: How long have you been here, dearest? How long have you made this house a house of roses?

GRACE: What a nice way to put it! Why, of course! I've been your secretary for fifteen years.

CORNELIA: Fifteen years my companion! A rose for every year, a year for every rose!

GRACE: What a charming sort of way to—observe the—occasion.

CORNELIA: First I thought "pearls" and then I thought, No, roses, but perhaps I should have given you something golden, ha ha! Silence is golden, they say.

GRACE: Oh, dear, that stupid machine is playing the same record over.

CORNELIA: Let it, let it; I like it.

GRACE: Just let me . . .

CORNELIA: Sit down!—It was fifteen years ago this very morning, on the sixth day of November, that someone very sweet and gentle and silent—a shy, little, quiet little widow!—arrived for the first time at Seven Edgewater Drive. The season was autumn. I had been raking dead leaves over the rose bushes to protect them from frost when I heard footsteps on the gravel; light, quick, delicate footsteps like spring coming in the middle of autumn; and looked up, and sure enough, there spring was! A little person so thin that light shone through her as if she were made of the silk of a white parasol! (GRACE *utters a short, startled laugh. Wounded,* CORNELIA *speaks harshly.*) Why did you laugh? Why did you laugh like that?

GRACE: It sounded—ha ha!—it sounded like the first paragraph of a woman's magazine story.

CORNELIA: What a cutting remark!

GRACE: I didn't mean it that way, I . . .

CORNELIA: What other way could you mean it?

GRACE: Cornelia, you know how I am! I'm always a little embarrassed by sentiment, aren't I?

CORNELIA: Yes, frightened of anything that betrays some feeling.

GRACE: People who don't know you well, nearly all people we know, would be astounded to hear you, Cornelia Scott, that grave and dignified lady, expressing herself in such a lyrical manner.

CORNELIA: People who don't know me well are everybody! Yes, I think even *you!*

GRACE: Cornelia, you must admit that sentiment isn't like you.

CORNELIA: *Is nothing like me but silence?* (*The clock ticks loudly.*) *Am I sentenced to silence for a lifetime?*

GRACE: It's just not like you to . . .

CORNELIA: Not like me, not like me; what do you know what's like me or not like me?

GRACE: You may deny it, Cornelia, as much as you please, but it's evident to me that you are completely unstrung by your anxieties over the Confederate Daughters' election.

CORNELIA: Another thinly veiled insult?

GRACE: Oh, Cornelia, please!

CORNELIA (*imitating her gesture*): "Oh, Cornelia, please!!"

GRACE: If I've said anything wrong, I beg your pardon. I offer my very humble apologies for it.

CORNELIA: I don't want apologies from you.

(*There is a strained silence. The clock ticks. Suddenly* GRACE *reaches across to touch the veined jewelled hand of* CORNELIA. CORNELIA *snatches her own hand away as though the touch had burned her.*)

GRACE: Thank you for the roses.

CORNELIA: I don't want thanks from you either. All that I want is a little return of affection, not much, but sometimes a little.

GRACE: You have that always, Cornelia.

CORNELIA: And one thing more: a little outspokenness, too.

GRACE: Outspokenness?

CORNELIA: Yes, outspokenness, if that's not too much to ask from such a proud young lady.

GRACE (*rising from the table*): I am not proud and I am not young, Cornelia.

CORNELIA: Sit down! Don't leave the table!

GRACE: Is that an order?

CORNELIA: I don't give orders to you; I make requests.

GRACE: Sometimes the requests of an employer are hard to distinguish from orders. (*She sits down.*)

CORNELIA: Please turn off the victrola. (GRACE *rises and stops the machine.*) Grace!—Don't you feel there's—*something unspoken* between us?

GRACE: No. No, I don't.

CORNELIA: I do. I've felt for a long time something unspoken between us.

GRACE: Don't you think there is always something unspoken between two people?

CORNELIA: I see no reason for it.

GRACE: But don't a great many things exist without reason?

CORNELIA: Let's not turn this into a metaphysical discussion.

GRACE: All right. But you mystify me.

CORNELIA: It's very simple. It's just that I feel that there's something unspoken between us that ought to be spoken. . . . Why are you looking at me like that?

GRACE: How am I looking at you?

CORNELIA: With positive terror!

GRACE: Cornelia!

CORNELIA: You are, you are, but I'm not going to be shut up.

GRACE: Go on, continue, please, do!

CORNELIA: I'm going to, I will, I will, I . . . (*The phone rings and* GRACE *reaches for it.*) No, no, no, let it ring! (*It goes on ringing.*) Take it off the hook!

GRACE: Do just let me . . .

CORNELIA: Off the hook, I told you!

(GRACE *takes the phone off the hook. A voice says: "Hello? Hello? Hello? Hello?"*)

GRACE (*suddenly sobbing*): I can't stand it!

CORNELIA: *Be* STILL! *Someone can hear you!*

VOICE: Hello? Hello? Cornelia? Cornelia Scott?

(CORNELIA *seizes the phone and slams it back into its cradle.*)

CORNELIA: Now stop that! Stop that silly little female trick!

GRACE: You say there's something unspoken. Maybe there is. I don't know. But I do know some things are better left unspoken. Also I know that when a silence between two people has gone on for a long time, it's like a wall that's impenetrable between them. Maybe between us there is such a wall. One that's impenetrable. Or maybe *you* can break it. I know I can't. I can't even attempt to. You're the strong one of us two and surely you know it. Both of us have turned gray!—But not the same kind of gray. In that velvet dressing gown you look like the Emperor Tiberius!—In his imperial toga! Your hair and your eyes are both the color of iron! Iron gray. Invincible looking! People nearby are all somewhat—frightened of you. They feel your force and they admire you for it. They come to you here for opinions on this or that. What plays are good on Broadway this season, what books are worth reading and what books are trash and what —what records are valuable and—what is the proper attitude toward—bills in Congress! Oh, you're a fountain of wisdom! And in addition to that, you have your—*wealth!* Yes, you have your—*fortune!* All of your real-estate holdings, your blue-chip stocks, your—bonds, your—mansion on Edgewater Drive, your—shy little—secretary, your—fabulous gardens that Pilgrims cannot go into . . .

CORNELIA: Oh, yes, now you are speaking, now you are speaking at last! Go on, please go on speaking.

GRACE: I am—very—different! Also turning gray, but my gray is different. Not iron, like yours, not imperial, Cornelia, but gray, yes, gray, the color of a . . . *cobweb* . . . (*She starts the record again, very softly.*) Something white getting soiled, the gray of something forgotten. (*The phone rings again. Neither of them seems to notice it.*) And that being the case, that being the difference between our two kinds of gray, yours and mine, you mustn't expect me to give bold answers to questions that make the house shake with silence! To speak out things that are fifteen years unspoken!—That long a time can make a silence a wall that nothing less than dynamite could break through and (*She picks up the phone.*) I'm not strong enough, bold enough, I'm not . . .

CORNELIA (*fiercely*): You're speaking into the phone!

GRACE (*into phone*): Hello? Oh, yes, she's here. It's Esmeralda Hawkins.

(CORNELIA *snatches the phone.*)

CORNELIA: What is it, Esmeralda? What are you saying; is the room full of women? Such a babble of voices! What are you trying to tell me? Have they held the election already? What, what, what? Oh, this is maddening! I can't hear a word that you're saying; it sounds like the Fourth of July, a great celebration! Ha, ha, now try once more with your mouth closer to the phone! What, what? Would I be willing to what? You can't be serious! Are you out of your mind? (*She speaks to* GRACE *in a panicky voice.*) She wants to know if I would be willing to serve as *vice*-Regent! (*into phone*) Esmeralda! Will you listen to me? What's going on? Are there some fresh defections? How does it look? Why did you call me again before the vote? Louder, please speak louder, and cup your mouth to the phone in case they're eavesdropping! Who asked if I would accept the vice-Regency, dear? Oh, Mrs. Colby, of course!—that treacherous witch! *Esmeralda!! Listen I—will accept—no office—except—the highest!* Did you understand that? *I—will accept no office except*—ESMERALDA! (*She drops the phone into its cradle.*)

GRACE: Have they held the election?

CORNELIA (*dazed*): What? No, there's a five-minute recess before the election begins.

GRACE: Things are not going well?

CORNELIA: "Would you accept the vice-Regency," she asked me, "if for some reason they don't elect you Regent?" Then she hung up as if somebody had snatched the phone away from her, or the house had—caught fire.

GRACE: You shouted so I think she must have been frightened.

CORNELIA: Whom can you trust in this world; whom can you ever rely on?

GRACE: I think perhaps you should have gone to the meeting.

CORNELIA: I think my not being there is much more pointed.

GRACE (*rising again*): May I be excused, now?

CORNELIA: No! Stay here!

GRACE: If that is just a request, I . . .

CORNELIA: That's an order! (GRACE *sits down and closes her eyes.*) When you first came to this house, do you know I didn't expect you?

GRACE: Oh, but, Cornelia, you'd invited me here.

CORNELIA: We hardly knew each other.

GRACE: We'd met the summer before when Ralph was . . .

CORNELIA: Living! Yes, we met at Sewanee where he was a summer instructor.

GRACE: He was already ill.

CORNELIA: I thought what a pity that lovely, delicate girl hasn't found someone she could lean on, who could protect her! And two months later I heard through Clarabelle Drake that he was dead.

GRACE: You wrote me such a sweet letter, saying how lonely you were since the loss of your mother and urging me to rest here till the shock was over.

You seemed to understand how badly I needed to withdraw for a while from—old associations. I hesitated to come. I didn't until you wrote me a second letter . . .

CORNELIA: After I received yours. You wanted urging.

GRACE: I wanted to be quite sure I was really wanted. I only came intending to stay a few weeks. I was so afraid that I would outstay my welcome.

CORNELIA: How blind of you not to see how desperately I wanted to keep you here forever.

GRACE: Oh, I did see that you—(*The phone rings.*) Miss Scott's residence! Yes, she's here.

CORNELIA (*snatching the phone finally*): Cornelia Scott speaking! Oh. It's you, Esmeralda! Well, how did it come out? *I don't believe you! I simply don't believe you!* (GRACE *sits down quietly at the table.*) *Mrs. Hornsby elected?* Well, there's a dark horse for you! Less than a year in the Chapter . . . Did you —nominate—*me?* Oh, I see! But I told you to withdraw my name if . . . No, no, no, don't explain; it doesn't matter; I have too much already. You know I am going into the Daughters of the Barons of Runnymede. Yes, it's been established, I have a direct line to the Earl of . . . No, it's been straightened out; a clear line is established, and then of course I am also eligible for the Colonial Dames and for the Huguenot Society; and what with all my other activities and so forth, why, I couldn't *possibly* have taken it on if they'd—*wanted* . . . Of course I'm going to resign from the local chapter! Oh, yes, I am! My secretary is sitting right here by me. She has her pencil, her notebook! I'm going to dictate my letter of resignation from the local chapter the moment that I hang up on this conversation. Oh, no, no, no, I'm not mad, not outraged, at all. I'm just a little—ha ha! —a little—amused . . . *Mrs. Hornsby?* Nothing succeeds like mediocrity, does it? Thanks and good-bye, Esmeralda. (*She hangs up, stunned.* GRACE *rises.*)

GRACE: Notebook and pencil?

CORNELIA: Yes. Notebook and pencil. I have to—dictate a letter.

(GRACE *leaves the table. Just at the edge of the lighted area, she turns to glance at* CORNELIA's *rigid shoulders, and a slight, equivocal smile appears momentarily on her face; not quite malicious but not really sympathetic. Then she crosses out of the light. A moment later, her voice comes from the outer dark.*)

GRACE: What lovely roses! One for every year!

CURTAIN

Waiting for the Bus

RAMON DELGADO

Characters

EDITH
ANDREW
CYNTHIA
BENNY
FEATHERS (*imaginary*)
TOTO (*imaginary*)

Reading Guides

1. *Waiting for the Bus* is not a realistic play, but it deals with realistic problems. This technique is called abstraction. If you are aware that the playwright is abstracting, you will find more depth in the play.

2. Edith and Andrew imagine things in this play. For example, Toto and Feathers don't actually exist except in Andrew and Edith's minds. This is true of many of the things they refer to.

Waiting for the Bus

THE SCENE *is the city park. A bench left center faces the audience. A mail box stands in the down right corner; a street lamp right center. A zoo is not so far away, and the sounds of the animals can be heard, dimly, but distinctly.*

The stage is empty at the rise of the curtain, but shortly, EDITH *and* ANDREW *hobble in down right, each trying to support the other, each failing miserably, because at the same time they are rolling a baby buggy with a birdcage in it and pulling on a leash attached to an imaginary dog.*

Acting note: A presentational approach to the characters may help the actors achieve the style of the play more fully than a representational approach.

EDITH: The blind leading the blind—and when the blind lead the blind, they shall both fall in a ditch. You really ought to get your glasses changed, Andrew.

ANDREW: I can see well enough, my dear.

(ANDREW *stops right center a moment and begins wiping his shoes on the grass.*)

EDITH: What's the matter, Andrew?

ANDREW: Damn dogs, dumb animals, you can't educate them!

EDITH: You shouldn't curse, my love. Besides it isn't the dog's fault. It's your eyes. They're getting weaker, and you must take care of your eyes; they're the only ones you'll ever have.

ANDREW: Now, Edith, at my age new glasses are hardly worth the expense. And don't let the dogs get out of this either. They know where the grass is, and they can tell the difference between grass and sidewalk, but leave it to you to defend the dumbest animals.

EDITH: Wasn't that a lovely zoo we just passed, Andrew?

ANDREW: The animals smelled.

EDITH: Of course animals smell—that's part of being alive.

ANDREW: Not smell, then—stink. The animals stink—stinked? Stunk? Anyway, there were musky odors and rancid odors and rotten odors and moldy odors and reeking odors and effluvious odors and—

EDITH: Andrew, you must admit the animals have helped us many times.

ANDREW (*crossing to left end of bench*): Well, we have machines to do everything now.

EDITH (*crossing to right end of bench*): But we must be grateful to them for the dog sled, the mule team, the ox cart, the reindeer sled, the camel caravan, the ostrich buggy, the peace doves, and you must admit some of them are smart—trained seals, educated elephants, performing lions and tigers, dancing zebras, movie star porpoises, wrestling bears, fighting roosters, talking dogs, verbose parrots—

ANDREW: If they're so intelligent, then why haven't they shown more cooperation in the efforts for peace?

EDITH: Why, Andrew, didn't I tell you? Our little Toto, our own little snoopy dog, has learned to sit up on his hind paws and lift his front legs and beg.

ANDREW: That I can believe.

EDITH (*sitting on right end of bench*): Now you just watch. Come here, Toto. That's a nice little puppy. Now—sit. That's it—Now show Daddy what you can do.

ANDREW: Don't call me his daddy.

EDITH: Oh, Andrew, you've insulted Toto. Now he won't perform.

ANDREW: Just like an actor.

EDITH (*placing the birdcage on the bench between them*): Maybe Feathers will say a few of the words she has learned—Now don't insult her, too, Andrew.

ANDREW: I won't say it, but I'll think it.

EDITH: Think what, dear?

ANDREW: That Feathers isn't worth her parakeet seed.

EDITH: Now you've gone and done it. She's put her head under her wing. She loves to show off for friendly people. Look what you've done to her, Andrew. You've made an introvert of her.

ANDREW: My humble apologies.

EDITH: And just when she was getting along so nicely. She's getting much plainer, too. Why only yesterday she said—

ANDREW (*sitting left end of bench*): I'm not interested.

EDITH: But, Andrew, children must be loved.

ANDREW: But Toto and Feathers are not our children; besides we're at the bus station, and I don't want the people to stare.

EDITH: When our other children left home, you said we would take care of Toto and Feathers, and they could go everywhere we went.

ANDREW: I didn't say I'd adopt them.

EDITH: Two more wouldn't hurt. We've only had twenty-seven billion, six hundred and fifty-four million, three hundred and eighty-one thousand, one hundred and two. Two more won't make much difference.

ANDREW: I absolutely refuse to adopt them.

EDITH: You will take them on the bus though, won't you, Andrew?

ANDREW: They'll have to ride in the luggage compartment.

EDITH: They'll smother to death.

ANDREW: They can't sit in the seats with us. What will the bus driver say? And you're sure to poke someone in the eye with that birdcage.

EDITH: Well, you ask the ticket man if they can't go. He'll tell you.

ANDREW: However, if they do go, it would make a good anecdote for my memoirs.

EDITH: Ah, yes, your memoirs. Do let them go, Andrew.

ANDREW: Only if the ticket man and the bus driver agree, which is highly unlikely for any two men in such administrative positions.

EDITH: Maybe you could start writing your memoirs on the trip.

ANDREW: Bad roads.

EDITH: But if you don't start now, you may never finish.

ANDREW: I shall not start my memoirs until I am no longer able to travel, but in the meantime I shall continue to keep little notes of all the things that have happened to us.

EDITH: Your library is full of notebooks. What was the last count?

ANDREW (*standing*): Let me see, what did I do with that piece of paper? (*He takes out an imaginary bit of paper.*) I counted last week, and wrote it down. (*behind left end of bench*) Here it is—seventy-five billion, six hundred and thirty-nine million, eight hundred and twenty-three thousand, nine hundred and ninety-nine. And with the notes I shall make on this trip, we may pass the seventy-six billion mark.

EDITH: My, my, all those notes. And how many volumes of memoirs will that make?

ANDREW: Well, when I subtract the duplication of events, the unimportant incidents, the adventures we started and never finished, the inventions that were failures, the languages that are dead, the characters who are only names, it should come roughly to one small volume .

EDITH: I can hardly wait to get back and help you begin your organization.

ANDREW (*crossing behind* EDITH, *pats her on the shoulder*): You have always been a faithful secretary.

EDITH: If I can't help you, Andrew, I would die. We have enjoyed life together, haven't we?

ANDREW: Yes, we have enjoyed life more than the average, I would say.

EDITH: We have many more years together, don't you think, Andrew?

ANDREW (*a distant echo*): Many more years.

EDITH: I hope we don't die separately. I hope we are killed together in a bus accident.

ANDREW (*a distant echo*): Together in a bus accident.

EDITH: Maybe it will be this time—but I hope not, because you haven't written your memoirs. Where are we going today, Andrew?

ANDREW: The scenic route.

EDITH: I always enjoy the scenic routes. The long trip or the short one.

ANDREW (*right end of bench*): The short one. We must hurry back, you know.

EDITH: Yes, so you'll have plenty of time to write.

ANDREW (*in the manner of a train announcer*): We're going to Charleston, Charlotte, Roanoke, Richmond, Washington, Newark, Boston, Ottawa, Winnipeg, Nome, Vladivostok, Yokohama, Sydney, Shanghai, Calcutta, Nazareth, Alexandria, Cologne, Heidelberg, Liverpool, Dublin, Johannesburg, Santiago, Rio de Janeiro, San Jose, Havana, Miami, and Atlantis.

EDITH: My, my. That is the short trip. Now, when you buy the tickets, tell the ticket seller that you were once a general.

ANDREW: What for?

EDITH: That should impress him and make him give you the best seats on the bus.

ANDREW: I don't see what difference that would make.

EDITH: Oh, the prestige that goes with being a general! He will know that you should have been president, because everybody knows that generals make the best presidents.

ANDREW: I just wasn't popular enough.

EDITH: I was proud of you, dear. Even when you lost. But tell the ticket man what battles you were in. Tell him how well you fought, for, dear, that is the one thing you really do well; in fact, I would say you do that best of all.

ANDREW: Except my memoirs.

EDITH: Yes, your memoirs—they shall be even greater than your battles.

ANDREW: They were so long ago, and now I have only their memory—I am past fighting, past desire.

EDITH (*a distant echo*): Past, past desire.

ANDREW: Past hope.

EDITH (*a distant echo*): Past, past hope. (*scolding*) Andrew, don't say that!

ANDREW: It's true, dear. We're on our way downhill. We have just passed middle age only last year. Past hope, past desire.

EDITH: Nonsense, now you go get the tickets, and I'll wait right here for you. Go along now.

ANDREW: All right, but my heart isn't in it anymore. I do this just to keep my mind occupied. I'm too old for pretend.

EDITH: We're not old yet. Now do as I say.

ANDREW: You always take our games too seriously anyway.

EDITH: Well, a body's got to take something in life seriously, or he'd soon go crazy. Now run along with you.

ANDREW: All right, my dear, I'll keep up the game. As long as you can keep up your end, I'll keep up mine.

EDITH: Hurry along. We'll miss the bus. If we don't have our tickets, the bus will go right along without us.

(ANDREW *crosses to the mailbox down right, but on the way he bumps into the lamppost.*)

ANDREW: Pardon me, miss. I thought you were a lamppost.

EDITH: Andrew, you do need your glasses changed. Something dreadful is going to happen to you if you don't.

ANDREW: Dreadful if I don't.

(ANDREW *gets to the mailbox, and pantomimes a conversation with the invisible ticket man; he looks back at* EDITH *every once in a while; she smiles reassuringly. He continues.* EDITH *talks to* TOTO *and* FEATHERS.)

EDITH: Toto, you should be ashamed of yourself. After all the care we've given you. I know Andrew gets irritated every once in a while, but you could make him smile by doing your cute tricks. And Feathers, I can't imagine what has gotten into you. You were so chipper this morning when we started out. Now, don't you worry. I'm going to see that you get to go on the trip this time.

(ANDREW *returns and sits on left end of bench.*)

Well, what did he say? Did you get the tickets?

ANDREW: Left coat pocket.

EDITH: And the animals, can they go?

ANDREW: He said the only way the animals could go was for the bus driver to say okay.

EDITH: Did you tell the man about your being a general and all that?

ANDREW: I told him everything.

EDITH: What did he say?

ANDREW: He said the bus would be late.

EDITH: It always is.

ANDREW: All we can do is wait.

EDITH: We must play a game to pass the time. What shall we play, Andrew? You're good at games.

ANDREW: A game within a game.

EDITH: I don't understand, Andrew.

ANDREW: Nothing. It doesn't matter. What game do you want to play?

EDITH: Let's play—chase.

ANDREW: Too strenuous.

EDITH: Let's play—making wishes.

ANDREW: Too tame.

(*pause*)

EDITH (*as if reading something in front of her*): Nickels, quarters, dimes.

ANDREW: What's that?

EDITH: I say nickels, quarters, dimes.

ANDREW: Well, what are you saying it for? Is that the name of a new game?

EDITH: No, I was just reading the instructions on the cigarette machine. Nickels, quarters, and dimes only. But of course that isn't true, is it?

ANDREW: Of course not.

EDITH: Because there are also annas, centavos, pesos, lire, francs, sous, drachmas, kopeks, reis, sen, yen, farthings, florins, salt whiskey, wampum, ginger, and mites.

ANDREW: In God We Trust!

(*another pause*)

EDITH (*as if reading something in front of her*): Mild, very mild.

ANDREW: What's that.

EDITH: I say mild, very mild. The sign on the cigar box. You should never have given up smoking, Andrew.

ANDREW: Why not?

EDITH: You could blow the most perfect smoke rings.

ANDREW: Any circle is perfect.

EDITH: Oh, let's not bother about geometry today, or any other of the mathematics. I'm tired of figures. Let's think about words instead. (*rises, crosses behind* ANDREW) That's a wonderful idea, Andrew. We can pass the time by making up words.

ANDREW: You just don't make up words by thinking about it.

EDITH (*over his shoulders*): Why not? You've made up millions.

ANDREW: But only when the occasion arose that needed a new word.

EDITH: Have you ever seen those trees look just exactly like they look now?

ANDREW: No, not exactly, why?

EDITH: Well, then we need a word for it—frilting.

ANDREW: Frilting?

EDITH: Frilting! I frilt, you frilt, he, she, or it frilts. The trees are frilting.

ANDREW: And exactly what does that mean?

EDITH: It means exactly what the trees are doing right now—nothing more, nothing less. Goodness, if I could tell you what a word meant by using another word, there wouldn't be much use in having new words at all, would there?

ANDREW: I guess not, but how are you going to explain to someone else what you mean?

EDITH: Nothing simpler. Just bring the people here and show them the trees. You point to the trees and you say "frilting." It's really a very nice word

—and more fun to say than eating a chocolate-covered cherry. Come on, try it.

ANDREW: This is ridiculous!

EDITH: Try it. For me, Andrew.

ANDREW: Oh, all right. Frilting! Frilting! Frilting! Say, you're right.

EDITH: Strench!

ANDREW: How's that!

EDITH: Strench. That's what you experienced when we passed by the zoo—a strong stench—stench—oh, Andrew, this is fun. I don't know why we didn't start this game a long time ago.

ANDREW: If we had, the language would be cluttered up with thousands of useless words.

EDITH: Oh, you're just against progress. Besides, it passes the time.

ANDREW: Sitting and meditating passes the time, too.

(ANDREW *looks at* EDITH *sharply. She sits on right end of bench.*)
(*pause*)

EDITH: Oh, Andrew, I almost forgot to mail the letter to our last child, telling him where we're going.

ANDREW: The child won't care.

EDITH: What a thing to say! Our children always care.

ANDREW: They never write us back.

EDITH: That doesn't mean they don't care. They have their own worries and responsibilities. Down in my heart, I know they still love us.

ANDREW: There's a mailbox on the corner.

EDITH: I see it, dear, and *I* can even see it from here.

ANDREW: Well, go to it then.

EDITH (*rising*): Can I trust you with the animals?

ANDREW: Of course.

EDITH: They'd better be all right when I get back.

ANDREW: They'll be just as you left them.

EDITH (*putting birdcage in baby buggy*): Just the same, I think I'll take Feathers with me.

(EDITH *crosses to the mailbox, pushing the baby buggy with the birdcage in it. As she mails the imaginary letter, she gets her hand stuck in the vent on the mailbox.*)

Andrew, Andrew, help me.

ANDREW (*rising*): What's the matter, dear?

EDITH: My hand. The mailbox. Stuck, dear.

(ANDREW *crosses to* EDITH*'s left.*)

ANDREW: You should have let me mail the letter for you.

EDITH: You didn't offer to.

ANDREW: You should have asked me. I would have been happy to. There, is that better?

EDITH: Kiss it, and make it well.

(ANDREW *does.*)

Oh, Andrew, you have rescued me from danger so many times. You have saved me from the dragon, from the noose, from burning at the stake, from the guillotine, from the rack, from the famine, from the flood, from the cross, and from the lions. And now from the mailbox! My, my, how brave you still are! And why did you do all this, Andrew?

ANDREW: Must I say? Don't you know?

EDITH: I never get tired of hearing you say it. You once had the voice of an orator, a politician, an opera baritone, an actor, a prince, and even now I can hear that voice. Tell me as you always tell me when you rescue me.

ANDREW: My dearest, I love you.

EDITH: And there has never been another?

ANDREW: Never.

EDITH: And there will never be another?

ANDREW: Never.

EDITH: How comforting to know that. For I am extremely jealous of you. You know that, don't you?

ANDREW: The people are staring, Edith.

EDITH: Let them stare. What do they know of our deep romance. I don't care if the world knows that you are my husband. I am proud to be your wife.

ANDREW: Past desire—past hope.

EDITH: Kiss me, Andrew.

ANDREW: Right here, in public?

EDITH: In the eyes of God!

ANDREW: On the mouth?

EDITH: On my trembling lips!

ANDREW: I can't. Not out in the open like this.

EDITH: Many other people do.

ANDREW: Well—I don't want to be too different from other people.

(ANDREW *kisses* EDITH.)

EDITH: Mild, very mild.

(BENNY, *the black shoeshine boy, enters down left.*)

Oh, look, Andrew.

BENNY (*left center*): Shine, mister?

EDITH: Andrew, he's talking to you.

ANDREW: Sons of Ham, cursed by Noah, servants of Shem.

EDITH: He only wants to shine your shoes.

ANDREW (*crossing behind lamppost*): I don't want to have them shined.

EDITH (*crossing to* BENNY, *down left center*): Why, Andrew, look at the child—I do believe he's one of ours.

ANDREW: Don't be unreasonable.

EDITH: Tell me, little boy, what's your name?

BENNY: I's named Benny, mam.

EDITH: Andrew, we had a Benny once. A-B-C-D—yes, right between Abel and Cain. Do you suppose it's the same one?

ANDREW: Sons of Ham, cursed by—

EDITH: Tell me, little boy, are we your parents?

BENNY: I don't know. I don't know what parents is.

EDITH: Poor little thing. He hasn't any parents. (*crossing to* ANDREW*'s left*) Andrew, we could adopt him. Make him our very own.

ANDREW: Servants of Shem.

EDITH: Now that's no way to talk. If the child is an orphan, the least we can do is be foster parents to him.

BENNY: Don't want no foster parents. I'm a shoeshine boy. Shoeshine boys shine shoes. They don't need no parents.

(BENNY *exits down right.*)

EDITH (*crossing down right*): Wait, little boy.

ANDREW (*crossing to left end of bench*): Let him go.

EDITH (*crossing to* ANDREW*'s right*): Andrew, you've no right to turn him away like that.

ANDREW: Sons of Ham, cursed by Noah, servants of Shem.

EDITH: Andrew, you must remember that even if he isn't our son he's a close relative.

ANDREW: Over my dead body.

EDITH: Maybe you don't keep track of the family. But I do, and one way or another, we're all related. We're related by aunts and great-grandmothers and second cousins, and uncles and fourth cousins twice removed and great-great-great-grandaddies and marriages among families and marriages between families and marriages outside of families. You never know when you meet a person that he might not be closer related to you than your own children, and that's a fact.

ANDREW: I don't see it that way.

EDITH: The trouble with you is you just don't see well at all.

(ANDREW *starts out down left.*)

And where are you going, may I ask?

ANDREW: The comfort station, if you have to know.

EDITH: I thought you'd been acting mighty fidgety. Well go ahead, don't let me stop you.

(ANDREW *exits down left.*)

EDITH (*crossing down right to get baby carriage*): Come, my pretty Feathers. You mustn't shiver like that. It's not cold. (*crossing to right end of bench*) In fact, it's a rather pleasant day. There, that's better. Now you look like my baby should—perk and lively. Are you going to talk for Mama? (*sits, right end of bench*) Well, Toto, of course I love you, too. I love all my children. Now, now, you mustn't mind what Andrew says. Andrew is just like a child, too, in so many ways. Of course he's done some very remarkable things, his inventions, his languages, his wars, his notes for his memoirs. Just wait until he gets his memoirs published. Then you'll see it hasn't all been in vain. He's tired now, and this last trip will be a great relaxation before the grind of writing; so you mustn't be too upset if he seems irritated. I love Andrew. I have always loved Andrew, and I shall love him forever—if I last that long. What's that, Feathers? Why, Feathers, how wonderful! It's clear. It's distinct. You will say that for Andrew when he comes, won't you? For my sake? And Toto, you're sitting up perfectly. Here's a milk bone. Mama bought it for you. That's a fine boy, a fine boy. Mama is proud of you both. Why, Feathers, how did you learn to say that? Will miracles never cease? All by yourself? You picked it up? Wait till Andrew hears—just wait till he hears.

(CYNTHIA *enters down right, crosses to left end of bench.*)

Oh, hello. How do you do.

CYNTHIA: Fine, sister. How about yourself.

EDITH: Rather well, thank you.

CYNTHIA (*sitting*): Mind if I sit down?

EDITH: Not a bit. Be careful of Toto.

CYNTHIA: Who?

EDITH: Our dog.

CYNTHIA: Where?

EDITH: Right here, on the end of the leash.

CYNTHIA (*uneasily*): Oh—sure. Pretty, ain't he?

EDITH: I don't know that you'd exactly call him pretty. Unique would be more correct.

CYNTHIA: Yeah, that's what I mean—a pretty unique dog. (*pause*) My name's Cynthia. What's yours?

EDITH: My name is Edith, and my husband's name is Andrew.

CYNTHIA (*nostalgically*): I knew an Andrew once—in Germany.

EDITH (*warily*): In Germany—you don't say. When was that?

CYNTHIA: Near the close of the war.

EDITH: Which one? There have been so many through Germany.

CYNTHIA: I don't guess it was the same Andrew.

EDITH: He's been a soldier a good long time.

CYNTHIA: Well, I've been going around from country to country for a good long time, too.

EDITH: And from man to man?

CYNTHIA: What makes you say that?

EDITH: I know your type. I can tell by the thick makeup. I've never understood that. Why does a woman in your "profession" cover herself with such heavy paint?

CYNTHIA: We have to work past our prime.

EDITH: Was it my Andrew you knew in Germany?

CYNTHIA: How do I know whether it was your Andrew or not. Men come and men go, and they don't leave their calling cards. There are Andrews all over the world.

EDITH: Did he tell you that he loved you?

CYNTHIA: They all say that.

EDITH: All of them?

CYNTHIA (*wistfully*): They used to.

EDITH: My Andrew wouldn't. He wouldn't even look at you.

CYNTHIA: Lady, I'm not going to argue with you. I don't know your Andrew from Adam's house cat, and if I weren't so dog tired, I'd walk on to find another bench.

EDITH: You had been running, hadn't you?

CYNTHIA: I'm always running—from something or to something.

EDITH: You don't have to, you know. You could get married.

CYNTHIA: I'd rather run.

EDITH: On the average, marriage is good for people.

CYNTHIA: When you've seen as many unfaithful men as I have, you don't have much faith in marriage.

EDITH: But the family is the foundation of our society, and without marriage—

CYNTHIA: Look, lady, you ain't gonna reform me. I heard all the gospel I could stand in the last Graham crusade.

EDITH: Just the same—

(ANDREW *enters down left, giggling to himself.*)
(EDITH *rises.*)

Andrew, I want you to tell this woman—(*crosses to* ANDREW*'s right*) Andrew, what is the matter with you? Stop that silly giggling.

ANDREW: I've seen it—the writing on the wall.

EDITH: On the wall?

ANDREW: The verses and quotations, the scriptures and passages, the jokes and songs on the wall of the comfort station.

EDITH: Andrew, be serious. I want you to—

ANDREW: And I have made an important decision.

EDITH: Andrew, this woman—

ANDREW: And I am sure that history will prove that all important decisions were made by some great man sitting on the john.

EDITH: Andrew, that isn't very nice.

ANDREW: Hello—who is this?

EDITH: Her name is Cynthia. Will you please tell her to go away?

ANDREW (*crossing to* CYNTHIA*'s left*): No, indeed. Didn't you tell me we were all related? She may be my kissing cousin.

EDITH: Past desire, past hope?

ANDREW: Past desire, but not past hope.

EDITH: You mustn't even look at such a woman.

ANDREW (*crossing to right end of bench*): It doesn't do any harm to look.

EDITH (*crossing to* CYNTHIA*'s left and tugging her up by her arm*): Run along, miss. Our bus will be here in just a little while.

CYNTHIA: I've got just as much right to be here as you have.

EDITH: We don't want you.

ANDREW (*crossing to* CYNTHIA*'s right*): Well, I want her. I want her to go on the bus trip with us. She would be delightful company.

CYNTHIA: See, lady, they're all alike.

EDITH: Miss, my dog needs walking. Would you be so kind.

CYNTHIA: I don't see why I shou—

EDITH (*giving* CYNTHIA *the leash*): Here, take his leash and come back later. (*shoving* CYNTHIA *out down left*) Take him on a long walk.

CYNTHIA: Well, you don't have to shove.

EDITH: Go along with you.

CYNTHIA: All right, but I'll be back, and take my place on the bench. I've got just as much right as the rest of you.

(CYNTHIA *exits with* TOTO*'s leash down left.*)

EDITH (*crossing to left end of bench*): Andrew, you should be ashamed. A man your age staring at lewd women.

ANDREW (*sitting right end of bench*): I don't see anything wrong—

EDITH (*crossing behind bench to* ANDREW*'s right*): Did you know her in Germany?

ANDREW: In Germany? I don't think so.

EDITH: She said she knew an Andrew in Germany during the war.

ANDREW: There are hundreds—

EDITH: I know. Did you know her?

ANDREW (*rising*): Now, love, you've been with me every time I went to Germany.

(EDITH *starts crying.*)

Now what's the matter?

EDITH: I've never been to Germany. I've given you the best years of my life, and you have been unfaithful to me. And not only were you unfaithful, but you want her to go on the bus with us on our last trip together.

ANDREW: Now, now, Edith.

EDITH: And we had planned on it for so long.

ANDREW: There's not any good reason to get upset.

EDITH: And after this you were going to write your memoirs.

ANDREW: Now, Edith—

EDITH: And I was going to be your faithful secretary—just like I have always been your faithful secretary.

ANDREW: If you don't want her, she shan't go.

EDITH: And you'll promise never to think of her again.

ANDREW: I promise.

EDITH: I knew you wouldn't let her beguile you. I had faith in you, Andrew, only I—

ANDREW: What is it, my pet?

EDITH: I became suspicious because I was so jealous—you will forgive me for that, won't you?

ANDREW: Certainly, my dear.

EDITH: Because we must stick together, Andrew.

ANDREW: Yes, we must.

(ANDREW *takes* EDITH*'s hands, sits her beside him on the bench,* ANDREW *left,* EDITH *right.*)

EDITH: Because we haven't got anybody else but each other.

ANDREW: Only each other.

EDITH: And Toto and Feathers.

ANDREW: And Toto and Feathers. But, look, Edith, would it really matter if I told her she could go on the bus with us?

EDITH: Andrew, you mustn't let yourself think like that.

ANDREW: Of course not.

EDITH (ANDREW *glows with each adjective*): Because that woman is a wicked, evil, sinful, lustful Jezebel!

ANDREW: Yes!

EDITH: Andrew!

ANDREW: I've changed my mind. If you aren't willing to let her on the bus, I shall not be willing to take my last trip.

(CYNTHIA *enters with the leash, down left.*)

EDITH: That wasn't a very long walk.

CYNTHIA (*crossing with leash to down left end of bench*): Your dog wasn't very anxious to exercise.

ANDREW (*rising*): Oh, miss, I have decided to tell you that you can go with us on the trip.

CYNTHIA: What does your wife say?

ANDREW: It doesn't matter what she says.

EDITH (*rising*): Oh, yes, it does. Our marriage is fifty-fifty. Miss, you cannot go.

CYNTHIA: If your husband says I can, I'm going just to prove to you that he isn't as faithful as you say he is.

EDITH (*stepping down to* CYNTHIA): We've never had any use for women like you. I don't know why you continue to hang around.

CYNTHIA: The supply is to meet the demand.

EDITH: There would be no demand, if you would get married and behave yourselves like sensible women.

CYNTHIA: If the world depended on sensible women, what use would it have for nonsense like you!

EDITH: The supply is to meet the demand!

ANDREW (*trying to step between* EDITH *and* CYNTHIA): Ladies—

CYNTHIA (*rebuffing* ANDREW): Don't go barking my words back at me!

EDITH: You taught them to me.

CYNTHIA: I taught you everything you know, and look what good it's done you.

ANDREW: Ladies—

EDITH: Past desire? Past hope?

ANDREW: Edith!

CYNTHIA: So you might as well throw in the rouge and lipstick. I'm taking over now.

EDITH: Oh, no, you're not! Andrew and I haven't come this far together to be separated by something like you!

CYNTHIA: Separation began years ago—in Germany!

EDITH (*as she begins to attack* CYNTHIA *physically*): We'll see whose Germany came between us.

CYNTHIA (*fighting*): Oh, yeah!

EDITH: Yeah!

ANDREW: Edith! Cynthia!

EDITH: Leave us alone, Andrew. We've got to settle this ourselves.

CYNTHIA (*to* ANDREW): Yeah, you were the cause of it all, but we've got to settle this ourselves.

ANDREW: Ladies, please! (*He tries to separate the women.*) Please! Please! (*He stands between them, propping them apart.*) I can't keep it up any longer. I'm old, I'm tired—past desire—past hope.

EDITH: You must never say past hope, Andrew.

ANDREW: I can't let you women fight like this.

EDITH: Andrew, this has got to be settled.

ANDREW: But it doesn't make any sense. Don't you remember, Edith, you started this all over a bus trip.

EDITH: You started it! Over *our* bus trip! Our *last* bus trip!

ANDREW: But it's senseless, Edith. There is no bus.

EDITH: No bus?

ANDREW: No bus!

EDITH: You jest.

ANDREW: No, Edith, there is no bus. It was all a game. You know it, and I know it. We just have our little game every Saturday morning to pass the time. But I can't let you take it this seriously. There is no bus station. This is the city park. There is no ticket seller—his office window is the mailbox. There is no bus, and we're not going anywhere.

EDITH: Why, Andrew, how dare you say such a thing.

ANDREW: And what's more, we've never gone anywhere, and never will go anywhere—I just keep up the game because you love to sit and wait for the bus. A fight between you women is useless.

EDITH: I am surprised at you, Andrew, I really am surprised. After this trip you were going to write your memoirs.

ANDREW: I decided while in the comfort station that it is useless. There is nothing to write.

EDITH: But your notebooks.

ANDREW: There aren't any notebooks.

EDITH: And your battles in memory.

ANDREW: I was never anything but a private for two years.

EDITH: No, Andrew, you fought in the Battle of Old Baldy, in the invasion of Iwo Jima, the Battle of Argonne Forest; you led the troops at Waterloo and Saratoga. You defeated the Spanish Armada; you helped Saint Joan at Orleans; you fought in the Battle of Hastings, the Battle of Tours, the Battle of Metaurus, the Battle of Marathon, and the Battle of Jericho.

ANDREW: Not I.

EDITH: Yes, you, Andrew. And think of all the things you invented—the wheel, the lever, the telescope, the printing press with movable type, the slide rule, the steam engine, the jet plane, the lawn mower, the hydrogen bomb, television, the space satellite, the mousetrap, the electric train, the electronic brain, penicillin, the underwater fountain pen, the zipper, and the hairpin that holds everything together.

ANDREW: Fancy—deception—illusion—dust.

EDITH: You must write your memoirs for those who come after.

ANDREW: There'll be no one to read them.

EDITH: You're wrong, Andrew. There's the orangutan, the gibbon, the passenger pigeon, the panda, the polar bear, the possum, the whale, the dodo, the angleworm, the salmon, the brontosaurus, the ostrich, the auk, the lyrebird, the tortoise, the buzzard, the hydra, the beetle, the scorpion, and the ant—remember the ant, Andrew, how wise, how frugal, how industrious—you always did underestimate the ant.

ANDREW: You can see, she's quite mad.

EDITH: Then there are the children. We mustn't give up for their sake—the white ones, the pink ones, the yellow ones, the red ones, the brown ones, the mulatto ones, the burnt sienna ones, the black ones, the gray ones, and the olive ones.

ANDREW: We haven't any children really.

EDITH: You mustn't give up now, Andrew. Just when things are looking up. Toto did his trick when you left. Come show him, Toto.

ANDREW: Toto isn't there either.

CYNTHIA: I know. Pitiful, isn't it.

EDITH: And Feathers spoke while you were gone, not in just one language, but many—in English, French, German, Latin, Lithuanian, Czechoslovakian, Russian, Chinese, Korean, Japanese, Arabic, Hebrew, Greek, Egyptian,

Sanscrit, hieroglyphics, Braille, lipreading, Morse code, semaphore, and one hundred and eighty-seven Indian dialects, and you know what she said in every language—"God is love." That's what Feathers said—"God is love," in every language in the world. And that's why you can't give up, Andrew. You must write your memoirs. This may only seem a game to you, but it's a *real* game!

ANDREW: She's quite harmless. I think she's had too much sun today.

EDITH: Andrew, it's time for the bus. We mustn't miss it. Will you step to the curb and see if it's coming?

CYNTHIA: I guess you should humor her.

ANDREW: That's the best way. (*to* EDITH) Of course, my dear.

(ANDREW *starts out down right.*)

EDITH: But be careful.

ANDREW: Certainly, I am always careful.

(ANDREW *exits down right.*)

EDITH: I guess that shows you whom he listens to.

CYNTHIA: I don't want him.

(*There is the sound of screeching brakes, and the thud of a vehicle against a soft, heavy object. Crowd noises increase.*)

EDITH: What was that?

CYNTHIA: I'll go see.

(CYNTHIA *exits down right.*)

EDITH (*crossing to bench*): Toto, let me straighten your bow for the trip. There, Feathers, settle down for the bus ride.

(CYNTHIA *returns down right.*)

CYNTHIA: Lady, your husband—

EDITH: Andrew?

CYNTHIA: He's dead. The bus killed him.

(EDITH *is stunned a moment, then sits on the bench.*)

EDITH (*hesitant, tearfully*): I told Andrew something would happen if he didn't get his glasses changed. Who will ever take his place?

(EDITH *is answered only by the sounds of the animals in the zoo,* TOTO, *the dog, and* FEATHERS, *the parakeet, who seem to be saying "God is Love," in all the languages of the world.*)

CURTAIN

The Governor's Lady

DAVID MERCER

Characters

- Lady Harriet Boscoe
- Amolo
- Charmian Maudsley
- Sir Gilbert Boscoe
- John Maudsley
- Police Sergeant

Reading Guides

1. Although *The Governor's Lady* is separated into scenes, it is still a one-act play. As Mr. Mercer indicates, the scenes are for punctuation of the action. They also serve as time breaks.
2. You must remember (Harriet can't) that Gilbert is dead. Harriet is living in a very realistic nightmare (daymare). For this reason, you must pay special attention to the stage directions beginning with SCENE TWO.

The Governor's Lady

THE PLAY *is in one continuous act punctuated by blackouts or fades.*

Exterior and interior of a bungalow in Africa surrounded by jungle.

The main stage is a composite set, with the sitting room right with a round tea table and two upright chairs.

On the left of the stage is the bedroom area, with a large double bed covered with a white mosquito net.

On the left of the bed is a very high, tall cupboard.

The forestage is a verandah area on which are two rush chairs and a drinks table.

On the right the jungle encroaches, and from one of the tall trees hangs a swing.

SCENE ONE

AFTERNOON BEFORE TEA

African music.

(HARRIET *is seated at the tea table. She is writing in her diary.*)

HARRIET: May 15th . . . I cannot resist the temptation to anticipate Charmian's visit this afternoon, for the pleasure of writing my insights now and feeling them vindicated when she has gone. (*pause*) Some women should not live in Africa, and Charmian is one of them. The heat withers her skin and the boredom withers her spirit . . . yet she still inspires in me that weary affection which passes for a bond between old women. (*pause*) I wonder . . . I have no doubt she and John consider it eccentric of us to take this house on the plateau . . . what was it John said? Practically the jungle. (*pause*) She will drive herself here in that ghastly what is it? Jeep? (*pause*) And harass me with her inanities for two hours or more . . .

AMOLO: Mrs. Maudsley, Madam—

HARRIET: Surely not! What time is it?

CHARMIAN: Harriet, darling . . . I know I'm too early—

HARRIET: Of course not. How nice to see you. Such a wretched drive out here in the middle of the afternoon. Let's have tea at once, shall we? Amolo —tea. And you're just the person to help me, Charmian.

CHARMIAN: Help you?

HARRIET: I can't find Gilbert's gun.

CHARMIAN: I can't think why you should want Gilbert's gun. Are you going to attack somebody or are you expecting to *be* attacked? Anyway, how should I know where it is? (*pause*) I came for tea, darling, since you invited me for tea.

HARRIET: You know you've always had a flair for finding Gilbert's things when he loses them—

CHARMIAN: That is true, but it is a flair of no practical value in the circumstances.

HARRIET: Circumstances?

CHARMIAN: Harriet, how could Gilbert lose *anything,* when Gilbert is dead?

(*pause*)

HARRIET: Did I ask Amolo to bring in the tea? I am a good shot, you know, Charmian. And I feel safer when I have the means to protect myself. There *was* a time when a white woman in this colony could dispense with such vulgarities. Now, however—

CHARMIAN: One doesn't say "this colony" any longer, Harriet. Times have changed, my dear. Since they won their precious freedom you have to be careful what you say.

HARRIET: I have always thought . . . and I always shall think . . . that the natives are children. I know I am an old-fashioned woman, a stubborn old woman—

CHARMIAN: But you want to die in full possession of all your prejudices?

HARRIET: What's that, Charmian?

CHARMIAN: I said—

HARRIET: But I fail to see why they should wish to exchange their simplicity and innocence for *our* vices and machines. (*pause*) Leave the trolley, Amolo . . . I shall not need you.

AMOLO: Yes, Madam.

HARRIET: I agree with Gilbert. Independence at this stage would mean anarchy. (*pause*) Lemon?

CHARMIAN: Please. (*pause*) Dear Harriet!

HARRIET: Why, Charmian . . . you are almost in tears!

CHARMIAN: Listen, darling. You're quite sure you know when and where you are?

HARRIET: But why on earth shouldn't I?

CHARMIAN: Harriet, it is one year since this colony became independent. And six months since Gilbert died. Harriet, you are not the Governor's wife . . . You are the ex-Governor's widow. (*pause*) I've . . . I—can't go on pretending I don't notice that your mind is . . . wandering. There, I've said it. I've tried and tried to think of a kinder way of putting it. But there isn't one. Harriet, John and I think . . . we think you should consider going home. Have you seen a doctor?

HARRIET: My dear Charmian, I *am* at home. And I am perfectly well, thank you. (*pause*) I think the drive must have tired you out. (*pause*) And yet, it is so lovely up here. It has its compensations. Gilbert says that it is always five degrees cooler up here than anywhere else in the colony.

(*pause*)

CHARMIAN: I meant—London, Harriet.

HARRIET: You don't know what you are saying, my dear. Leave Karalinga now? (*pause*) You know, Charmian, Gilbert feels—and I couldn't agree with him more—that it is precisely now when they need us most. When they have to choose between *us* and those awful little demagogues of theirs with a degree from Manchester or wherever it is.

CHARMIAN: You can quote Gilbert till you're blue in the face, darling, but it won't do me a bit of good. And it makes *them* fractious. (*pause*) Peter says they've got us by the short and curlies—

HARRIET: By the *what?*

CHARMIAN: It does sound ghastly, doesn't it? Children are so mature nowadays. John says when he was Peter's age he spent all his time reading Shelley and worrying about self-abuse. Thank God we only have one grandchild. I'd be prostrate by now if Tim and Mary had any more like Peter.

HARRIET: Short and curly indeed! A boy of sixteen—

CHARMIAN: Curlies, Harriet.

HARRIET: Well, I ask you!

CHARMIAN: It has a certain crude vigor, as dormitory language goes—

HARRIET: My dear Charmian, a boy who can be as facetious as that at sixteen can be a Socialist at twenty-one!

CHARMIAN: I don't *quite* see the connection—

HARRIET: From the moment they came to power in 1945, Gilbert noticed the prevailing tone in their dealings with him was one of disrespect . . . a, a want of feeling and discretion.

CHARMIAN: Well, darling, you remember what the Permanent Under Secretary said at the time—

HARRIET: I don't believe I do.

CHARMIAN: Uneasy lies the Red that wears a crown! (*laughs*) No, Harriet, it won't do. Gilbert failed to adapt, and people who fail to adapt—especially in colonial matters—are, as I have no doubt Peter would say, sitting ducks.

HARRIET: I shall never understand you, Charmian. You talk as though it is all over and done with.

CHARMIAN: But isn't it?

(*pause*)

HARRIET: So long as Gilbert is Governor of Karalinga, it is the *colony* that must learn to adapt.

CHARMIAN: Harriet—

HARRIET: Will you have some more tea?

CHARMIAN: Harriet—

HARRIET (*petulantly*): Now what is it?

CHARMIAN: Gilbert is dead.

HARRIET: Then I have nothing more to say on the subject. We all have our, our idiosyncrasies, Charmian. You must cling to yours, and I must cling to mine.

CHARMIAN: I would hardly call it an idiosyncrasy, to ignore the fact that Gilbert caught pneumonia, and died, and has been buried nearly six months.

(*pause*)

HARRIET: *I* was speaking of the subtleties of colonial administration, Charmian.

(*pause*)

CHARMIAN: Look, darling, why not let John and me come and help you to pack? Have everything sent off by sea, and book you an air passage to London? (*pause*) This house is too lonely, Harriet. Anything could happen to you out here, and none of us would know. (*pause*) Living out here with two or three native servants . . . not even a telephone . . . must you, Harriet? At least, come and stay with us for a while—

HARRIET (*sharply*): Do *not* insist on treating me as if I were mentally infirm, Charmian. (*pause*) Amolo can reach the town on his bicycle in forty minutes. Should I need you in any way during Gilbert's absence, I am grateful to think you would come if I sent for you.

(*pause*)

CHARMIAN: Well, if you will insist on being indomitable—

(*pause*)

HARRIET: Not indomitable, Charmian. Independent.

CHARMIAN (*jungle noises start*): Well, it's nice to know you're not entirely without faith in independence! (*pause*) I think I'd better be going. Come out and see what I did, to the jeep thing on the way up here—

(*exit both; blackout.*)

SCENE TWO

MORNING: BREAKFAST

Fade-in Mozart piano concerto.

(AMOLO *is serving breakfast.* HARRIET *enters.*)

HARRIET: Good morning, Amolo. No, leave it. . . . I'll see to it myself. You can go now.

AMOLO: Yes, Madam.

HARRIET: Amolo—

AMOLO: Yes, Madam?

HARRIET: Where is that music coming from?

AMOLO: My nephew, Madam. He is visiting. Has gramophone.

HARRIET: I see. Your nephew is fond of Mozart?

AMOLO: Fond of all music, Madam. (*with pride*) He is a student.

HARRIET: A music student?

AMOLO: Go for engineer, Madam.

HARRIET: Ah! At Manchester College I suppose—

AMOLO: No, Madam. (*pause*) Moscow.

(*pause*)

HARRIET: That will be all, Amolo.

AMOLO: Yes, Madam.

HARRIET (*peevishly*): And ask him to turn the gramophone down, will you?

AMOLO: Yes, Madam.

(AMOLO *goes out. The music stops.*)

HARRIET: Absurd. Poor Charmian. (*pours tea*) She does not understand that they are . . . how can one put it? Biologically remote from us. Charmian will ramble. She rambles and rambles, which always infuriated Gilbert. I remember once during a lull at a Memorial Service in Westminster, she brayed out "When are you going to get that paunch of yours knighted, Gilbert?" So cruel! So unjust! (*She slices at an egg.*) The way a person slices an egg can be most revealing. There. Poor little embryo. I wonder if I—

(*Jungle noises as* GILBERT *enters. He is in full Governor's regalia.*)

GILBERT: Morning, Harriet.

HARRIET: Why, Gilbert! What time did you get back last night? I didn't hear you.

GILBERT: Small hours. No reason to wake you. Slept in the dressing room.

HARRIET: Will you have an egg?

GILBERT: I think, a banana.

HARRIET: A fresh egg—

GILBERT (*picks up an egg*): Frankly, I've always considered eggs to be messy things. (*Smashes it on the table.*) All that sog inside. No more eggs.

HARRIET: Did you have a good trip?

GILBERT: Arrived in Bonda just after a ritual murder. And in Kadun too early for the trials. All this rushing round from one province to another, ridiculous. A Governor should be . . . remote. Pass the bananas, will you, Harriet?

(HARRIET *passes the bananas. Noisy eating punctuated by snorts and grunts.*)

HARRIET: You must be very hungry, Gilbert.

GILBERT (*a growling belch*).

HARRIET: Really! Let me give you some tea. (*tea poured*)

GILBERT (*slurping*): They've actually asked me to let them have a report on the colony's fitness for self-government. Thoughtful of them, isn't it? Especially when they'll go straight ahead with it whatever I say. (*pause*)

HARRIET: Charmian was here yesterday. For tea.

(GILBERT *knocks a cup off the table clumsily—it breaks.*)

Gilbert! What an extraordinary thing to do! That was one of my mother's breakfast cups. Gilbert, you deliberately broke it. Amolo!

GILBERT: Very odd, that. Had a sort of . . . impulse.

HARRIET: And a very cruel one, if I may say so.

GILBERT: Now, Harriet—

HARRIET: My mother bought those cups in—

GILBERT: Oh, damn your mother's cups.

HARRIET: Gilbert!

GILBERT: You loathe those cups. You've said so before.

HARRIET: Civilization, Gilbert, is the art of tolerating what we loathe.

GILBERT: Prissy old devil.

HARRIET: I think I shall go to my room and write some letters. You must have been out in the sun. We shall say no more about it.

(GILBERT *knocks off another cup.*)

GILBERT: Oh, God! Now, that *was* an accident—

HARRIET: Was it, Gilbert? (*pause*) Where *is* Amolo? (*pause*) It has suddenly gone very quiet—

GILBERT: I've never liked that boy. Imagine . . . imagine Amolo voting. Can you? Ridiculous.

(HARRIET *is uneasy.*)

HARRIET: It's so quiet, Gilbert.

GILBERT: Subhuman. Subhuman, the lot of them. Can't help it, but no use ignoring. It's a matter of evolution, Harriet. Brain pan's too small. (*pause*) Ever seen one?

(HARRIET *goes to the door.*)

HARRIET: I believe . . . I believe there's no one there, Gilbert.

GILBERT: Now, what's the weight of the average human brain? In ounces. A *white* human brain.

HARRIET: Is there such a thing as a *black* human brain?

GILBERT: Ho-ho, you old liberal, you!

(HARRIET *comes back to him.*)

HARRIET: Gilbert, do not be jocose. I am trying to tell you that the servants, the servants have all disappeared.

GILBERT: Damn good riddance.

HARRIET: I don't know what it is, but I have the distinct impression that you are not yourself today. And what are we going to do for servants?

GILBERT: Get some more, Harriet. Get some more.

HARRIET: If it were not nine o'clock in the morning, I should say you had been drinking.

GILBERT: How like a woman!

HARRIET: We are too old for scenes, Gilbert.

GILBERT: Too old for too many things, if one listened to you!

HARRIET: I hope you are not going to raise *that* subject again.

GILBERT: What subject?

HARRIET: That subject.

GILBERT: You know, I sometimes wonder if you aren't getting just a bit senile, Harriet.

HARRIET: I shall go to my room. I will not listen to this.

GILBERT: And the servants?

HARRIET: I have managed your domestic affairs efficiently for forty years, Gilbert . . . I am not a spiteful woman, but what would you like me to do? Chase into the bush after them?

GILBERT: Don't think of it, Harriet. Don't think of it. (*pause*) The proper setting for a colonial administrator's wife is, of course, a garden. Where everything is pruned . . . and sprayed . . . and kept under control. (*pause*) So stick to the garden, there's a good woman.

HARRIET: Your mind is wandering, Gilbert. You ought to see a doctor. (*pause*) Do stop scratching! It's hardly . . . Take a bath or whatever you like, but do not scratch. Gilbert!

GILBERT: It's that damned headman in Bonda. The feller's crawling. Now, you run along and write your letters, m'dear.

HARRIET: Perhaps by lunchtime you will be more yourself—(*exits*)

GILBERT: I hope so, Harriet. If that will please you. I hope so.

(*Fade-out.*)

SCENE THREE

EVENING

Fade-in nocturnal jungle sounds.
(HARRIET *at table writing*)

HARRIET: May 16th. The situation is maddening. The servants ran away this morning, for some inexplicable reason, and nothing will induce Gilbert to take the matter seriously. (*pause*) An extraordinary change has come over my husband. He seems . . . coarsened. Almost brutal, at times. It is perhaps one of the inevitable trials of old age that human dignity should prove so vulnerable to the malfunctionings of body and mind. (*pause*) Gilbert is waging a struggle with himself in which I can take no part, except insofar as I can, and must, share his humiliations. (*pause*) How one longs for white servants at moments like these; and despite one's love for Africa, there is always that sense of emergence from the primordial . . . that nostalgia for reason and order, which these poor people cannot achieve—no, not in a hundred years.

(*pause; creaking; silence; creaking; silence; creaking; silence*)

Gilbert . . . (*louder*) Gilbert—Gilbert, where are you? (*sound as of some kind of ring being thrown onto a post*)

(GILBERT *on wardrobe*)

GILBERT: Now where the devil would you *expect* me to be?

(*pause*)

HARRIET: *Not* on top of the wardrobe! And *not* rifling my jewel case! (*pause*) What are my necklaces doing on this bedpost, might I ask?

(*Creak.* GILBERT *is throwing necklaces onto the bedpost.*)

Gilbert, come down here at once! Give me my jewel case. Come along. Give it to me.

(*creak; rattle*)

GILBERT (*irritated*): Nearly missed that time! Go away, Harriet. Go away and write your blessed diary.

HARRIET: Not until you come down off that wardrobe and . . . (*crying*) Oh, Gilbert!

GILBERT: Harriet, you are trivializing our relationship—

HARRIET: Won't you come down? Just for me?

GILBERT: I can't imagine why you should think *you* are any sort of temptation!

HARRIET: Come down, my dear—

GILBERT: Ha! *My dear* now, are we?

HARRIET: Oh, this is futile.

GILBERT: You're not the woman I married, Harriet.

HARRIET: I am not, indeed! I should like to think that nearly half a century had brought a little wisdom. Common sense, at least.

GILBERT: Who the devil wants wisdom in a woman? What about your woman's instincts, eh? What about them?

HARRIET: I have noticed before, that when you begin to talk like a character out of a Russian novel, it is best to leave you to your own devices.

GILBERT: A Russian novel? Me? I've never read one of those damned things in me life! All those vitches and ovnas . . . ukins and inskys.

HARRIET: It is your loss.

GILBERT: But, you wouldn't say I'm an *uncultured* man, would you, Harriet?

HARRIET: Until recently—no.

GILBERT: Now, they can say what they like but these people . . . these wretched natives . . . they're *all* instinct. Primitive. (*pause*) I can admire instinct in a white woman of gentle birth. We have, we have centuries of slow, painful refinement behind us. But oh, my God, the unadulterated thing! The *thing* itself! Chaos! Absolute chaos! (*pause*) If they knew what I really think about this situation . . . why, they'd have me out. Have me out, Harriet.

HARRIET: Gilbert . . . I do believe . . .

GILBERT: What's that? What?

HARRIET: Gilbert, are you—

GILBERT: Am I *what?*

HARRIET: A trick of the light.

GILBERT: Trick?

HARRIET: I had the distinct impression you were . . . salivating.

GILBERT: Salivating? What the devil do you think I am? *Animals* salivate, Harriet. Human beings spit. There's a world of difference.

HARRIET: Well, are you?

GILBERT: Or drool, I suppose.

HARRIET: There has never been the slightest confusion in *my* mind. A person who drools is not a person. (*pause*) Which are *you* doing, Gilbert?

(*pause*)

GILBERT: I'm spitting, Harriet. I'm spitting. I spit when I get carried away.

HARRIET: Then be good enough to regain control of yourself.

GILBERT: You know, there's something bloody odd about you this evening.

HARRIET: I have never known you lose control of yourself in forty years of Government service.

GILBERT: There's a difference between losing control and getting carried away. (*pause*) In any case, the point is an academic one since I am not prone to either, when publicly fulfilling my obligations as a servant of Her Majesty's Government.

(*pause*)

HARRIET: What *resonance* there was in that phrase . . . once.

GILBERT: Oh, the *resonance* has gone, right enough!

HARRIET: When there was order in the world—

GILBERT: Law and order. Nowadays it's all, wha'do they call it? Pragmatism. Oh, there are people who regard me as a sort of living fossil! I know. I'm an enemy of pragmatism, you see. And it doesn't do these days, Harriet. It doesn't do.

HARRIET: It is satisfying to think that our kind have always acted . . . disinterestedly. That the instincts have been . . . sublimated.

GILBERT: You always were a clever woman, Harriet.

HARRIET: Do come down, my dear—

GILBERT: What about a nightcap?

HARRIET: On the balcony? As we . . . used to?

GILBERT: Right. I'm coming down then.

HARRIET: It's a lovely night— (*pause*) Let me help you down, my dear!

(*Chattering of monkeys.* GILBERT *pours drinks.*)

GILBERT: It's a long time since we did this. (*pause*) Life's too long, really. Ought to be cut off in the prime. (*goes down to verandah in front*)

HARRIET: I am not sure that a woman knows what . . . or when . . . her prime is.

GILBERT: Different for a woman.

HARRIET: That was how my father explained away a great deal in his declining years. Everything was . . . different for a woman. But he never mentioned his prime.

GILBERT: Great diplomat, your father. (*pause*) The middle classes can run the Empire, he used to say, but it takes an aristocrat to run the middle classes. (*pause*) Wouldn't recognize things as they are today.

HARRIET: I remember . . . at a weekend house party once, he encountered that Lawrence person—

GILBERT: T.E.?

HARRIET: David Herbert—

GILBERT: Ugh!

HARRIET: We were strolling in the garden before dinner. Someone was talking about the Weimar Republic. Lawrence was being most tiresome, and my father said to him: Mister Lawrence, you stick to your solar plexus and leave Germany to the politicians—

GILBERT: Oh, splendid! (*pause*)

HARRIET: Lawrence was a venomous little man, you know. He despised people like my father. He despised what we all stood for. But he lacked wit—

GILBERT: Worlds apart—

HARRIET: His reply must have been unexceptional, because I can't remember what it was.

GILBERT: Your father was in his prime then.

(*Chattering of monkeys outside*)

HARRIET: He was not a bigoted man.

(*pause*)

GILBERT: These young men *now* . . . They talk about the first war marking the end of an epoch. . . . They've no real idea what there, what there *was.*

(*pause*)

HARRIET: And yet . . . I sometimes think, Europe was besotted with sex after 1919.

GILBERT: Europe was in its prime, just before the First World War.

HARRIET: Well, we enjoyed some of the last of it, Gilbert—

(*pause*)

GILBERT: That's a pretty bowl—

HARRIET: Really! We have had that bowl for over twenty years.

GILBERT: Oh, it's pretty all right!

HARRIET: You gave it to me yourself.

GILBERT: Did I now? Did I?

HARRIET: You have always had exquisite taste, Gilbert.

GILBERT: Curious . . . don't remember it.

HARRIET: We have so many fine things. (*pause*) I sometimes . . . even after all these years I still think how it would have been to have had children. Someone to pass these things on to. The sense of . . . continuity. It becomes more important as one grows older. (*pause*) I don't like to think it might be . . . as if we had never existed.

GILBERT: Getting morbid, Harriet.

HARRIET: And these things will pass into the world after we are gone, and they will be . . . anonymous.

GILBERT: Morbid!

HARRIET: Oh, our lives have been rich, and full. I am grateful for that. (*pause*)

GILBERT: Well, who mentioned not having children? Did I? Did I say anything about it? No. You raised the subject. (*pause*) There's something . . . obscene about an old woman maundering over her sterility.

HARRIET: The question of whose incapacity was involved was never settled.

GILBERT: And why not? What in God's name is science *for,* then?

HARRIET: I have often put the same question to myself. Science illuminates, but it fails to explain. I believe that was the gist of *your* refusal to undergo a medical examination.

GILBERT: All this beating about the bush—

HARRIET: Gilbert, since you came home yesterday, I have had a strangely . . . cutoff feeling. Almost . . . almost the sensation that you wish to do me harm, Gilbert. Or, to put it another way, that you wish harm might come to me. (*pause*) Everything was perfectly normal when you went away—

GILBERT: Everything is perfectly normal now, Harriet. Perfectly normal.

HARRIET: But, we don't appear to have quite the relationship that we had before. (*pause*) The relationship that we have enjoyed since we were young people.

GILBERT: You mustn't allow yourself to feel guilty, Harriet. One has to adjust, as one gets older.

HARRIET: Guilty?

GILBERT: A more passionate woman might have . . . so to speak, disturbed the balance.

(*pause*)

HARRIET: You are spitting again, Gilbert. Wipe your chin.

GILBERT: I'm going to shave this damned beard off. It gets . . . matted.

HARRIET: It is very distinguished. (*pause*) You didn't tell me that you intended to grow one whilst you were away. (*pause*) An imperial suits you.

GILBERT: It compensates somewhat for the waning authority of the Crown, don't you think? If Queen Victoria had had a beard the Empire would have lasted for a thousand years! (*pause*) Still, they do . . . tend . . . to get . . . matted.

HARRIET: Never mind. It will photograph so much better than a . . . what does one say? A *naked* face? A bare face?

GILBERT: Nude face?

HARRIET: Most certainly not.

GILBERT: There, that's the last of the whisky.

HARRIET: Surely not? There was . . . surely, half a bottle?

GILBERT: Then Amolo must have been at it.

HARRIET: *Not* the sort of behavior that goes with political maturity!

GILBERT: Ought to get back up in the trees, where they belong.

HARRIET: Oh!

GILBERT: Now you're shocked.

HARRIET: I *am* shocked.

GILBERT: I can just tolerate the hypothesis that Amolo and I have a common ancestor in the lemur. Where I diverge from enlightened opinion is in the crass assertion that Amolo and I are the same beneath the skin. My remark was an attempt to be graphic about the divergence.

HARRIET: Nonetheless, it was the sort of remark one hears from gutter racialists—

GILBERT: Admirably put, Harriet, but you know me better than that.

HARRIET: I know you are not a racialist, Gilbert. (*pause*) That I could *not* bear.

GILBERT: But you women . . . *you* know there's . . . something different about them. Now don't you? Something . . . attractive.

(*pause*)

HARRIET: Attractive?

GILBERT: What do you mean, "attractive"?

HARRIET: You said: "something attractive."

GILBERT: I said repellent, Harriet.

HARRIET: I heard you distinctly. You said: "attractive."

GILBERT: And equally distinctly, I heard myself say repellent.

HARRIET: That must be what you intended to say.

GILBERT: Dammit, *I* know what I said!

HARRIET: Then we cannot profitably discuss the matter any further.

GILBERT: I *intended* to say "attractive," and I *said* "attractive."

(*pause*)

HARRIET: There you go again!

(*pause*)

GILBERT: You know, Harriet, it's just possible . . . it's just possible that *you* find them attractive!

HARRIET: I find them repellent.

GILBERT: Ah!

HARRIET: You needn't sound so pleased about it.

GILBERT (*shouting*): I am *not* pleased.

HARRIET: Oh? Aren't you?

GILBERT: I mean . . . I don't know where the devil all this is leading—

HARRIET: In my case—to bed. In your case, Gilbert, perhaps . . . up on the wardrobe, where you belong?

(*monkeys; fade-out*)

SCENE FOUR

(*Fade-in* HARRIET)

HARRIET: March 18th. I must force myself to put it down in writing: Gilbert is going insane. The evidence is overwhelming. He is gratuitously violent—so far, thank heaven, directed elsewhere, than at my own person. He has willfully broken every bowl and vase in the house, and most of the cups. He appears to be losing control of his bodily functions and has also evolved the distressing habit of vomiting forth his bananas, then eating his vomit! In my last entry I spoke of sharing his humiliations! I see now that I was trying to conceal the truth from myself, for Gilbert and I are beyond sharing. . . . He has gone where I cannot reach him, and is so far in this that I cannot, I dare not, hope for his return. (*pause*) Yet, such is the resilience of human nature that I have already taken certain practical steps. (*pause*) My poor Gilbert! I have unearthed the picnic basket which Charmian gave us last year, and I propose from now on to serve him his meals on plastic plates and his tea and coffee in a plastic beaker. (*pause*) I found a set of clean dungarees in Amolo's room which, after some persuasion and cajoling, Gilbert consented to wear . . . until I can have his ruined suits cleaned and pressed. When I look at Gilbert, my whole instinct is to weep and weep. (*pause*) This must be conquered like any other.

(*Fade-out* HARRIET. *A long-drawn-out yell. Fade-up into bedroom area.* GILBERT, *in semidarkness—a great hulking figure in dungarees. He is strangling* AMOLO. *The body thuds onto the stage.* GILBERT *scuttles off.* HARRIET *enters, frightened. Enter* GILBERT *humming "The Teddy Bears' Picnic." He now has gorilla hands.*)

GILBERT: What's this?
HARRIET: Amolo . . . I think . . . I think his neck is broken.
GILBERT: Good God! (*pause*) Dead as mutton.
HARRIET: His *neck* is broken—
GILBERT: Came sneaking back for the rest of the whisky, I suppose.
HARRIET: And broke his own neck?
GILBERT: One of the others did—
HARRIET: But why? Why?
GILBERT: This damned colony's seething. *Seething.* Tribal feuds . . . politics . . . communist agitators—
HARRIET: Not *Amolo*—
GILBERT: I shall declare a state of emergency throughout the province.
HARRIET: But—
GILBERT: Arrest the ringleaders . . . declare a curfew . . . soon put a stop to all *this.*
HARRIET: But Amolo—
GILBERT: What's that?
HARRIET: Wasn't mixed up in anything like that, Gilbert.
GILBERT: My dear Harriet, they are *all* mixed up in things like that.
HARRIET: What are we going to do . . . with Amolo's . . . body?
GILBERT: Have to be buried immediately, of course. Be stinking within twelve hours, poor fellow.

(*pause*)

HARRIET: Do *you* intend to bury him, Gilbert?
GILBERT: *I?*
HARRIET: There is no one else—
GILBERT: I think I'll have a little swing, and think about it.
HARRIET: A swing?
GILBERT: You know what a *swing* is, Harriet! A wooden seat suspended by two ropes from a—

HARRIET: Yes . . . I know what a swing is.

GILBERT: Then what are you looking so vacant about?

HARRIET: Nothing . . . nothing.

GILBERT: Nothing in that tone of voice means *something.* (*pause*) This is not the time to be perversely feminine!

HARRIET: I think we had better go out into the garden. Amolo's body—

GILBERT: I've never thought of you as a *squeamish* woman, Harriet! The garden—

(*She exits fast out to garden and swing.* GILBERT *follows and sits on swing.* GILBERT *on swing, pushed by* HARRIET.)

GILBERT: Come on, Harriet, push me. Harder, Harriet! Push harder—

HARRIET: This is ridiculous—

GILBERT: Push, Harriet—

HARRIET: I am exhausted.

GILBERT: Feeble old woman!

HARRIET: I can bear no more.

GILBERT: Why, Harriet! Come now, I'll *stop* swinging—if you like.

HARRIET: Yes—do. For goodness' sake stop.

GILBERT: Didn't *you* ever like to swing?

HARRIET: Oh, yes! I liked to swing. Nearly sixty years ago!

GILBERT: In the privacy of one's own garden, Harriet . . . there are no limits.

(*pause*)

HARRIET: I think it is time you pulled yourself together and faced reality, Gilbert. The situation is intolerable. First the servants run away, then Amolo is killed—and you do nothing. Nothing. (*pause*) For all we know, we are completely cut off. And once the killing begins—

GILBERT: They can tear themselves to pieces for all I care.

HARRIET: And what if they should tear *us* to pieces?

GILBERT: They wouldn't dare to lay a finger on us.

HARRIET: Revenge takes no account of the consequences.

GILBERT: Revenge? Good God, woman, what have we done to them except bring them a . . . a civilization? Schools, roads, hospitals, technicians . . . government, Harriet. (*pause*) If they remain savages, as they very obviously do —despite their gramophones and briefcases—then it is not a question of revenge, but of blind, gratuitous violence. And I know how to deal with that!

HARRIET: *Do* you, Gilbert?

GILBERT: Haven't I dealt with it before?

HARRIET: You have certainly shown that you know how to *eliminate* it. (*pause*) Whether you have *dealt* with it, except in a very limited sense of the word . . . I don't know.

(*pause; distant sound of drums*)

Listen—

(*pause*)

GILBERT: Listen to what? Can't hear a thing.

HARRIET: Sure . . . drums?

GILBERT: Nonsense.

HARRIET: I can hear drums—

(*drumming stepped up slightly*)

GILBERT: Blood pressure, more likely!

HARRIET: If I were the sort of person who hears things, Gilbert, I would know it!

GILBERT: Drums!

HARRIET: You *must* hear them.

GILBERT: But . . . I don't.

(*pause; drumming*)

HARRIET: I am going into the house—

GILBERT: Well, then, you'd better be the one to bury Amolo . . . because I'm going for a walk.

HARRIET: I? Dig a *grave?* Bury *Amolo?* (*pause*) How *can* you!

GILBERT: Harriet, you know perfectly well that I can't touch dead things. It's one of my, one of my . . . phobias. (*pause*) On the other hand, you could simply let him rot—

HARRIET: Gilbert!

GILBERT: Leave him to the ants—

HARRIET: But . . . but Amolo is a *Christian!*

GILBERT: I shouldn't think the ants will mind, Harriet. Besides, being a Christian doesn't logically entitle anyone to a burial, now does it?

(*pause*)

HARRIET: *We* are Christian, too.

GILBERT: Come now. Not *really* Christians. Eh? (*pause*) There are other things besides being a Christian, you know.

HARRIET: Are you no longer a Christian, Gilbert?

GILBERT: Oh, come, come, come. I really thought we were more sophisticated than that, Harriet! (*pause*) Just a minute. What's that? Listen?

(*pause. silence*)

HARRIET: Why . . . the drums have stopped.

GILBERT: *Your* drums may have stopped. (*pause*) *Mine* have just started—

HARRIET: But . . . it's perfectly *quiet!*

(*pause*)

GILBERT: I think you'd better get started on that grave. On that *Christian's* grave.

HARRIET: I am sorry, Gilbert. . . . I will not do such a thing. How can you seem to . . . to expect—

GILBERT: You've had the poor devil at your beck and call for the last eight years . . . the least you can do is to bury him!

HARRIET (*moaning*): Gilbert . . . Gilbert . . . I won't, I can't—

GILBERT: I wish they'd stop those bloody drums. (*pause*) Now Harriet, I'll find you a nice spade. I tell you what; I'll find some big stones as well. To put on top. If you don't, the hyenas'll get him, you know. (HARRIET *sobbing quietly*) Come along . . . that's right give me your arm . . . must get it done before sundown—

(*fade-out* HARRIET *crying*)

SCENE FIVE

LATER THAT EVENING

(*Fade-in* HARRIET *reading her diary. Muted drumming.*)

HARRIET: For what sin has my awful punishment been devised? (*pause*) And what woman, grown old and experienced in the world, has had to take pen and record such vile assault on her whole being as I have endured today? (*pause*) And Gilbert . . . Gilbert stood over me whilst I dug a grave. Under the hot sun, I took a spade, and measured the ground . . . and dug a grave for Amolo, whilst Gilbert watched . . . half smiling. (*pause*) I half dragged, half carried the body to the grave, wrapped in a sheet. I read from the Book of Common Prayer (I cannot remember what) and lowered

Amolo in, as gently as I could. (*pause*) I was drenched with perspiration —and trembling . . . almost ready to die *then,* and have Gilbert bury *me.* (*pause*) We came back to the house, and have not spoken since. . . . I feel . . . fanciful though it might be . . . that in burying that poor native boy, I have buried some angry devouring thing in my husband. (*pause*) Now I must go to bed, for I ache both in body and heart . . . and the drumming out there in the hills is like the beat of evil itself. (*pause*) Perhaps . . . we should give them their country, and go. (*pause*) I can write no more. (*pause*) God bring us peace with the morning light.

(*gets into bed*)
(*fade-out*)

SCENE SIX

(*Fade-up bed in semidarkness. Low muted drumming. A clock strikes three. There is a scream, and we see* GILBERT *trying to climb into a bed. He does so, and* HARRIET *pleads with him.*)

HARRIET (*in bed; mosquito net over bed*): What are you doing? (*pause*) Gilbert? Is that you? (*creaking springs*) What are you . . . no, no . . . go back to your own bed and go to sleep. (*pause. silence*) Gilbert? (*pause. creaking springs*) Gilbert . . . we are old people. . . . This is . . . This is . . . you *shall* not! (*pause*) Please . . . please, Gilbert—(GILBERT *grunts several times.*) How *dare* you, dare you attempt this disgusting behavior! (*pause*) Gilbert? (*pause*) Be good enough to return to your own bed, and molest me no further. (*pause*) It was . . . it was beastliness when we were young . . . and it would be . . . degraded beastliness now. Gilbert? You cannot. You must not. It was . . . *always* loathesome. There was never any response in me. You know that, don't you? (*pause*) Never in me. *That* was not in me. (*pause*) Gilbert? (*pause*) Gilbert, I shall get up, and cross the room, and go out through that door . . . and *lock* it. I shall lock you up. Lock you in. (*pause*) Lock you in alone with yourself, where you belong. (*pause*) And perhaps tomorrow . . . if you are good . . . I shall let you out . . . and we shall say no more about it? Shall we? Not another word.

(*massive jungle cacophony. fade-out on bed.*)

SCENE SEVEN

NEXT MORNING: BREAKFAST

(*Long pause. Fade-up* HARRIET *at breakfast. She has a rifle by her chair. Enter* GILBERT.)

GILBERT: Morning, Harriet. (*pause*) I said Good morning, Harriet—

HARRIET: Yes. I heard you.

GILBERT: Well then?

HARRIET: You will understand if I find it difficult to engage in pleasantries this morning!

(*pause*)

GILBERT: Dammit, you unlocked the door, didn't you?

HARRIET: As your presence at breakfast testifies!

GILBERT: Then we'll say no more about it.

HARRIET: *You* say that! (*pause*) If it will reassure you . . . I do not propose to make an issue of what happened last night.

GILBERT: How are your drums?

HARRIET: I . . . I can't hear them this morning.

GILBERT: Mine have stopped, too. (*pause*) It's a bit . . . ominous, isn't it? (*pause*) The calm before the . . . attack . . . and all that.

HARRIET: Gilbert, why are you trying to frighten me? (*pause*) What are you trying to do to me? (*pause*) What have you become, Gilbert?

GILBERT: Now, Harriet, you unlocked the door of your own free will!

HARRIET: I unlocked the door . . . out of respect for *your* free will—

GILBERT: And why should *I* wish to frighten *you?*

HARRIET: If I knew . . . *I* would know how to help *you*—

GILBERT: The truth is, of course, that you are a cold, arrogant woman, Harriet. Something disturbs you . . . you find its source in me. And yet, when it comes to the natives you are . . . equivocal. If I were to put them down ruthlessly you would applaud me. Yet, secretly, you know that to have what you really want is an act of aggression against yourself. (*pause*) I hope I am being lucid?

(*pause*)

HARRIET: I . . . do not know you . . . any longer, Gilbert.

GILBERT: Which is why, I suppose, you are carrying that gun!

(*pause*)

HARRIET: I . . . I am so tired of all this. (*pause*) Do you remember what we were when we first came out here? Do you think I have not the pride of knowing that a few great families in one small country held out as long as they did? (*pause*) Our motives have always been . . . beyond reproach.

And to suggest that we were moved by the hungers and lusts which characterize *these* people is to put yourself . . . on the wrong side of the boundary of sanity.

(*pause*)

GILBERT: A . . . few . . . great . . . families! What a felicitous way of understanding fifty years' precarious authority! (*pause*) Isn't it time we did what we really want for a change? (*pause*) Since we are virtually an extinct class . . . since we've let the *merchants* and *managers* and *technicians* capture the roost . . . we might as *well* go out with a bang! (*pause*) And admit . . . that we are grateful . . . for the modest privilege of . . . destroying . . . each other!

(GILBERT *exits.*)

HARRIET: Where are you going? (*pause*) Come *back,* Gilbert! (*pause*) It's no use running off into the bush, you know—they'll catch you and tear you to pieces! You are behaving in a ridiculous manner, Gilbert. (*pause*) You cannot possibly climb that tree. (*pause*) Come down at once. Very well, then. If you will not—

GILBERT: There are some fine coconuts up here, Harriet . . . try one.

(*pause; crash of breaking coconut*)

HARRIET: I warn you, Gilbert—

GILBERT: Try another—

(*coconut*)

HARRIET: Oh, I wish they could all see you now . . . in your tree, Gilbert. Like the beast you are. (*coconuts thick and fast*) Like the ugly, monstrous creature you always have been. That is what I have lived with all these years, a monster! I have the gun, Gilbert. (*pause*) Come down, or I shall shoot . . . oh, I've wanted to, you know. I've wanted to. *Wanted* to shoot you. *Will* you come down or must I . . . (*She fires. Loud crash. Scream from* HARRIET.)

(*blackout*)

SCENE EIGHT

LATER THE SAME EVENING

(*Chattering monkeys. Fade-in. Breakfast things still there. Fade-up sound of jeep. We hear it stop—its lights swing across the stage and come to rest. In half shadow there is a tree with the body of a huge gorilla lying beneath it. Voices off:* CHARMIAN, JOHN (*her husband*), *and a* NATIVE POLICEMAN.)

CHARMIAN (*off*): The place looks deserted.
JOHN (*off*): You take the back, Sergeant. I'll take the front.

(*They enter; the* POLICEMAN *first, carrying an electric torch, then* JOHN *and* CHARMIAN *together.*)

POLICEMAN: Mr. Maudsley—*you* will take the back.
JOHN (*irritated*): It's hardly an occasion for quibbling about protocol—
CHARMIAN (*frightened*): Poor Harriet—
JOHN: What do you mean? How do we know? She's probably in bed and asleep.
POLICEMAN: In Karalinga, Mrs. Maudsley, bad things no longer happen. We are not savages. Know how to behave. I am afraid, sir, this was not always the same with your own people.
JOHN: Oh, let's get on with it!

(JOHN *goes off. The* POLICEMAN *comes downstage flashing his torch, followed by* CHARMIAN. *He is near the tree.*)

CHARMIAN: I'm sure something's happened—
POLICEMAN: These men from the place of Lady Boscoe—good men, Mrs. Maudsley. Not liars. Thieves. They didn't have to come to me. Good cook, good houseboy.

(JOHN *enters. He takes* CHARMIAN's *arm. The* POLICEMAN *is wandering near the tree with his torch.*)

JOHN: She's on the verandah. Dead.

(*With a gasp,* CHARMIAN *makes to go toward the verandah.* JOHN *holds her back. Nods at the* POLICEMAN.)

JOHN: Best let him go first. His self-esteem, and all that. It's nothing violent. A heart attack, I should say.

(*The* POLICEMAN *has at last trained his torch on the gorilla.*)

POLICEMAN: Mr. Maudsley—

(JOHN *goes to him, followed by* CHARMIAN—*they look, and* CHARMIAN *screams.*)

JOHN: My God!

POLICEMAN: I have heard it said many times, Mr. Maudsley, they are the most intelligent, cunning of creatures. (*pause*) And is it not known, sir, by your Darwin that they are our forefathers? Ancestors of black and white, red and yellow?

CHARMIAN: It's *huge!*

JOHN: And Harriet alone—

POLICEMAN (*slyly*): Perhaps he was a friendly fellow, sir—

JOHN: That's quite enough, Sergeant! Don't you realize what might have happened? Good God! Come away, Charmian. Ugly brute. (*pause*) Gilbert told me himself . . . ages ago . . . the last, the last gorilla shot in these parts it was . . . surely it was before independence, wasn't it?

THE END

About Death

Death comes to everyone, as does love, and because it does, it is subject to much speculation, is a basis of much philosophy, and is a major concern in most religions. Yet, because death is understood only by the dead, we essentially know nothing about it.

Because we know nothing about death, we are constantly trying to learn. We read articles about death in newspapers and magazines, we watch television news reports concerning death, we stop at the scene of automobile accidents, and we listen with morbid fascination to personal experiences with death. It is both fascinating and repugnant.

Death as a theme is particularly fascinating in the theater. The characters are portrayed by real people (actors) who recreate a conception of a real situation. In the theater death is not a personal threat, and we can, for the moment, satisfy our fascination, knowing that an actor will "die" again the following night.

Death can be torturously unexpected, as in the mystery *Sorry, Wrong Number.* It can be totally devastating, as in *Riders to the Sea.* It can be looked at almost intellectually, as in *Pullman Car Hiawatha.* The Young Man in *Hello Out There* needs love in order to face his fate with strength and pride. (You might turn to an earlier play, *Coming Through the Rye,* for another interesting view of death.)

One might say that all plays about life are, in one way or another, plays about death; for just as birth marks the beginning of life so death marks its close. In a sense physical life without death to define its length is unthinkable. Yet, we often don't see it that way—in life we see a future—in death we see only the end. The four plays in this section, on one level, do no more than reaffirm that death comes to us all. On another level, since death as well as life defines character, we see the inner-self of the characters revealed in the manner in which they face death.

Sorry, Wrong Number

LUCILLE FLETCHER

Characters

- MRS. STEVENSON
- FIRST OPERATOR
- FIRST MAN
- SECOND MAN (*George*)
- CHIEF OPERATOR
- SECOND, THIRD, FOURTH, AND FIFTH OPERATORS
- INFORMATION
- HOSPITAL RECEPTIONIST
- WESTERN UNION
- SERGEANT DUFFY
- A LUNCHROOM COUNTER ATTENDANT

Reading Guides

1. Because *Sorry, Wrong Number* is a murder mystery, details are extremely important. Read the stage directions carefully.
2. Technically, this is a difficult play. Your visualizations of the constant changes of telephone conversants is extremely important.

SCENE: *As curtain rises, we see a divided stage, only the center part of which is lighted and furnished as* MRS. STEVENSON'S *bedroom. Expensive, rather fussy furnishings. A large bed, on which* MRS. STEVENSON, *clad in bed jacket, is lying. A night table close by, with phone, lighted lamp, and pill bottles. A mantel, with clock, right. A closed door, right. A window, with curtains closed, rear. The set is lit by one lamp on night table. It is enclosed by three flats. Beyond this central set, the stage, on either side, is in darkness.*

MRS. STEVENSON *is dialing a number on phone, as curtain rises. She listens to phone, slams down receiver in irritation. As she does so, we hear sound of a train roaring by in the distance. She reaches for her pill bottle, pours herself a glass of water, shakes out pill, swallows it, then reaches for phone again, dials number nervously.* SOUND: *Number being dialed on phone, busy signal.*

MRS. STEVENSON (*a querulous, self-centered neurotic*): Oh—*dear!* (*Slams down receiver. Dials* OPERATOR.)

(SCENE: *A spotlight, left of side flat, picks up out of peripheral darkness, figure of* FIRST OPERATOR, *sitting with headphones at small table. If spotlight not available, use flashlight, clicked on by* FIRST OPERATOR, *illumining her face.*)

OPERATOR: Your call, please?

MRS. STEVENSON: Operator? I have been dialing Murray Hill 4-0098 now for the last three-quarters of an hour, and the line is always busy. But I don't see how it *could* be busy that long. Will you try it for me, please?

OPERATOR: Murray Hill 4-0098? One moment, please.

(SCENE: *She makes gesture of plugging in call through a switchboard.*)

MRS. STEVENSON: I don't see how it could be busy all this time. It's my husband's office. He's working late tonight, and I'm all alone here in the house. My health is very poor—and I've been feeling so nervous all day. . . .

OPERATOR: Ringing Murray Hill 4-0098. . . . (SOUND: *Phone buzz. It rings three times. Receiver is picked up at other end*). (SCENE: *Spotlight picks up figure of a heavy-set man, seated at desk with phone on right side of dark periphery of stage. He is wearing a hat. Picks up phone, which rings three times.*)

MAN: Hello.

MRS. STEVENSON: Hello . . . ? (*a little puzzled*) Hello. Is Mr. Stevenson there?

MAN (*into phone, as though he had not heard*): Hello. . . . (*louder*) Hello. (SCENE: *Spotlight on left now moves from* OPERATOR *to another man,* GEORGE. *A killer type, also wearing hat, but standing as in a phone booth. A three-sided screen may be used to suggest this.*)

SECOND MAN (*slow heavy quality, faintly foreign accent*): Hello.

FIRST MAN: Hello. George?

GEORGE: Yes, sir.

MRS. STEVENSON (*louder and more imperious, to phone*): Hello. Who's this? What number am I calling, please?

FIRST MAN: We have heard from our client. He says the coast is clear for to-night.

GEORGE: Yes, sir.

FIRST MAN: Where are you now?

GEORGE: In a phone booth.

FIRST MAN: Okay. You know the address. At eleven o'clock the private patrolman goes around to the bar on Second Avenue for a beer. Be sure that all the lights downstairs are out. There should be only one light visible from the street. At eleven-fifteen a subway train crosses the bridge. It makes a noise in case her window is open, and she should scream.

MRS. STEVENSON (*shocked*): Oh—HELLO! What number is this, please?

GEORGE: Okay. I understand.

FIRST MAN: Make it quick. As little blood as possible. Our client does not wish to make her suffer long.

GEORGE: A knife okay, sir?

FIRST MAN: Yes. A knife will be okay. And remember—remove the rings and bracelets and the jewelry in the bureau drawer. Our client wishes it to look like simple robbery.

GEORGE: Okay—I get— (SCENE: *Spotlight suddenly goes out on* GEORGE.) (SOUND: *A bland buzzing signal*). (SCENE: *Spotlight goes off on* FIRST MAN.)

MRS. STEVENSON (*clicking phone*): Oh . . . ! (*Bland buzzing signal continues. She hangs up.*) How awful! How unspeakably . . . (SCENE: *She lies back on her pillows, overcome for a few seconds, then suddenly pulls herself together, reaches for phone*). (SOUND: *Dialing. Phone buzz*). (SCENE: *Spotlight goes on at* FIRST OPERATOR'S *switchboard.* FIRST *and* SECOND MAN *exit as unobtrusively as possible, in darkness.*)

OPERATOR: Your call, please?

MRS. STEVENSON (*unnerved and breathless, into phone*): Operator. I—I've just been cut off.

OPERATOR: I'm sorry, madam. What number were you calling?

MRS. STEVENSON: Why—it was supposed to be Murray Hill 4-0098, but it wasn't. Some wires must have crossed—I was cut into a wrong number —and—I've just heard the most dreadful thing—a—a murder—and— (*imperiously*). Operator, you'll simply have to retrace that call at once.

OPERATOR: I beg your pardon, madam—I don't quite—

MRS. STEVENSON: Oh—I know it was a wrong number, and I had no business listening—but these two men—they were cold-blooded fiends—and they were going to murder somebody—some poor innocent woman—who was all alone—in a house near a bridge. And we've got to stop them—we've got to—

OPERATOR (*patiently*): What number were you calling, madam?

MRS. STEVENSON: That doesn't matter. This was a *wrong* number. And *you* dialed it. And we've got to find out what it was—immediately!

OPERATOR: But—madam—

MRS. STEVENSON: Oh—why are you so stupid? Look—it was obviously a case of some little slip of the finger. I told you to try Murray Hill 4-0098 for me —you dialed it but your finger must have slipped—and I was connected with some other number—and I could hear them, but they couldn't hear me. Now, I simply fail to see why you couldn't make that same mistake again—on purpose—why you couldn't *try* to dial Murray Hill 4-0098 in the same careless sort of way. . . .

OPERATOR (*quickly*): Murray Hill 4-0098? I will try to get it for you, madam.

MRS. STEVENSON (*sarcastically*): *Thank* you. (SCENE: *She bridles, adjusts herself on her pillows, reaches for handkerchief, wipes forehead, glancing uneasily for a moment toward window, while still holding phone.*) (*sound of ringing: busy signal.*)

OPERATOR: I am sorry. Murray Hill 4-0098 is busy.

MRS. STEVENSON (*frantically clicking receiver*): Operator. Operator.

OPERATOR: Yes, Madam.

MRS. STEVENSON (*angrily*): You *didn't* try to get that wrong number at all. I asked explicitly. And all you did was dial correctly.

OPERATOR: I am sorry. What number were you calling?

MRS. STEVENSON: Can't you, for once, forget what number I was calling, and do something specific? Now I want to trace that call. It's my civic duty—it's *your* civic duty—to trace that call . . . and to apprehend those dangerous killers—and if *you* won't . . .

OPERATOR (*glancing around wearily*): I will connect you with the Chief Operator.

MRS. STEVENSON: *Please!* (*sound of ringing*) (SCENE: OPERATOR *puts hand over mouthpiece of phone, gestures into darkness. A half whisper:*)

OPERATOR: Miss Curtis. Will you pick up on 17, please?

(MISS CURTIS, *Chief Operator, enters. Middle-aged, efficient type, pleasant, wearing headphones*)

MISS CURTIS: Yes, dear. What's the trouble?

OPERATOR: Somebody wanting a call traced. I can't make head nor tail of it. . . .

MISS CURTIS (*sitting down at desk, as* OPERATOR *gets up*): Sure, dear. 17? (*She makes gesture of plugging in her headphone, coolly and professionally*). This is the Chief Operator.

MRS. STEVENSON: Chief Operator? I want you to trace a call. A telephone call. Immediately. I don't know where it came from, or who was making it, but it's absolutely necessary that it be tracked down. Because it was about a murder. Yes, a terrible, cold-blooded murder of a poor innocent woman —tonight—at eleven-fifteen.

CHIEF OPERATOR: I see.

MRS. STEVENSON (*high-strung, demanding*): Can you trace it for me? Can you track down those men?

CHIEF OPERATOR: It depends, madam.

MRS. STEVENSON: Depends on what?

CHIEF OPERATOR: It depends on whether the call is still going on. If it's a live call, we can trace it on the equipment. If it's been disconnected, we can't.

MRS. STEVENSON: Disconnected?

CHIEF OPERATOR: If the parties have stopped talking to each other.

MRS. STEVENSON: Oh—but—but of course they must have stopped talking to each other by *now.* That was at least five minutes ago—and they didn't sound like the type who would make a long call.

CHIEF OPERATOR: Well, I can try tracing it. (SCENE: *She takes pencil out of her hair-do.*) Now—what is your name, madam?

MRS. STEVENSON: Mrs. Stevenson. Mrs. Elbert Stevenson. But—listen—

CHIEF OPERATOR (*writing it down*): And your telephone number?

MRS. STEVENSON (*more irritated*): Plaza 4-2295. But if you go on wasting all this time— (SCENE: *She glances at clock on mantel.*)

CHIEF OPERATOR: And what is your reason for wanting this call traced?

MRS. STEVENSON: My reason? Well—for Heaven's sake—isn't it obvious? I overhear two men—they're killers—they're planning to murder this woman —it's a matter for the police.

CHIEF OPERATOR: Have you told the police?

MRS. STEVENSON: No. How could I?

CHIEF OPERATOR: You're making this check into a private call purely as a private individual?

MRS. STEVENSON: Yes. But meanwhile—

CHIEF OPERATOR: Well, Mrs. Stevenson—I seriously doubt whether we could make this check for you at this time just on your say-so as a private individual. We'd have to have something more official.

MRS. STEVENSON: Oh—for Heaven's sake! You mean to tell me I can't report a murder without getting tied up in all this redtape? Why—it's perfectly idiotic. All right, then. I *will* call the police. (*She slams down receiver.*) (SCENE: *Spotlight goes off on two* OPERATORS.) Ridiculous! (*sound of dialing*). (SCENE: MRS. STEVENSON *dials numbers on phone, as two* OPERATORS *exit unobtrusively in darkness.*) (*On right of stage, spotlight picks up a* SECOND OPERATOR, *seated like first, with headphones at table* [*same one vacated by* FIRST MAN].)

SECOND OPERATOR: Your call, please?

MRS. STEVENSON (*very annoyed*): The Police Department—*please.*

SECOND OPERATOR: Ringing the Police Department. (*ring twice. Phone is picked up.*) (SCENE: *Left stage, at table vacated by* FIRST *and* CHIEF OPERATOR, *spotlight now picks up* SERGEANT DUFFY, *seated in a relaxed position. Just entering beside him is a young man in cap and apron, carrying a large brown paper parcel, delivery boy for a local lunch counter. Phone is ringing.*)

YOUNG MAN: Here's your lunch, Sarge. They didn't have no jelly doughnuts, so I give you French crullers. Okay, Sarge?

SERGEANT DUFFY: French crullers. I got ulcers. Whyn't you make it apple pie? (*picks up phone, which has rung twice*) Police department. Precinct 43. Duffy speaking. (SCENE: LUNCHROOM ATTENDANT, *anxiously.* We don't have no apple pie, either, Sarge—)

MRS. STEVENSON: Police Department? Oh. This is Mrs. Stevenson—Mrs. Elbert Smythe Stevenson of 53 North Sutton Place. I'm calling up to report a murder. (SCENE: DUFFY *has been examining lunch, but double-takes suddenly on above.*)

DUFFY: Eh?

MRS. STEVENSON: I mean—the murder hasn't been committed yet. I just overheard plans for it over the telephone . . . over a wrong number that the operator gave me. (SCENE: DUFFY *relaxes, sighs, starts taking lunch from bag*). I've been trying to trace down the call myself, but everybody is so stupid—and I guess in the end you're the only people who could *do* anything.

DUFFY (*not too impressed*): (SCENE: ATTENDANT, *who exits.*) Yes, ma'am.

MRS. STEVENSON (*trying to impress him*): It was a perfectly *definite* murder. I heard their plans distinctly. (SCENE: DUFFY *begins to eat sandwich, phone at his ear.*) Two men were talking, and they were going to murder some woman at eleven-fifteen tonight—she lived in a house near a bridge.

DUFFY: Yes, ma'am.

MRS. STEVENSON: And there was a private patrolman on the street. He was going to go around for a beer on Second Avenue. And there was some third man —a client, who was paying to have this poor woman murdered—they were going to take her rings and bracelets—and use a knife . . . well, it's unnerved me dreadfully—and I'm not well. . . .

DUFFY: I see. (SCENE: *Having finished sandwich, he wipes mouth with paper napkin.*) When was all this, ma'am?

MRS. STEVENSON: About eight minutes ago. Oh . . . (*relieved*) Then you *can* do something? You *do* understand—

DUFFY: And what is your name, ma'am? (SCENE: *He reaches for pad.*)

MRS. STEVENSON (*impatiently*): Mrs. Stevenson. Mrs. Elbert Stevenson.

DUFFY: And your address?

MRS. STEVENSON: 53 North Sutton Place. *That's* near a bridge. The Queensboro Bridge, you know—and *we* have a private patrolman on *our* street—and Second Avenue—

DUFFY: And what was that number you were calling?

MRS. STEVENSON: Murray Hill 4-0098. (SCENE: DUFFY *writes it down.*) But—that wasn't the number I overheard. I mean Murray Hill 4-0098 is my husband's office. (SCENE: DUFFY, *in exasperation, holds pencil poised.*) He's working late tonight, and I was trying to reach him to ask him to come home. I'm an invalid, you know—and it's the maid's night off—and I *hate* to be alone—even though he says I'm perfectly safe as long as I have the telephone right beside my bed.

DUFFY (*stolidly*): (SCENE: *He has put pencil down, pushes pad away.*) Well—we'll look into it, Mrs. Stevenson—and see if we can check it with the telephone company.

MRS. STEVENSON (*getting impatient*): But the telephone company said they couldn't check the call if the parties had stopped talking. I've already taken care of *that.*

DUFFY: Oh—yes? (SCENE: *He yawns slightly.*)

MRS. STEVENSON (*high-handed*): Personally I feel you ought to do something far more immediate and drastic than just check the call. What good does checking the call do, if they've stopped talking? By the time you track it down, they'll already have committed the murder.

DUFFY (SCENE: *He reaches for paper cup of coffee.*): Well—we'll take care of it, lady. Don't worry. (SCENE: *He begins to take off paper top of coffee container.*)

MRS. STEVENSON: I'd say the whole thing calls for a search—a complete and thorough search of the whole city. (SCENE: DUFFY *puts down phone for a moment, to work on cup, as her voice continues.*) I'm very near a bridge, and I'm not far from Second Avenue. And I know *I'd* feel a whole lot better if you sent around a radio car to *this* neighborhood at once.

DUFFY (SCENE: *picks up phone again, drinks coffee*): And what makes you think the murder's going to be committed in your neighborhood, ma'am?

MRS. STEVENSON: Oh—I don't know. The coincidence is so horrible. Second Avenue—the patrolman—the bridge . . .

DUFFY (SCENE: *He sips coffee.*): Second Avenue is a very long street, ma'am. And do you happen to know how many bridges there are in the city of New York alone? Not to mention Brooklyn, Staten Island, Queens, and the Bronx? And how do you know there isn't some little house out on Staten Island—on some little Second Avenue you never heard about? (SCENE: *A long gulp of coffee*) How do you know they were even talking about New York at all?

MRS. STEVENSON: But I heard the call on the New York dialing system.

DUFFY: How do you know it wasn't a long-distance call you overheard? Telephones are funny things. (SCENE: *He sets down coffee.*) Look, lady, why don't you look at it this way? Supposing you hadn't broken in on that telephone call? Supposing you'd got your husband the way you always do? Would this murder have made any difference to you then?

MRS. STEVENSON: I suppose not. But it's so inhuman—so cold-blooded . . .

DUFFY: A lot of murders are committed in this city every day, ma'am. If we could do something to stop 'em, we would. But a clue of this kind that's so vague isn't much more use to us than no clue at all.

MRS. STEVENSON: But, surely—

DUFFY: Unless, of course, you have some reason for thinking this call is phoney —and that someone may be planning to murder *you?*

MRS. STEVENSON: *Me?* Oh—no—I hardly think so. I—I mean—why should anybody? I'm alone all day and night—I see nobody except my maid Eloise —she's a big two-hundred-pounder—she's too lazy to bring up my breakfast tray—and the only other person is my husband Elbert—he's crazy about me—adores me—waits on me hand and foot—he's scarcely left my side since I took sick twelve years ago—

DUFFY: Well—then—there's nothing for you to worry about, is there? (SCENE: LUNCHCOUNTER ATTENDANT *has entered. He is carrying a piece of apple pie on a plate. Points it out to* DUFFY *triumphantly*). And now—if you'll just leave the rest of this to us—

MRS. STEVENSON: But what will you *do?* It's so late—it's nearly eleven o'clock.

DUFFY (*firmly*) (SCENE: *He nods to* ATTENDANT, *pleased*): We'll take care of it, lady.

MRS. STEVENSON: Will you broadcast it all over the city? And send out squads? And warn your radio cars to watch out—especially in suspicious neighborhoods like mine? (SCENE: ATTENDANT, *in triumph, has put pie down in front of* DUFFY. *Takes fork out of his pocket, stands at attention, waiting.*)

DUFFY (*more firmly*): Lady, I *said* we'd take care of it. (SCENE: *Glances at pie.*) Just now I've got a couple of other matters here on my desk that require my immediate—

MRS. STEVENSON: Oh! (*She slams down receiver hard.*) Idiot. (SCENE: DUFFY, *listening at phone, hangs up. Shrugs. Winks at* ATTENDANT *as though to say, "What a crazy character!" Attacks his pie as spotlight fades out*). (MRS. STEVENSON, *in bed, looking at phone nervously*). Now—why did I do that? Now—he'll think I *am* a fool. (SCENE: *She sits there tensely, then throws herself back against pillows, lies there a moment, whimpering with self-pity.*) Oh—why doesn't Elbert come home? *Why* doesn't he? (SCENE: *We hear sound of train roaring by in the distance. She sits up reaching for phone.*) (*sound of dialing operator*) (SCENE: *spotlight picks up* SECOND OPERATOR, *seated right.*)

OPERATOR: Your call, please?

MRS. STEVENSON: Operator—for Heaven's sake—will you ring that Murray Hill 4-0098 number again? I can't think what's keeping him so long.

OPERATOR: Ringing Murray Hill 4-0098. (*rings; busy signal*) The line is busy. Shall I—

MRS. STEVENSON (*nastily*): I can hear it. You don't have to tell me. I know it's busy. (*slams down receiver*) (SCENE: *Spotlight fades off on* SECOND OPERATOR.) (SCENE: MRS. STEVENSON *sinks back against pillows again, whimpering to herself fretfully. She glances at clock, then turning, punches her pillows up, trying to make herself comfortable. But she isn't. Whimpers to herself as she squirms restlessly in bed.*) If I could only get out of this bed for a little while. If I could get a breath of fresh air—or just lean out the window—and see the street. . . . (SCENE: *She sighs, reaches for pill bottle, shakes out a pill. As she does so:*) (*The phone rings. She darts for it instantly.*) Hello. Elbert? Hello. Hello. Hello. Oh—what's the *matter* with this phone? HELLO? HELLO? (*slams down the receiver*) (SCENE: *She stares at it, tensely.*) (*The phone rings again. Once. She picks it up.*) Hello? Hello. . . . Oh—for Heaven's sake—who *is* this? Hello. Hello. HELLO. (*Slams down receiver. Dials operator.*) (SCENE: *Spotlight comes on left, showing* THIRD OPERATOR, *at spot vacated by* DUFFY.)

THIRD OPERATOR: Your call, please?

MRS. STEVENSON (*very annoyed and imperious*): Hello. Operator. I don't know what's the matter with this telephone tonight, but it's positively driving me crazy. I've never seen such inefficient, miserable service. Now, look. I'm an invalid, and I'm very nervous, and I'm *not* supposed to be annoyed. But if this keeps on much longer . . .

THIRD OPERATOR (*a young sweet type*): What seems to be the trouble, madam?

MRS. STEVENSON: Well—everything's wrong. The whole world could be murdered, for all you people care. And now—my phone keeps ringing. . . .

OPERATOR: Yes, madam?

MRS. STEVENSON: Ringing and ringing and ringing every five seconds or so, and when I pick it up, there's no one there.

OPERATOR: I am sorry, madam. If you will hang up, I will test it for you.

MRS. STEVENSON: I don't want you to test it for me. I want you to put through that call—whatever it is—at once.

OPERATOR (*gently*): I am afraid that is not possible, madam.

MRS. STEVENSON (*storming*): Not possible? And why—may I ask?

OPERATOR: The system is automatic, madam. If someone is trying to dial your number, there is no way to check whether the call is coming through the system or not—unless the person who is trying to reach you complains to his particular operator—

MRS. STEVENSON: Well, of all the stupid, complicated . . . ! And meanwhile *I've* got to sit here in my bed, *suffering* every time that phone rings—imagining everything. . . .

OPERATOR: I will try to check it for you, madam.

MRS. STEVENSON: Check it! Check it! That's all anybody can do. Of all the stupid, idiotic . . . ! (*She hangs up.*) Oh—what's the use . . . (SCENE: THIRD OPERATOR *fades out of spotlight, as*) (*Instantly* MRS. STEVENSON's *phone rings again. She picks up receiver. wildly*) Hello. HELLO. Stop ringing, do you hear me? Answer me? What do you want? Do you realize you're driving me crazy? (SCENE: *Spotlight goes on right. We see a* MAN *in eye-shade and shirt-sleeves, at desk with phone and telegrams.*) Stark, staring . . .

MAN (*dull, flat voice*): Hello. Is this Plaza 4-2295?

MRS. STEVENSON (*catching her breath*): Yes. Yes. This is Plaza 4-2295.

WESTERN UNION: This is Western Union. I have a telegram here for Mrs. Elbert Stevenson. Is there anyone there to receive the message?

MRS. STEVENSON (*trying to calm herself*): I am Mrs. Stevenson.

WESTERN UNION (*reading flatly*): The telegram is as follows: "Mrs. Elbert Stevenson. 53 North Sutton Place, New York, New York. Darling. Terribly sorry. Tried to get you for last hour, but line busy. Leaving for Boston eleven p. m. tonight on urgent business. Back tomorrow afternoon. Keep happy. Love. Signed. Elbert."

MRS. STEVENSON (*breathlessly, aghast, to herself*): Oh . . . no . . .

WESTERN UNION: That is all, madam. Do you wish us to deliver a copy of the message?

MRS. STEVENSON: No—no, thank you.

WESTERN UNION: Thank you, madam. Good night. (*He hangs up phone.*) (SCENE: *Spotlight on* WESTERN UNION *immediately out.*)

MRS. STEVENSON (*mechanically, to phone*): Good night. (*She hangs up slowly. suddenly bursting into*) No—no—it isn't true! He couldn't do it! Not when he knows I'll be all alone. It's some trick—some fiendish . . . (SCENE: *We hear sound of train roaring by outside. She half rises in bed, in panic, glaring toward curtains. Her movements are frenzied. She beats with her knuckles on bed, then suddenly stops, and reaches for phone.*) (*She dials operator.*) (SCENE: *Spotlight picks up* FOURTH OPERATOR, *seated left.*)

OPERATOR (*coolly*): Your call, please?

MRS. STEVENSON: Operator—try that Murray Hill 4-0098 number for me just once more, please.

OPERATOR: Ringing Murray Hill 4-0098. (*Call goes through. We hear ringing at other end. ring after ring*) (SCENE: *If telephone noises are not used audibly, have* OPERATOR *say after a brief pause: "They do not answer."*)

MRS. STEVENSON: He's gone. Oh—Elbert, how could you? How could you . . . ? (*She hangs up phone, sobbing pityingly to herself, turning restlessly*). (SCENE: *Spotlight goes out on* FOURTH OPERATOR.) But I can't be alone tonight. I can't. If I'm alone one more second . . . (SCENE: *She runs hands wildly through hair.*) I don't care what he says—or what the expense is—I'm a sick woman—I'm entitled . . . (SCENE: *With trembling fingers she picks up receiver again.*) (*She dials* INFORMATION) (SCENE: *The spotlight picks up* INFORMATION OPERATOR, *seated right.*)

INFORMATION: This is Information.

MRS. STEVENSON: I want the telephone number of Henchley Hospital.

INFORMATION: Henchley Hospital? Do you have the address, madam?

MRS. STEVENSON: No. It's somewhere in the 70's, though. It's a very small, private, and exclusive hospital where I had my appendix out two years ago. Henchley. H-E-N-C—

INFORMATION: One moment, please.

MRS. STEVENSON: Please—hurry. And please—what *is* the time?

INFORMATION: I do not know, madam. You may find out the time by dialing Meridan 7-1212.

MRS. STEVENSON (*irritated*): Oh—for Heaven's sake! Couldn't you—?

INFORMATION: The number of Henchley Hospital is Butterfield 7-0105, madam.

MRS. STEVENSON: Butterfield 7-0105. (*She hangs up before she finishes speaking, and immediately dials number as she repeats it.*) (SCENE: *Spotlight goes out on* INFORMATION.) (*Phone rings.*) (SCENE: *Spotlight picks up* WOMAN *in nurse's uniform, seated at desk, left.*)

WOMAN (*middle-aged, solid, firm, practical*): Henchley Hospital, good evening.

MRS. STEVENSON: Nurses' Registry.

WOMAN: Who was it you wished to speak to, please?

MRS. STEVENSON (*high-handed*): I want the Nurses' Registry at once. I want a trained nurse. I want to hire her immediately. For the night.

WOMAN: I see. And what is the nature of the case, madam?

MRS. STEVENSON: Nerves. I'm very nervous. I need soothing—and companionship. My husband is away—and I'm—

WOMAN: Have you been recommended to us by any doctor in particular, madam?

MRS. STEVENSON: No. But I really don't see why all this catechizing is necessary. I want a trained nurse. I was a patient in your hospital two years ago. And after all, I *do* expect to *pay* this person—

WOMAN: We quite understand that, madam. But registered nurses are very scarce just now—and our superintendent has asked us to send people out only on cases where the physician in charge feels it is absolutely necessary.

MRS. STEVENSON (*growing hysterical*): Well—it *is* absolutely necessary. I'm a sick woman. I—I'm very upset. Very. I'm alone in this house—and I'm an invalid—and tonight I overheard a telephone conversation that upset me dreadfully. About a murder—a poor woman who was going to be murdered at eleven-fifteen tonight—in fact, if someone doesn't come at once —I'm afraid I'll go out of my mind. . . . (*almost off handle by now*)

WOMAN (*calmly*): I see. Well—I'll speak to Miss Phillips as soon as she comes in. And what is your name, madam?

MRS. STEVENSON: Miss Phillips. And when do you expect her in?

WOMAN: I really don't know, madam. She went out to supper at eleven o'clock.

MRS. STEVENSON: Eleven o'clock. But it's not eleven yet. (*She cries out.*) Oh, my clock *has* stopped. I thought it was running down. What time is it? (SCENE: WOMAN *glances at wristwatch.*)

WOMAN: Just fourteen minutes past eleven. . . . (*sound of phone receiver being lifted on same line as* MRS. STEVENSON'S; *a click*)

MRS. STEVENSON (*crying out*): What's *that?*

WOMAN: What was what, madam?

MRS. STEVENSON: That—that click just now—in my own telephone? As though someone had lifted the receiver off the hook of the extension phone downstairs. . . .

WOMAN: I didn't hear it, madam. Now—about this . . .

MRS. STEVENSON (*scared*): But I *did.* There's someone in this house. Someone downstairs in the kitchen. And they're listening to me now. They're . . . (SCENE: *She puts hand over her mouth.*) (*hangs up phone*) (SCENE: *She sits there, in terror, frozen, listening.*) (*in a suffocated voice*) I won't pick it up, I won't let them hear me. I'll be quiet—and they'll think . . . (*with growing terror*) But if I don't call someone now—while they're still down there—there'll be no time. . . . (*She picks up receiver. bland buzzing signal. She dials operator. ring twice*) (SCENE: *On second ring, spotlight goes on right. We see* FIFTH OPERATOR.)

OPERATOR (*fat and lethargic*): Your call, please?

MRS. STEVENSON (*a desperate whisper*): Operator—I—I'm in desperate trouble . . . I—

OPERATOR: I cannot hear you, madam. Please speak louder.

MRS. STEVENSON (*still whispering*): I don't dare. I—there's someone listening. Can you hear me now?

OPERATOR: Your call, please? What number are you calling, madam?

MRS. STEVENSON (*desperately*): You've got to hear me. Oh—please. You've got to help me. There's someone in this house. Someone who's going to murder me. And you've got to get in touch with the . . . (*Click of receiver being put down on* MRS. STEVENSON'S *line. bursting out wildly*) Oh—there it is . . . he's put it down . . . he's coming . . . (*She screams.*) he's coming up the stairs . . . (SCENE: *She thrashes in bed, phone cord catching in lamp wire, lamp topples, goes out. darkness*) (*hoarsely*) Give me the Police Department. . . . (SCENE: *We see on the dark center stage, the shadow of door opening.*) (*screaming.*) The police! . . . (SCENE: *On stage, swift rush of a shadow, advancing to bed—sound of her voice is choked out, as*)

OPERATOR: Ringing the Police Department. (*Phone is rung. We hear sound of a train beginning to fade in. On second ring,* MRS. STEVENSON *screams again, but roaring of train drowns out her voice. For a few seconds we hear nothing but roaring of train, then dying away, phone at police headquarters ringing.*) (SCENE: *Spotlight goes on* DUFFY, *left stage.*)

DUFFY: Police Department. Precinct 43. Duffy speaking. (*pause*) (SCENE: *Nothing visible but darkness on center stage*). Police Department. Duffy speaking. (SCENE: *A flashlight goes on, illuminating open phone to one side of* MRS. STEVENSON'S *bed. Nearby, hanging down, is her lifeless hand. We see the second man,* GEORGE, *in black gloves, reach down and pick up phone. He is breathing hard.*)

GEORGE: Sorry. Wrong number. (*hangs up*) (SCENE: *He replaces receiver on hook quietly, exits, as* DUFFY *hangs up with a shrug, and* CURTAIN falls.)

Hello Out There

WILLIAM SAROYAN

Characters

YOUNG MAN
THE GIRL (*Emily*)
THE MAN
THE WOMAN
ANOTHER MAN
THIRD MAN

Reading Guides

1. *Hello Out There* is a very easy play to read. Yet, very subtle things happen between the two people. If you read the play aloud, you will become aware of the subtlety.

2. There is a real terror in both Emily and the Young Man. You should look for it and be aware of it in order to identify more fully with the two characters.

Hello Out There

SCENE: *There is a fellow in a small-town prison cell, tapping slowly on the floor with a spoon. After tapping half a minute, as if he were trying to telegraph words, he gets up and begins walking around the cell. At last he stops, stands at the center of the cell, and doesn't move for a long time. He feels his head, as if it were wounded. Then he looks around. Then he calls out dramatically, kidding the world.*

YOUNG MAN: Hello—out there! (*pause*) Hello—out there! Hello—out there! (*long pause*) Nobody out there. (*still more dramatically, but more comically, too*) Hello—out there! Hello—out there!

(*A* GIRL'S VOICE *is heard, very sweet and soft.*)

THE VOICE: Hello.

YOUNG MAN: Hello—out there.

THE VOICE: Hello.

YOUNG MAN: Is that you, Katey?

THE VOICE: No—this here is Emily.

YOUNG MAN: Who? (*swiftly*) Hello out there.

THE VOICE: Emily.

YOUNG MAN: Emily who? I don't know anybody named Emily. Are you that girl I met at Sam's in Salinas about three years ago?

THE VOICE: No—I'm the girl who cooks here. I'm the cook. I've never been in Salinas. I don't even know where it is.

YOUNG MAN: Hello out there. You say you cook here?

THE VOICE: Yes.

YOUNG MAN: Well, why don't you study up and learn to cook? How come I don't get no Jell-O or anything good?

THE VOICE: I just cook what they tell me to. (*pause*) You lonesome?

YOUNG MAN: Lonesome as a coyote. Hear me hollering? Hello out there!

THE VOICE: Who you hollering to?

YOUNG MAN: Well—nobody, I guess. I been trying to think of somebody to write a letter to, but I can't think of anybody.

THE VOICE: What about Katey?

YOUNG MAN: I don't know anybody named Katey.

THE VOICE: Then why did you say, Is that you, Katey?

YOUNG MAN: Katey's a good name. I always did like a name like Katey. I never *knew* anybody named Katey, though.

THE VOICE: *I* did.

YOUNG MAN: Yeah? What was she like? Tall girl, or little one?

THE VOICE: Kind of medium.

YOUNG MAN: Hello out there. What sort of a looking girl are *you?*

THE VOICE: Oh, I don't know.

YOUNG MAN: Didn't anybody ever tell you? Didn't anybody ever talk to you that way?

THE VOICE: What way?

YOUNG MAN: You know. Didn't they?

THE VOICE: No, they didn't.

YOUNG MAN: Ah, the fools—they should have. I can tell from your voice you're OK.

THE VOICE: Maybe I am and maybe I ain't.

YOUNG MAN: I never missed yet.

THE VOICE: Yeah, I know. That's why you're in jail.

YOUNG MAN: The whole thing was a mistake.

THE VOICE: They claim it was rape.

YOUNG MAN: No—it wasn't.

THE VOICE: That's what they claim it was.

YOUNG MAN: They're a lot of fools.

THE VOICE: Well, you sure are in trouble. Are you scared?

YOUNG MAN: Scared to death. (*suddenly*) Hello out there!

THE VOICE: What do you keep saying that for all the time?

YOUNG MAN: I'm lonesome. I'm as lonesome as a coyote. (*a long one.*) Hello—out there!

(THE GIRL *appears, over to one side. She is a plain girl in plain clothes.*)

THE GIRL: I'm kind of lonesome, too.

YOUNG MAN (*turning and looking at her*): Hey—No fooling? Are you?

THE GIRL: Yeah—I'm almost as lonesome as a coyote myself.

YOUNG MAN: Who *you* lonesome for?

THE GIRL: I don't know.

YOUNG MAN: It's the same with me. The minute they put you in a place like this you remember all the girls you ever knew, and all the girls you didn't get to know, and it sure gets lonesome.

THE GIRL: I bet it does.

YOUNG MAN: Ah, it's awful. (*pause*) You're a pretty kid, you know that?

THE GIRL: You're just talking.

YOUNG MAN: No, I'm not just talking—you *are* pretty. Any fool could see that. You're just about the prettiest kid in the whole world.

THE GIRL: I'm not—and you know it.

YOUNG MAN: No—you are. I never saw anyone prettier in all my born days, in all my travels. I knew Texas would bring me luck.

THE GIRL: Luck? You're in jail, aren't you? You've got a whole gang of people all worked up, haven't you?

YOUNG MAN: Ah, that's nothing. I'll get out of this.

THE GIRL: Maybe.

YOUNG MAN: No, I'll be all right—*now.*

THE GIRL: What do you mean—now?

YOUNG MAN: I mean after seeing you. I got something now. You know for a while there I didn't care one way or another. Tired. (*pause*) Tired of trying for the best all the time and never getting it. (*suddenly*) Hello out there!

THE GIRL: Who you calling now?

YOUNG MAN: You.

THE GIRL: Why, I'm right here.

YOUNG MAN: I know. (*calling*) Hello out there!

THE GIRL: Hello.

YOUNG MAN: Ah, you're sweet. (*pause*) I'm going to marry *you.* I'm going away with *you.* I'm going to take you to San Francisco or some place like that. I *am,* now. I'm going to win myself some real money, too. I'm going to study 'em real careful and pick myself some winners, and we're going to have a lot of money.

THE GIRL: Yeah?

YOUNG MAN: Yeah. Tell me your name and all that stuff.

THE GIRL: Emily.

YOUNG MAN: I know that. What's the rest of it? Where were you born? Come on, tell me the whole thing.

THE GIRL: Emily Smith.

YOUNG MAN: Honest to God?

THE GIRL: Honest. That's my name—Emily Smith.

YOUNG MAN: Ah, you're the sweetest girl in the whole world.

THE GIRL: Why?

YOUNG MAN: I don't know why, but you are, that's all. Where were you born?

THE GIRL: Matador, Texas.

YOUNG MAN: Where's that?

THE GIRL: Right here.

YOUNG MAN: Is this Matador, Texas?

THE GIRL: Yeah, it's Matador. They brought you here from Wheeling.

YOUNG MAN: Is that where I was—Wheeling?

THE GIRL: Didn't you even know what town you were in?

YOUNG MAN: All towns are alike. You don't go up and ask somebody what town you're in. It doesn't make any difference. How far away is Wheeling?

THE GIRL: Sixteen or seventeen miles. Didn't you know they moved you?

YOUNG MAN: How could I know, when I was out—cold? Somebody hit me over the head with a lead pipe or something. What'd they hit me for?

THE GIRL: Rape—that's what they *said.*

YOUNG MAN: Ah, that's a lie. (*amazed, almost to himself*) She wanted me to give her money.

THE GIRL: Money?

YOUNG MAN: Yeah, if I'd have known she was a woman like that—well, by God, I'd have gone on down the street and stretched out in a park somewhere and gone to sleep.

THE GIRL: Is that what she wanted—money?

YOUNG MAN: Yeah. A fellow like me hopping freights all over the country, trying to break his bad luck, going from one poor little town to another, trying to get in on something good somewhere, and she asks for money. I thought she was lonesome. She *said* she was.

THE GIRL: Maybe she was.

YOUNG MAN: She was *something.*

THE GIRL: I guess I'd never see you, if it didn't happen, though.

YOUNG MAN: Oh, I don't know—maybe I'd just mosey along this way and see you in this town somewhere. I'd recognize you, too.

THE GIRL: Recognize me?

YOUNG MAN: Sure, I'd recognize you the minute I laid eyes on you.

THE GIRL: Well, who would I be?

YOUNG MAN: Mine, that's who.

THE GIRL: Honest?

YOUNG MAN: Honest to God.

THE GIRL: You just say that because you're in jail.

YOUNG MAN: No, I mean it. You just pack up and wait for me. We'll high-roll the hell out of here to Frisco.

THE GIRL: You're just lonesome.

YOUNG MAN: I been lonesome all my life—there's no cure for that—but you and me—we can have a lot of fun hanging around together. You'll bring me luck. I know it.

THE GIRL: What are you looking for luck for all the time?

YOUNG MAN: I'm a gambler. I don't work. I've *got* to have luck, or I'm a bum. I haven't had any decent luck in years. Two whole years now—one place to another. Bad luck all the time. That's why I got in trouble back there in Wheeling, too. That was no accident. That was my bad luck following me around. So here I am, with my head half busted. I guess it was her old man that did it.

THE GIRL: You mean her father?

YOUNG MAN: No, her husband. If I had an old lady like that, I'd throw her out.

THE GIRL: Do you think you'll have better luck, if I go with you?

YOUNG MAN: It's a cinch. I'm a good handicapper. All I need is somebody good like you with me. It's no good always walking around in the streets for anything that might be there at the time. You got to have somebody staying with you all the time—through winters when it's cold, and springtime when it's pretty, and summertime when it's nice and hot and you can go swimming—through *all* the times—rain and snow and all the different kinds of weather a man's got to go through before he dies. You got to have somebody who's right. Somebody who knows you, from away back. You got to have somebody who even knows you're wrong but likes you just the same. I know I'm wrong, but I just don't want anything the hard way, working like a dog, or the *easy* way, working like a dog—working's the hard way and the easy way both. All I got to do is beat the price, always—and then I don't feel lousy and don't hate anybody. If you go along with me, I'll be the finest guy anybody ever saw. I won't be wrong any more. You know when you get enough of that money, you *can't* be wrong any more—you're right because the money says so. I'll have a lot of money and you'll be just about the prettiest, most wonderful kid in the whole world. I'll be proud walking around Frisco with you on my arm and people turning around to look at us.

THE GIRL: Do you think they will?

YOUNG MAN: Sure they will. When I get back in some decent clothes, and you're on my arm—well, Katey, they'll turn around and look, and they'll see something, too.

THE GIRL: Katey?

YOUNG MAN: Yeah—that's your name from now on. You're the first girl I ever called Katey. I've been saving it for you. OK?

THE GIRL: OK.

YOUNG MAN: How long have I been here?

THE GIRL: Since last night. You didn't wake up until late this morning, though.

YOUNG MAN: What time is it now? About nine?

THE GIRL: About ten.

YOUNG MAN: Have you got the key to this lousy cell?

THE GIRL: No. They don't let me fool with any keys.

YOUNG MAN: Well, can you get it?

THE GIRL: No.

YOUNG MAN: Can you *try?*

THE GIRL: They wouldn't let me get near any keys. I cook for this jail, when they've got somebody in it. I clean up and things like that.

YOUNG MAN: Well, I want to get out of here. Don't you know the guy that runs this joint?

THE GIRL: I know him, but he wouldn't let you out. They were talking of taking you to another jail in another town.

YOUNG MAN: Yeah? Why?

THE GIRL: Because they're afraid.

YOUNG MAN: What are they afraid of?

THE GIRL: They're afraid these people from Wheeling will come over in the middle of the night and break in.

YOUNG MAN: Yeah? What do they want to do that for?

THE GIRL: Don't *you* know what they want to do it for?

YOUNG MAN: Yeah, I know all right.

THE GIRL: Are you scared?

YOUNG MAN: Sure I'm scared. Nothing scares a man more than ignorance. You can argue with people who ain't fools, but you can't argue with fools—they just go to work and do what they're set on doing. Get me out of here.

THE GIRL: How?

YOUNG MAN: Well, go get the guy with the key, and let me talk to him.

THE GIRL: He's gone home. Everybody's gone home.

YOUNG MAN: You mean I'm in this little jail all alone?

THE GIRL: Well—yeah—except me.

YOUNG MAN: Well, what's the big idea—doesn't anybody stay here all the time?

THE GIRL: No, they go home every night. I clean up and then I go, too. I hung around tonight.

YOUNG MAN: What made you do that?

THE GIRL: I wanted to talk to you.

YOUNG MAN: Honest? What did you want to talk about?

THE GIRL: Oh, I don't know. I took care of you last night. You were talking in your sleep. You liked me, too. I didn't think you'd like me when you woke up, though.

YOUNG MAN: Yeah? Why not?

THE GIRL: I don't know.

YOUNG MAN: Yeah? Well, you're wonderful, see?

THE GIRL: Nobody ever talked to me that way. All the fellows in town—(*pause*)

YOUNG MAN: What about 'em? (*pause*) Well, what about 'em? Come on—tell me.

THE GIRL: They laugh at me.

YOUNG MAN: Laugh at *you?* They're fools. What do they know about anything? You go get your things and come back here. I'll take you with me to Frisco. How old are you?

THE GIRL: Oh, I'm of age.

YOUNG MAN: How old are you?—Don't lie to me! Sixteen?

THE GIRL: I'm seventeen.

YOUNG MAN: Well, bring your father and mother. We'll get married before we go.

THE GIRL: They wouldn't let me go.

YOUNG MAN: Why not?

THE GIRL: I don't know, but they wouldn't. I know they wouldn't.

YOUNG MAN: You go tell your father not to be a fool, see? What is he, a farmer?

THE GIRL: No—nothing. He gets a little relief from the government because he's supposed to be hurt or something—his side hurts, he says. I don't know what it is.

YOUNG MAN: Ah, he's a liar. Well, I'm taking you with me, see?

THE GIRL: He takes the money I earn, too.

YOUNG MAN: He's got no right to do that.

THE GIRL: I know it, but he does it.

YOUNG MAN (*almost to himself*): This world stinks. You shouldn't have been born in this town, anyway, and you shouldn't have had a man like that for a father, either.

THE GIRL: Sometimes I feel sorry for him.

YOUNG MAN: Never mind feeling sorry for him. (*pointing a finger*) I'm going to talk to your father some day. I've got a few things to tell that guy.

THE GIRL: I know you have.

YOUNG MAN (*suddenly*): Hello—out there! See if you can get that fellow with the keys to come down and let me out.

THE GIRL: Oh, I couldn't.

YOUNG MAN: Why not?

THE GIRL: I'm nobody here—they give me fifty cents every day I work.

YOUNG MAN: How much?

THE GIRL: Fifty cents.

YOUNG MAN (*to the world*): You see? They ought to pay money to *look* at you. To breathe the *air* you breathe. I don't know. Sometimes I figure it never is going to make sense. Hello—out there! I'm scared. You try to get me out of here. I'm scared them fools are going to come here from Wheeling and go crazy, thinking they're heroes. Get me out of here, Katey.

THE GIRL: I don't know what to do. Maybe I could break the door down.

YOUNG MAN: No, you couldn't do that. Is there a hammer out there or anything?

THE GIRL: Only a broom. Maybe they've locked the broom up, too.

YOUNG MAN: Go see if you can find anything.

THE GIRL: All right. (*She goes.*)

YOUNG MAN: Hello—out there! Hello—out there! (*pause*) Hello—out there! Hello—out there! (*pause*) Putting me in jail. (*with contempt*) Rape! Rape? *They* rape everything good that was ever born. His side hurts. They laugh at her. Fifty cents a day. Little punk people. Hurting the only good thing that ever came their way. (*suddenly*) Hello—out there!

THE GIRL (*returning*): There isn't a thing out there. They've locked everything up for the night.

YOUNG MAN: Any cigarettes?

THE GIRL: Everything's locked up—all the drawers of the desk, all the closet doors—everything.

YOUNG MAN: I ought to have a cigarette.

THE GIRL: I could get you a package maybe, somewhere. I guess the drug store's open. It's about a mile.

YOUNG MAN: A mile? I don't want to be alone that long.

THE GIRL: I could run all the way, and all the way back.

YOUNG MAN: You're the sweetest girl that ever lived.

THE GIRL: What kind do you want?

YOUNG MAN: Oh, any kind—Chesterfields or Camels or Lucky Strikes—any kind at all.

THE GIRL: I'll go get a package. (*She turns to go.*)

YOUNG MAN: What about the money?

THE GIRL: I've got some money. I've got a quarter I been saving. I'll run all the way. (*She is about to go.*)

YOUNG MAN: Come here.

THE GIRL (*going to him*): What?

YOUNG MAN: Give me your hand. (*He takes her hand and looks at it, smiling. He lifts it and kisses it.*) I'm scared to death.

THE GIRL: I am, too.

YOUNG MAN: I'm not lying—I don't care what happens to me, but I'm scared nobody will ever come out here to this godforsaken broken-down town and find you. I'm scared you'll get used to it and not mind. I'm scared you'll never get to Frisco and have 'em all turning around to look at you. Listen—go get me a gun, because if they come, I'll kill 'em! They don't understand. Get me a gun!

THE GIRL: I could get my father's gun. I know where he hides it.

YOUNG MAN: Go get it. Never mind the cigarettes. Run all the way. (*pause, smiling but seriously*) Hello, Katey.

THE GIRL: Hello. What's *your* name?

YOUNG MAN: Photo-Finish is what they *call* me. My races are always photo-finish races. You don't know what that means, but it means they're very close. So close the only way they can tell which horse wins is to look at a photograph after the race is over. Well, every race I bet turns out to be a photo-finish race, and my horse never wins. It's my bad luck, all the time. That's why they call me Photo-Finish. Say it before you go.

THE GIRL: Photo-Finish.

YOUNG MAN: Come here. (THE GIRL *moves close and he kisses her.*) Now, hurry. Run all the way.

THE GIRL: I'll run. (THE GIRL *turns and runs. The* YOUNG MAN *stands at the center of the cell a long time.* THE GIRL *comes running back in. Almost crying.*) I'm afraid. I'm afraid I won't see you again. If I come back and you're not here, I—

YOUNG MAN: Hello—out there!

THE GIRL: It's so lonely in this town. Nothing here but the lonesome wind all the time, lifting the dirt and blowing out to the prairie. I'll stay *here.* I won't *let* them take you away.

YOUNG MAN: Listen, Katey. Do what I tell you. Go get that gun and come back. Maybe they won't come tonight. Maybe they won't come at all. I'll hide the gun and when they let me out you can take it back and put it where you found it. And then we'll go away. But if they come, I'll kill 'em! Now, hurry—

THE GIRL: All right. (*pause*) I want to tell you something.

YOUNG MAN: OK.

THE GIRL (*very softly*): If you're not here when I come back, well, I'll have the gun and I'll know what to do with it.

YOUNG MAN: You know how to handle a gun?

THE GIRL: I know how.

YOUNG MAN: Don't be a fool. (*takes off his shoe, brings out some currency*) Don't be a fool, see? Here's some money. Eighty dollars. Take it and go to Frisco. Look around and find somebody. Find somebody alive and halfway human, see? Promise me—if I'm not here when you come back, just throw the gun away and get the hell to Frisco. Look around and find somebody.

THE GIRL: I don't *want* to find anybody.

YOUNG MAN (*swiftly, desperately*): Listen, if I'm not here when you come back, how do you know I haven't gotten away? Now, do what I tell you. I'll meet you in Frisco. I've got a couple of dollars in my other shoe. I'll see you in San Francisco.

THE GIRL (*with wonder*): San Francisco?

YOUNG MAN: That's right—San Francisco. That's where you and me belong.

THE GIRL: I've always wanted to go to *some* place like San Francisco—but how could I go alone?

YOUNG MAN: Well, you're not alone any more, see?

THE GIRL: Tell me a little what it's like.

YOUNG MAN (*very swiftly, almost impatiently at first, but gradually slower and with remembrance, smiling, and* THE GIRL *moving closer to him as he speaks*): Well, it's on the Pacific to begin with—ocean water all around. Cool fog and seagulls. Ships from all over the world. It's got seven hills. The little streets go up and down, around and all over. Every night the foghorns bawl. But they won't be bawling for you and me.

THE GIRL: What else?

YOUNG MAN: That's about all, I guess.

THE GIRL: Are people different in San Francisco?

YOUNG MAN: People are the same everywhere. They're different only when they love somebody. That's the only thing that makes 'em different. More people in Frisco love somebody, that's all.

THE GIRL: Nobody anywhere loves anybody as much as I love you.

YOUNG MAN (*shouting, as if to the world*): You see? Hearing you say that, a man could die and still be ahead of the game. Now, hurry. And don't forget, if I'm not here when you come back, get the hell to San Francisco where you'll have a chance. Do you hear me?

(THE GIRL *stands a moment looking at him, then backs away, turns and runs. The* YOUNG MAN *stares after her, troubled and smiling. Then he turns away from the image of her and walks about like a lion in a cage. After a while he sits down suddenly and buries his head in his hands. From a distance the sound of several automobiles approaching is heard. He listens a moment, then ignores the implications of the sound, whatever they may be. Several automobile doors are slammed. He ignores this also. A wooden door is opened with a key and closed, and footsteps are heard in a hall. Walking easily, almost casually and yet arrogantly, a* MAN *comes in.*)

YOUNG MAN (*jumps up suddenly and shouts at* THE MAN, *almost scaring him*): What the hell kind of a jailkeeper are you, anyway? Why don't you attend to your business? You get paid for it, don't you? Now, get me out of here.

THE MAN: But I'm not the jailkeeper.

YOUNG MAN: Yeah? Well, who are you, then?

THE MAN: I'm the husband.

YOUNG MAN: What husband you talking about?

THE MAN: You know what husband.

YOUNG MAN: Hey! (*pause, looking at* THE MAN) Are you the guy that hit me over the head last night?

THE MAN: I am.

YOUNG MAN (*with righteous indignation*): What do you mean going around hitting people over the head?

THE MAN: Oh, I don't know. What do you *mean* going around—the way you do?

YOUNG MAN (*rubbing his head*): You hurt my head. You got no right to hit anybody over the head.

THE MAN (*suddenly angry, shouting*): Answer my question! What do you mean?

YOUNG MAN: Listen, you—don't be hollering at me just because I'm locked up.

THE MAN (*with contempt, slowly*): You're a dog!

YOUNG MAN: Yeah, well, let me tell you something. You *think* you're the husband. You're the husband of nothing. (*slowly*) What's more, your wife—if you want to call her that—is a tramp. Why don't you throw her out in the street where she belongs?

THE MAN (*draws a pistol*): Shut up!

YOUNG MAN: Yeah? Go ahead, shoot—(*softly*) and spoil the fun. What'll your pals think? They'll be disappointed, won't they. What's the fun hanging a man who's already dead? (THE MAN *puts the gun away.*) That's right, because now you can have some fun yourself, telling me what you're going to do. That's what you came here for, isn't it? Well, you don't need to tell me. I *know* what you're going to do. I've read the papers and I know. They have fun. A mob of 'em fall on one man and beat him, don't they? They tear off his clothes and kick him, don't they? And women and little children stand around watching, don't they? Well, before you go on *this* picnic, I'm going to tell you a few things. Not that that's going to send you home with your pals—the other heroes. No. You've been outraged. A stranger has come to town and violated your women. Your pure, innocent, virtuous women. You fellows have got to set this thing right. You're men, not mice. You're homemakers, and you beat your children. (*suddenly*) Listen, you—I didn't know she was your wife. I didn't know she was anybody's wife.

THE MAN: You're a liar!

YOUNG MAN: Sometimes—when it'll do somebody some good—but not this time. Do you want to hear about it? (THE MAN *doesn't answer.*) All right, I'll tell you. I met her at a lunch counter. She came in and sat next to me. There was plenty of room, but she sat next to me. Somebody had put a nickel in the phonograph and a fellow was singing *New San Antonio Rose.* Well, she got to talking about the song. I thought she was talking to the waiter, but *he* didn't answer her, so after a while *I* answered her. That's how I met her. I didn't think anything of it. We left the place together and started walking. The first thing I knew she said, This is where I live.

THE MAN: You're a dirty liar!

YOUNG MAN: Do you want to hear it? Or not? (THE MAN *does not answer.*) OK. She asked me to come in. Maybe she had something in mind, maybe she didn't. Didn't make any difference to me, one way or the other. If she was lonely, all right. If not, all right.

THE MAN: You're telling a lot of dirty lies!

YOUNG MAN: I'm telling the truth. Maybe your wife's out there with your pals. Well, call her in. I got nothing against her, or you—or any of you. Call her in, and ask her a few questions. Are you in love with her? (THE MAN *doesn't answer.*) Well, that's too bad.

THE MAN: What do you mean, too bad?

YOUNG MAN: I mean this may not be the first time something like this has happened.

THE MAN (*swiftly*): Shut up!

YOUNG MAN: Oh, you know it. You've always known it. You're afraid of your pals, that's all. She asked me for money. That's all she wanted. I wouldn't be here now if I had given her the money.

THE MAN (*slowly*): How much did she ask for?

YOUNG MAN: I didn't ask her how much. I told her I'd made a mistake. She said she would make trouble if I didn't give her money. Well, I don't like bargaining, and I don't like being threatened, either. I told her to get the hell away from me. The next thing I knew she'd run out of the house and was hollering. (*pause*) Now, why don't you go out there and tell 'em they took me to another jail—go home and pack up and leave her. You're a pretty good guy; you're just afraid of your pals.

(THE MAN *draws his gun again. He is very frightened. He moves a step toward the* YOUNG MAN, *then fires three times. The* YOUNG MAN *falls to his knees.* THE MAN *turns and runs, horrified.*)

YOUNG MAN: Hello—out there! (*He is bent forward.*)

(THE GIRL *comes running in, and halts suddenly, looking at him.*)

THE GIRL: There were some people in the street, men and women and kids—so I came in through the back, through a window. I couldn't find the gun. I looked all over but I couldn't find it. What's the matter?

YOUNG MAN: Nothing—nothing. Everything's all right. Listen. Listen, kid. Get the hell out of here. Go out the same way you came in and run—run like hell—run all night. Get to another town and get on a train. Do you hear me?

THE GIRL: What's happened?

YOUNG MAN: Get away—just get away from here. Take any train that's going—you can get to Frisco later.

THE GIRL (*almost sobbing*): I don't want to go any place without you.

YOUNG MAN: I can't go. Something's happened. (*He looks at her.*) But I'll be with you always—God damn it. Always!

(*He falls forward.* THE GIRL *stands near him, then begins to sob softly, walking away. She stands over to one side, stops sobbing, and stares out. The excitement of the mob outside increases.* THE MAN, *with two of his pals, comes running in.* THE GIRL *watches, unseen.*)

THE MAN: Here's the son of a bitch!

ANOTHER MAN: OK. Open the cell, Harry.

(*The* THIRD MAN *goes to the cell door, unlocks it, and swings it open.*)
(*A* WOMAN *comes running in.*)

THE WOMAN: Where is he? I want to see him. Is he dead? (*Looking down at him, as the* MEN *pick him up.*) There he is. (*pause*) Yeah, that's him.

(*Her husband looks at her with contempt, then at the dead man.*)

THE MAN (*trying to laugh*): All right—let's get it over with.
THIRD MAN: Right you are, George. Give me a hand, Harry.

(*They lift the body.*)

THE GIRL (*suddenly, fiercely*): Put him down!
THE MAN: What's this?
SECOND MAN: What are you doing here? Why aren't you out on the street?
THE GIRL: Put him down and go away.

(*She runs toward the* MEN.)
(THE WOMAN *grabs her.*)

THE WOMAN: Here—where do you think *you're* going?
THE GIRL: Let me go. You've no right to take him away.
THE WOMAN: Well, listen to her, will you? (*She slaps* THE GIRL *and pushes her to the floor.*) Listen to the little slut, will you?

(*They all go, carrying the* YOUNG MAN'S *body.* THE GIRL *gets up slowly, no longer sobbing. She looks around at everything, then looks straight out, and whispers.*)

THE GIRL: Hello—out—there! Hello—out there!

CURTAIN

Pullman Car Hiawatha

THORNTON WILDER

Characters

STAGE MANAGER
COMPARTMENT THREE, *an insane woman, male attendant, trained nurse*
COMPARTMENT TWO, *Philip*
COMPARTMENT ONE, *Harriet, his young wife*
LOWER ONE, *a maiden lady*
LOWER THREE, *a middle-aged doctor*
LOWER FIVE, *a stout, amiable woman of fifty*
LOWER SEVEN, *an engineer going to California*
LOWER NINE, *another engineer*
PORTER
GROVER'S CORNERS, OHIO
THE FIELD
A TRAMP
PARKERSBURG, OHIO
TWO WORKERS
A MECHANIC
TEN, ELEVEN, AND TWELVE O'CLOCK
GABRIEL AND MICHAEL, *two archangels*

Reading Guides

1. *Pullman Car Hiawatha* is very different from the other plays you have read. If you read carefully early in the play, you won't have problems later on. Understand that the Stage Manager controls everybody.

2. There is no set in this play, but there is a "scene," which Wilder leaves completely up to you to imagine.

Pullman Car Hiawatha

SCENE: *At the back of the stage is a balcony or bridge or runway leading out of sight in both directions. Two flights of stairs descend from it to the stage. There is no further scenery.*

At the rise of the curtain the STAGE MANAGER *is making lines with a piece of chalk on the floor of the stage by the footlights.*

THE STAGE MANAGER: This is the plan of a Pullman car. Its name is Hiawatha and on December twenty-first it is on its way from New York to Chicago. Here at your left are three compartments. Here is the aisle and five lowers. The berths are all full, uppers and lowers, but for the purposes of this play we are limiting our interest to the people in the lower berths on the further side only.

The berths are already made up. It is half-past nine. Most of the passengers are in bed behind the green curtains. They are dropping their shoes on the floor, or wrestling with their trousers, or wondering whether they dare hide their valuables in the pillow slips during the night.

All right! Come on, everybody!

The actors enter carrying chairs. Each improvises his berth by placing two chairs facing one another in his chalk-marked space. They then sit in one chair, profile to the audience, and rest their feet on the other. This must do for lying in bed. The passengers in the compartments do the same.
Reading from left to right we have:

COMPARTMENT THREE: *an insane woman with a male attendant and a trained nurse.*
COMPARTMENT TWO: PHILIP *and*
COMPARTMENT ONE: HARRIET, *his young wife.*
LOWER ONE: *a maiden lady.*
LOWER THREE: *a middle-aged doctor.*
LOWER FIVE: *a stout, amiable woman of fifty.*
LOWER SEVEN: *an engineer going to California.*
LOWER NINE: *another engineer.*

LOWER ONE: Porter, be sure and wake me up at quarter of six.
PORTER: Yes, ma'am.
LOWER ONE: I know I shan't sleep a wink, but I want to be told when it's quarter of six.

PORTER: Yes, ma'am.

LOWER SEVEN (*putting his head through the curtains*): Hsst! Porter! Hsst! How the hell do you turn on this other light?

PORTER (*fussing with it*): I'm afraid it's outa order, suh. You'll have to use the other end.

THE STAGE MANAGER (*falsetto, substituting for some woman in an upper berth*): May I ask if someone in this car will be kind enough to lend me some aspirin?

PORTER (*rushing about*): Yes, ma'am.

LOWER NINE (*one of the engineers, descending the aisle and falling into Lower Five*): Sorry, lady, sorry. Made a mistake.

LOWER FIVE (*grumbling*): Never in all my born days!

LOWER ONE (*in a shrill whisper*): Porter! Porter!

PORTER: Yes, ma'am.

LOWER ONE: My hot-water bag's leaking. I guess you'll have to take it away. I'll have to do without it tonight. How awful!

LOWER FIVE (*sharply to the passenger above her*): Young man, you mind your own business, or I'll report you to the conductor.

STAGE MANAGER (*substituting for* UPPER FIVE): Sorry, ma'am, I didn't mean to upset you. My suspenders fell down and I was trying to catch them.

LOWER FIVE: Well, here they are. Now go to sleep. Everybody seems to be rushing into my berth tonight.

(*She puts her head out.*)

Porter! Porter! Be a good soul and bring me a glass of water, will you? I'm parched.

LOWER NINE: Bill!

(*No answer.*)

Bill!

LOWER SEVEN: Ye'? Wha' d'y'a want?

LOWER NINE: Slip me one of those magazines, willya?

LOWER SEVEN: Which one d'y'a want?

LOWER NINE: Either one. *Detective Stories.* Either one.

LOWER SEVEN: Aw, Fred. I'm just in the middle of one of'm in *Detective Stories.*

LOWER NINE: That's all right. I'll take the Western. Thanks.

THE STAGE MANAGER (*to the actors*): All right! Sh! Sh! Sh—

(*To the audience*)

Now I want you to hear them thinking.

(*There is a pause and then they all begin a murmuring—swishing noise, very soft. In turn each one of them can be heard above the others.*)

LOWER FIVE (*the lady of fifty*): Let's see: I've got the doll for the baby. And the slip-on for Marietta. And the fountain pen for Herbert. And the subscription to *Time* for George . . .

LOWER SEVEN (*Bill*): God! Lillian, if you don't turn out to be what I think you are, I don't know what I'll do. I guess it's bad politics to let a woman know that you're going all the way to California to see her. I'll think up a song and dance about a business trip or something. Was I ever as hot and bothered about anyone like this before? Well, there was Martha. But that was different. I'd better try and read or I'll go cuckoo. "How did you know it was ten o'clock when the visitor left the house?" asked the detective. "Because at ten o'clock," answered the girl, "I always turn out the lights in the conservatory and in the back hall. As I was coming down the stairs I heard the master talking to someone at the front door. I heard him say, 'Well, good night . . .' "—Gee, I don't feel like reading; I'll just think about Lillian. That yellow hair. Them eyes! . . .

LOWER THREE: *The* DOCTOR *reads aloud to himself from a medical journal the most hair-raising material, every now and then punctuating his reading with an interrogative "So?"*

LOWER ONE (*the maiden lady*): I know I'll be awake all night. I might just as well make up my mind to it now. I can't imagine what got hold of that hot-water bag to leak on the train of all places. Well now, I'll lie on my right side and breathe deeply and think of beautiful things, and perhaps I can doze off a bit.

(*And lastly:*)

LOWER NINE (*Fred*): That was the craziest thing I ever did. It's set me back three whole years. I could have saved up thirty thousand dollars by now if I'd only stayed over here. What business had I got to fool with contracts with the goddam Soviets. Hell, I thought it would be interesting. Interesting, what the hell! It's set me back three whole years. I don't even know if the company'll take me back. I'm green, that's all. I just don't grow up.

(*The* STAGE MANAGER *strides toward them with lifted hand, crying "Hush," and their whispering ceases.*)

THE STAGE MANAGER: That'll do! Just one minute. Porter!

THE PORTER (*appearing at the left*): Yessuh.

THE STAGE MANAGER: It's your turn to think.

(THE PORTER *is very embarrassed.*)

Don't you want to? You have a right to.

THE PORTER (*torn between the desire to release his thoughts and his shyness*): Ah . . . ah . . . I'm only thinkin' about my home in Chicago and . . . and my life insurance.

THE STAGE MANAGER: That's right.

THE PORTER: . . . well, thank you . . . thank you.

(*He slips away, blushing violently, in an agony of self-consciousness and pleasure.*)

THE STAGE MANAGER (*to the audience*): He's a good fellow, Harrison is. Just shy.

(*To the actors again*)

Now the compartments, please.

(*The berths fall into shadow.*)
(PHILIP *is standing at the door connecting his compartment with his wife's.*)

PHILIP: Are you all right, angel?

HARRIET: Yes. I don't know what was the matter with me during dinner.

PHILIP: Shall I close the door?

HARRIET: Do see whether you can't put a chair against it that will hold it half open without banging.

PHILIP: There. Good night, angel. If you can't sleep, call me, and we'll sit up and play Russian bank.

HARRIET: You're thinking of that awful time when we sat up every night for a week . . . But at least I know I shall sleep tonight. The noise of the wheels has become sort of nice and homely. What state are we in?

PHILIP: We're tearing through Ohio. We'll be in Indiana soon.

HARRIET: I know those little towns full of horse blocks.

PHILIP: Well, we'll reach Chicago very early. I'll call you. Sleep tight.

HARRIET: Sleep tight, darling.

(*He returns to his own compartment. In Compartment Three, the male attendant tips his chair back against the wall and smokes a cigar. The trained nurse knits a stocking. The insane woman leans her forehead against the windowpane; that is, stares into the audience.*)

THE INSANE WOMAN (*Her words have a dragging, complaining sound but lack any conviction.*): Don't take me there. Don't take me there.

THE FEMALE ATTENDANT: Wouldn't you like to lie down, dearie?

THE INSANE WOMAN: I want to get off the train. I want to go back to New York.

THE FEMALE ATTENDANT: Wouldn't you like me to brush your hair again? It's such a nice feeling.

THE INSANE WOMAN (*going to the door*): I want to get off the train. I want to open the door.

THE FEMALE ATTENDANT (*taking one of her hands*): Such a noise! You'll wake up all the nice people. Come and I'll tell you a story about the place we're going to.

THE INSANE WOMAN: I don't want to go to that place.

THE FEMALE ATTENDANT: Oh, it's lovely! There are lawns and gardens everywhere. I never saw such a lovely place. Just lovely.

THE INSANE WOMAN (*lies down on the bed*): Are there roses?

THE FEMALE ATTENDANT: Roses! Red, yellow, white . . . just everywhere.

THE MALE ATTENDANT (*after a pause*): That musta been Cleveland.

THE FEMALE ATTENDANT: I had a case in Cleveland once. Diabetes.

THE MALE ATTENDANT (*after another pause*): I wisht I had a radio here. Radios are good for *them.* I had a patient once that had to have the radio going every minute.

THE FEMALE ATTENDANT: Radios are lovely. My married niece has one. It's always going. It's wonderful.

THE INSANE WOMAN (*half rising*): I'm not beautiful. I'm not beautiful as she was.

THE FEMALE ATTENDANT: Oh, I think you're beautiful! Beautiful. Mr. Morgan, don't you think Mrs. Churchill is beautiful?

THE MALE ATTENDANT: Oh, fine lookin'! Regular movie star, Mrs. Churchill.

(*She looks inquiringly at them and subsides.*)

(HARRIET *groans slightly. Smothers a cough. She gropes about with her hand and finds the bell.*)

(*The* PORTER *knocks at her door.*)

HARRIET (*whispering*): Come in. First, please close the door into my husband's room. Softly. Softly.

PORTER (*a plaintive porter*): Yes, ma'am.

HARRIET: Porter, I'm not well. I'm sick. I must see a doctor.

PORTER: Why, ma'am, they ain't no doctor . . .

HARRIET: Yes, when I was coming out from dinner I saw a man in one of the seats on *that* side reading medical papers. Go and wake him up.

PORTER (*flabbergasted*): Ma'am, I cain't wake anybody up.

HARRIET: Yes, you can. Porter. Porter. Now don't argue with me. I'm very sick. It's my heart. Wake him up. Tell him it's my heart.

PORTER: Yes, ma'am.

(*He goes into the aisle and starts pulling the shoulder of the man in Lower Three.*)

LOWER THREE: Hello. Hello. What is it? Are we there?

(*The* PORTER *mumbles to him.*)

I'll be right there. Porter, is it a young woman or an old one?

PORTER: I dono, suh. I guess she's kinda old, suh, but not so very old.

LOWER THREE: Tell her I'll be there in a minute and to lie quietly.

(*The* PORTER *enters* HARRIET'S *compartment. She has turned her head away.*)

PORTER: He'll be here in a minute, ma'am. He says you lie quiet.

(LOWER THREE *stumbles along the aisle muttering.*)

LOWER THREE: Damn these shoes!

SOMEONE'S VOICE: Can't we have a little quiet in this car, please?

LOWER NINE: Oh, shut up!

(*The* DOCTOR *passes the* PORTER *and enters* HARRIET'S *compartment. He leans over her, concealing her by his stooping figure.*)

LOWER THREE: She's dead, Porter. Is there anyone on the train traveling with her?

PORTER: Yessuh. Dat's her husband in dere.

LOWER THREE: Idiot! Why didn't you call him? I'll go in and speak to him.

(*The* STAGE MANAGER *comes forward.*)

THE STAGE MANAGER: All right. So much for the inside of the car. That'll be enough of that for the present. Now for its position geographically, meteorologically, astronomically, theologically considered.
Pullman Car Hiawatha, ten minutes of ten. December twenty-first, 1930. All ready.

(*Some figures begin to appear on the balcony.*)

No, no. It's not time for the planets yet. Nor the hours.

(*They retire.*)
(*The* STAGE MANAGER *claps his hands. A grinning boy in overalls enters from the left behind the berths.*)

GROVER'S CORNERS, OHIO (*in a foolish voice as though he were reciting a piece at a Sunday School entertainment*): I represent Grover's Corners, Ohio—821 souls. "There's so much good in the worst of us and so much bad in the best of us, that it ill behooves any of us to criticize the rest of us." Robert Louis Stevenson. Thankya.

(*He grins and goes out right.*)
(*Enter from the same direction somebody in shirt sleeves. This is a field.*)

THE FIELD: I represent a field you are passing between Grover's Corners, Ohio, and Parkersburg, Ohio. In this field there are fifty-one gophers, two hundred six field mice, six snakes and millions of bugs, insects, ants, and spiders, all in their winter sleep. "What is so rare as a day in June? Then, if ever, come perfect days." *The Vision of Sir Launfal,* William Cullen—I mean James Russell Lowell. Thank you. (*exit*)

(*Enter a tramp.*)

THE TRAMP: I just want to tell you that I'm a tramp that's been traveling under this car Hiawatha, so I have a right to be in this play. I'm going from Rochester, New York, to Joliet, Illinois. It takes a lotta people to make a world.

> On the road to Mandalay
> Where the flying fishes play
> And the sun comes up like thunder
> Over China cross the bay.

Frank W. Service. It's bitter cold. Thank you.

(*Exit.*)

(*Enter a gentle old farmer's wife with three stringy young people.*)

PARKERSBURG, OHIO: I represent Parkersburg, Ohio—2604 souls. I have seen all the dreadful havoc that alcohol has done, and I hope no one here will ever touch a drop of the curse of this beautiful country.

(*She beats a measure and they all sing unsteadily.*)

"Throw out the life line! Throw out the life line! Someone is sinking today-ay . . ."

(THE STAGE MANAGER *moves them away tactfully.*)

(*Enter a workman.*)

THE WORKMAN: Ich bin der Arbeiter der hier sein Leben verlor. Bei der Sprengung für diese Brücke über die Sie in dem Moment fahren—

(*The engine whistles for a trestle crossing.*)

—erschlug mich ein Felsbock. Ich spiele jetzt als Geist in diesem Stuck mit. "Vor sieben und achtzig Jahren haben unsere Väter auf diesem Continent eine neue Nation hervorgebracht . . ."

THE STAGE MANAGER (*helpfully, to the audience*): I'm sorry; that's in German. He says that he's the ghost of a workman who was killed while they were building the trestle over which the car Hiawatha is now passing—

(*The engine whistles again.*)

—and he wants to appear in this play. A chunk of rock hit him while they were dynamiting. His motto you know: "Four score and seven years ago our fathers brought forth upon this continent a new nation dedicated," and so on. Thank you, Mr. Krüger.

(*Exit the ghost.*)

(*Enter another worker.*)

THIS WORKER: I'm a watchman in a tower near Parkersburg, Ohio. I just want to tell you that I'm not asleep and that the signals are all right for this train. I hope you all have a fine trip. "If you can keep your heads when all about you are losing theirs and blaming it on you . . ." Rudyard Kipling. Thank you. (*exit*)

(*The* STAGE MANAGER *comes forward.*)

THE STAGE MANAGER: All right. That'll be enough of that. Now the weather.

(*Enter a mechanic.*)

A MECHANIC: It is eleven degrees above zero. The wind is north-northwest, velocity, 57. There is a field of low barometric pressure moving eastward from Saskatchewan to the eastern coast. Tomorrow it will be cold with some snow in the Middle Western States and northern New York. (*exit*)

THE STAGE MANAGER: All right. Now for the hours.

(*helpfully to the audience*)

The minutes are gossips; the hours are philosophers; the years are theologians. The hours are philosophers with exception of Twelve O'clock who is also a theologian. Ready, Ten O'clock!

(*The hours are beautiful girls dressed like Elihu Vedder's Pleiades. Each carries a great gold roman numeral. They pass slowly across the balcony at the back, moving from right to left.*)

What are you doing, Ten O'clock? Aristotle?

TEN O'CLOCK: No, Plato, Mr. Washburn.

THE STAGE MANAGER: Good. "Are you not rather convinced that he who thus . . . "

TEN O'CLOCK: "Are you not rather convinced that he who sees beauty as only it can be seen will be specially favored? And since he is in contact not with images but with realities . . ."

(*She continues the passage in a murmur as* ELEVEN O'CLOCK *appears.*)

ELEVEN O'CLOCK: "What else can I, Epictetus, do, a lame old man, but sing hymns to God? If then I were a nightingale, I would do the nightingale's part. If I were a swan, I would do a swan's. But now I am a rational creature . . ."

(*Her voice, too, subsides to a murmur.* TWELVE O'CLOCK *appears.*)

THE STAGE MANAGER: Good. Twelve O'clock, what have you?

TWELVE O'CLOCK: Saint Augustine and his mother.

THE STAGE MANAGER: So. "And we began to say: If to any the tumult of the flesh were hushed . . ."

TWELVE O'CLOCK: "And we began to say: If to any the tumult of the flesh were hushed; hushed the images of earth; of waters and of air; . . ."

THE STAGE MANAGER: Faster. "Hushed also the poles of heaven."

TWELVE O'CLOCK: "Yea, were the very soul to be hushed to herself."

STAGE MANAGER: A little louder, Miss Foster.

TWELVE O'CLOCK (*a little louder*): "Hushed all dreams and imaginary revelations . . ."

THE STAGE MANAGER (*waving them back*): All right. All right. Now the planets. December twenty-first, 1930, please.

(*The hours unwind and return to their dressing rooms at the right. The planets appear on the balcony. Some of them take their place halfway on the steps. These have no words, but each has a sound. One has a pulsating, zinging sound. Another has a thrum. One whistles ascending and descending scales. Saturn does a slow, obstinate:*)

Louder, Saturn—Venus, higher. Good. Now, Jupiter. Now the Earth.

(*He turns to the beds on the train.*)

Come, everybody. This is the Earth's sound.

(*The towns, workmen, etc., appear at the edge of the stage. The passengers begin their "thinking" murmur.*)

Come, Grover's Corners. Parkersburg. You're in this. Watchman. Tramp. This is the Earth's sound.

(*He conducts it as the director of an orchestra would. Each of the towns and workmen does his motto.*)

(THE INSANE WOMAN *breaks into passionate weeping. She rises and stretches out her arms to the* STAGE MANAGER.)

THE INSANE WOMAN: Use me. Give me something to do.

(*He goes to her quickly, whispers something in her ear, and leads her back to her guardians. She is unconsoled.*)

THE STAGE MANAGER: Now sh-sh-sh! Enter the archangels. (*to the audience*) We have now reached the theological position of Pullman car Hiawatha.

(*The towns and workmen have disappeared. The planets, off stage, continue a faint music. Two young men in blue serge suits enter along the balcony and descend the stairs at the right. As they pass each bed the passenger talks in his sleep.* GABRIEL *points out* BILL *to* MICHAEL *who smiles with raised eyebrows. They pause before* LOWER FIVE, *and* MICHAEL *makes the sound of assent that can only be rendered, "Hn-Hn." The remarks that the characters make in their sleep are not all intelligible, being lost in the sound of sigh or groan or whisper by which they are conveyed. But we seem to hear:*)

LOWER NINE (*loud*): Some people are slower than others, that's all.

LOWER SEVEN: It's no fun, y'know. I'll try.

LOWER FIVE (*the lady of the Christmas presents, rapidly*): You know best, of course. I'm ready whenever you are. One year's like another.

LOWER ONE: I can teach sewing. I can sew.

(*They approach* HARRIET'S *compartment.*)

(THE INSANE WOMAN *sits up and speaks to them.*)

THE INSANE WOMAN: Me?

(THE ARCHANGELS *shake their heads.*)

THE INSANE WOMAN: What possible use can there be in my simply waiting? Well, I'm grateful for anything. I'm grateful for being so much better than I was. The old story, the terrible story, doesn't haunt me as it used to. A great load seems to have been taken off my mind. But no one understands me any more. At last I understand myself perfectly, but no one else understands a thing I say. So I must wait?

(THE ARCHANGELS *nod, smiling.*)

THE INSANE WOMAN (*resignedly, and with a smile that implies their complicity*): Well, you know best. I'll do whatever is best; but everyone is so childish, so absurd. They have no logic. These people are all so mad . . . These people are like children; they have never suffered.

(*She returns to her bed and sleeps.* THE ARCHANGELS *stand beside* HARRIET. *The doctor has drawn* PHILIP *into the next compartment and is talking to him in earnest whispers.*)

(HARRIET's *face has been toward the wall; she turns it slightly and speaks toward the ceiling.*)

HARRIET: I wouldn't be happy there. Let me stay dead down here. I belong here. I shall be perfectly happy to roam about my house and be near Philip. You know I wouldn't be happy there.

(GABRIEL *leans over and whispers into her ear. After a short pause she bursts into fierce tears.*)

I'm ashamed to come with you. I haven't done anything. I haven't done anything with my life. Worse than that: I was angry and sullen. I never realized anything. I don't dare go a step in such a place.

(*They whisper to her again.*)

But it's not possible to forgive such things. I don't want to be forgiven so easily. I want to be punished for it all. I won't stir until I've been punished a long, long time. I want to be freed of all that—by punishment. I want to be all new.

(*They whisper to her. She puts her feet slowly on the ground.*)

But no one else could be punished for me. I'm willing to face it all myself. I don't ask anyone to be punished for me.

(*They whisper to her again. She sits long and brokenly looking at her shoes and thinking it over.*)

It wasn't fair. I'd have been willing to suffer for it myself, if I could have endured such a mountain.

(*She smiles.*)

Oh, I'm ashamed! I'm just a stupid and you know it. I'm just another American. But then what wonderful things must be beginning now. You really want me? You really want me?

(*They start leading her down the aisle of the car.*)

Let's take the whole train. There are some lovely faces on this train. Can't we all come? You'll never find anyone better than Philip. Please, please, let's all go.

(*They reach the steps. The* ARCHANGELS *interlock their arms as a support for her as she leans heavily on them, taking the steps slowly. Her words are half singing and half babbling.*)

But look at how tremendously high and far it is. I've a weak heart. I'm not supposed to climb stairs. "I do not ask to see the distant scene; one step enough for me." It's like Switzerland. My tongue keeps saying things. I can't control it. Do let me stop a minute: I want to say good-by.

(*She turns in their arms.*)

Just a minute, I want to cry on your shoulder.

(*She leans her forehead against* GABRIEL'S *shoulder and laughs long and softly.*)

Good-by, Philip. I begged him not to marry me, but he would. He believed in me just as you do. Good-by, 1312 Ridgewood Avenue, Oaksbury, Illinois. I hope I remember all its steps and doors and wallpapers forever. Good-by, Emerson Grammar School on the corner of Forbush Avenue and Wherry Street. Good-by, Miss Walker and Miss Cramer who taught me English and Miss Matthewson who taught me biology. Good-by, First Congregational Church on the corner of Meyerson Avenue and Sixth Street and Dr. McReady and Mrs. McReady and Julia. Good-by, Papa and Mama . . .

(*She turns.*)

Now I'm tired of saying good-by. I never used to talk like this. I was so homely I never used to have the courage to talk. Until Philip came. I see now. I see now. I understand everything now.

(*The* STAGE MANAGER *comes forward.*)

THE STAGE MANAGER (*to the actors*): All right. All right. Now we'll have the whole world together, please. The whole solar system, please.

(*The complete cast begins to appear at the edges of the stage. He claps his hands.*)

The whole solar system, please. Where's the tramp? Where's the moon?

(*He gives two raps on the floor, like the conductor of an orchestra attracting the attention of his forces, and slowly lifts his hand. The human beings murmur their thoughts; the hours discourse; the planets chant or hum.* HARRIET'S *voice finally rises above them all saying:*)

HARRIET: "I was not ever thus, nor asked that Thou
Shouldst lead me on . . . and spite of fears,
Pride ruled my will: remember not past years."

(*The* STAGE MANAGER *waves them away.*)

THE STAGE MANAGER: Very good. Now clear the stage, please. Now we're at Englewood Station, South Chicago. See the University's towers over there! The best of them all.

LOWER ONE (*the spinster*): Porter, you promised to wake me up at quarter of six.

PORTER: Sorry, ma'am, but it's been an awful night on this car. A lady's been terrible sick.

LOWER ONE: Oh! Is she better?

PORTER: No'm. She ain't one jot better.

LOWER FIVE: Young man, take your foot out of my face.

THE STAGE MANAGER (*again substituting for* UPPER FIVE): Sorry, lady, I slipped—

LOWER FIVE (*grumbling not unamiably*): I declare, this trip's been one long series of insults.

THE STAGE MANAGER: Just one minute, ma'am, and I'll be down and out of your way.

LOWER FIVE: Haven't you got anybody to darn your socks for you? You ought to be ashamed to go about that way.

THE STAGE MANAGER: Sorry, lady.

LOWER FIVE: You're too stuck up to get married. That's the trouble with you.

LOWER NINE: Bill! Bill!

LOWER SEVEN: Ye'? Wha' d'y'a want?

LOWER NINE: Bill, how much d'y'a give the porter on a train like this? I've been outa the country so long . . .

LOWER SEVEN: Hell, Fred, I don't know myself.

THE PORTER: CHICAGO, CHICAGO. All out. This train don't go no further.

(*The passengers jostle their way out and an army of old women with mops and pails enters and prepares to clean up the car.*)

CURTAIN

Riders to the Sea

JOHN M. SYNGE

Characters

MAURYA
BARTLEY, *her son*
CATHLEEN, *her daughter*
NORA, *her daughter*
MEN AND WOMEN

Reading Guides

1. The characters in *Riders to the Sea* use an Irish dialect. This makes for difficult reading, but after a page or two you will grow accustomed to it.
2. The people in this play make their livings from the sea, and they lose their lives to the sea. Naturally, the sea is their major topic of conversation. In fact, the sea is a major character—to them.

Riders to the Sea

SCENE. *An island off the west of Ireland.*

(*Cottage kitchen, with nets, oilskins, spinning wheel, some new boards standing by the wall, etc.* CATHLEEN, *a girl of about twenty, finishes kneading cake, and puts it down in the pot-oven by the fire; then wipes her hands, and begins to spin at the wheel.* NORA, *a young girl, puts her head in at the door.*)

NORA (*in a low voice*): Where is she?

CATHLEEN: She's lying down, God help her, and may be sleeping, if she's able. (NORA *comes in softly, and takes a bundle from under her shawl.*) (*Spinning the wheel rapidly.*) What is it you have?

NORA: The young priest is after bringing them. It's a shirt and a plain stocking were got off a drowned man in Donegal.

(CATHLEEN *stops her wheel with a sudden movement, and leans out to listen.*)

We're to find out if it's Michael's they are, some time herself will be down looking by the sea.

CATHLEEN: How would they be Michael's, Nora. How would he go the length of that way to the far north?

NORA: The young priest says he's known the like of it. "If it's Michael's they are," says he, "you can tell herself he's got a clean burial by the grace of God, and if they're not his, let no one say a word about them, for she'll be getting her death," says he, "with crying and lamenting."

(*The door which* NORA *half closed is blown open by a gust of wind.*)

CATHLEEN (*looking out anxiously*): Did you ask him would he stop Bartley going this day with the horses to the Galway fair?

NORA: "I won't stop him," says he, "but let you not be afraid. Herself does be saying prayers half through the night, and the Almighty God won't leave her destitute," says he, "with no son living."

CATHLEEN: Is the sea bad by the white rocks, Nora?

NORA: Middling bad, God help us. There's a great roaring in the west, and it's worse it'll be getting when the tide's turned to the wind. (*She goes over to the table with the bundle.*) Shall I open it now?

CATHLEEN: Maybe she'd wake up on us, and come in before we'd done. (*coming to the table*) It's a long time we'll be, and the two of us crying.

NORA (*goes to the inner door and listens*): She's moving about on the bed. She'll be coming in a minute.

CATHLEEN: Give me the ladder, and I'll put them up in the turf-loft, the way she won't know of them at all, and maybe when the tide turns she'll be going down to see would he be floating from the east.

(*They put the ladder against the gable of the chimney;* CATHLEEN *goes up a few steps and hides the bundle in the turf-loft.* MAURYA *comes from the inner room.*)

MAURYA (*looking up at* CATHLEEN *and speaking querulously*): Isn't it turf enough you have for this day and evening?

CATHLEEN: There's a cake baking at the fire for a short space (*throwing down the turf*) and Bartley will want it when the tide turns if he goes to Connemara.

(NORA *picks up the turf and puts it round the pot-oven.*)

MAURYA (*sitting down on a stool at the fire*): He won't go this day with the wind rising from the south and west. He won't go this day, for the young priest will stop him surely.

NORA: He'll not stop him, mother, and I heard Eamon Simon and Stephen Pheety and Colum Shawn saying he would go.

MAURYA: Where is he itself?

NORA: He went down to see would there be another boat sailing in the week, and I'm thinking it won't be long till he's here now, for the tide's turning at the green head, and the hooker's tacking from the east.

CATHLEEN: I hear someone passing the big stones.

NORA (*looking out*): He's coming now, and he in a hurry.

BARTLEY (*comes in and looks round the room; speaking sadly and quietly*): Where is the bit of new rope, Cathleen, was bought in Connemara?

CATHLEEN (*coming down*): Give it to him, Nora; it's on a nail by the white boards. I hung it up this morning, for the pig with the black feet was eating it.

NORA (*giving him a rope*): Is that it, Bartley?

MAURYA: You'd do right to leave that rope, Bartley, hanging by the boards. (BARTLEY *takes the rope.*) It will be wanting in this place, I'm telling you, if Michael is washed up tomorrow morning, or the next morning, or any morning in the week, for it's a deep grave we'll make him by the grace of God.

BARTLEY (*beginning to work with the rope*): I've no halter the way I can ride down on the mare, and I must go now quickly. This is the one boat going for two weeks or beyond it, and the fair will be a good fair for horses I heard them saying below.

MAURYA: It's a hard thing they'll be saying below if the body is washed up and there's no man in it to make the coffin, and I after giving a big price for the finest white boards you'd find in Connemara. (*She looks round at the boards.*)

BARTLEY: How would it be washed up, and we after looking each day for nine days, and a strong wind blowing a while back from the west and south?

MAURYA: If it wasn't found itself, that wind is raising the sea, and there was a star up against the moon, and it rising in the night. If it was a hundred horses, or a thousand horses you had itself, what is the price of a thousand horses against a son where there is one son only?

BARTLEY (*working at the halter, to* CATHLEEN): Let you go down each day, and see the sheep aren't jumping in on the rye, and if the jobber comes you can sell the pig with the black feet if there is a good price going.

MAURYA: How would the like of her get a good price for a pig?

BARTLEY (*to* CATHLEEN): If the west wind holds with the last bit of the moon let you and Nora get up weed enough for another cock for the kelp. It's hard set we'll be from this day with no one in it but one man to work.

MAURYA: It's hard set we'll be surely the day you're drown'd with the rest. What way will I live and the girls with me, and I an old woman looking for the grave?

(BARTLEY *lays down the halter, takes off his old coat, and puts on a newer one of the same flannel.*)

BARTLEY (*to* NORA): Is she coming to the pier?

NORA (*looking out*): She's passing the green head and letting fall her sails.

BARTLEY (*getting his purse and tobacco*): I'll have half an hour to go down, and you'll see me coming again in two days, or in three days, or maybe in four days if the wind is bad.

MAURYA (*turning round to the fire, and putting her shawl over her head*): Isn't it a hard and cruel man won't hear a word from an old woman, and she holding him from the sea?

CATHLEEN: It's the life of a young man to be going on the sea, and who would listen to an old woman with one thing and she saying it over?

BARTLEY (*taking the halter*): I must go now quickly. I'll ride down on the red mare, and the gray pony'll run behind me. . . . The blessing of God on you. (*He goes out.*)

MAURYA (*crying out as he is in the door*): He's gone now, God spare us, and we'll not see him again. He's gone now, and when the black night is falling I'll have no son left me in the world.

CATHLEEN: Why wouldn't you give him your blessing and he looking round in the door? Isn't it sorrow enough is on every one in this house without your sending him out with an unlucky word behind him, and a hard word in his ear?

(MAURYA *takes up the tongs and begins raking the fire aimlessly without looking round.*)

NORA (*turning towards her*): You're taking away the turf from the cake.

CATHLEEN (*crying out*): The Son of God forgive us, Nora, we're after forgetting his bit of bread. (*She comes over to the fire.*)

NORA: And it's destroyed he'll be going till dark night, and he after eating nothing since the sun went up.

CATHLEEN (*turning the cake out of the oven*): It's destroyed he'll be, surely. There's no sense left on any person in a house where an old woman will be talking for ever.

(MAURYA *sways herself on her stool.*)

(*cutting off some of the bread and rolling it in a cloth; to* MAURYA.) Let you go down to the spring well and give him this and he passing. You'll see him then and the dark word will be broken, and you can say "God speed you," the way he'll be easy in his mind.

MAURYA (*taking the bread*): Will I be in it as soon as himself?

CATHLEEN: If you go now quickly.

MAURYA (*standing up unsteadily*): It's hard set I am to walk.

CATHLEEN (*looking at her anxiously*): Give her the stick, Nora, or maybe she'll slip on the big stones.

NORA: What stick?

CATHLEEN: The stick Michael brought from Connemara.

MAURYA (*taking a stick* NORA *gives her*): In the big world the old people do be leaving things after them for their sons and children, but in this place it is the young men do be leaving things behind for them that do be old.

(*She goes out slowly.* NORA *goes over to the ladder.*)

CATHLEEN: Wait, Nora, maybe she'd turn back quickly. She's that sorry, God help her, you wouldn't know the thing she'd do.

NORA: Is she gone round by the bush?

CATHLEEN (*looking out*): She's gone now. Throw it down quickly, for the Lord knows when she'll be out of it again.

NORA (*getting the bundle from the loft*): The young priest said he'd be passing tomorrow, and we might go down and speak to him below if it's Michael's they are surely.

CATHLEEN (*taking the bundle*): Did he say what way they were found?

NORA (*coming down*): "There were two men," says he, "and they rowing round with poteen before the cocks crowed, and the oar of one of them caught the body, and they passing the black cliffs of the north."

CATHLEEN (*trying to open the bundle*): Give me a knife, Nora, the string's perished with the salt water, and there's a black knot on it you wouldn't loosen in a week.

NORA (*giving her a knife*): I've heard tell it was a long way to Donegal.

CATHLEEN (*cutting the string*): It is surely. There was a man in here a while ago—the man sold us that knife—and he said if you set off walking from the rocks beyond, it would be seven days you'd be in Donegal.

NORA: And what time would a man take, and he floating?

(CATHLEEN *opens the bundle and takes out a bit of a stocking. They look at them eagerly.*)

CATHLEEN (*in a low voice*): The Lord spare us, Nora! Isn't it a queer hard thing to say if it's his they are surely?

NORA: I'll get his shirt off the hook the way we can put the one flannel on the other. (*She looks through some clothes hanging in the corner.*) It's not with them, Cathleen, and where will it be?

CATHLEEN: I'm thinking Bartley put it on him in the morning, for his own shirt was heavy with the salt in it. (*pointing to the corner*) There's a bit of a sleeve was of the same stuff. Give me that and it will do.

(NORA *brings it to her and they compare the flannel.*)

It's the same stuff, Nora; but if it is itself aren't there great rolls of it in the shops of Galway, and isn't it many another man may have a shirt of it as well as Michael himself?

NORA (*who has taken up the stockings and counted the stitches, crying out*): It's Michael, Cathleen, it's Michael; God spare his soul, and what will herself say when she hears this story, and Bartley on the sea?

CATHLEEN (*taking the stocking*): It's a plain stocking.

NORA: It's the second one of the third pair I knitted, and I put up three score stitches, and I dropped four of them.

CATHLEEN (*counts the stitches*): It's that number is in it. (*crying out*) Ah, Nora, isn't it a bitter thing to think of him floating that way to the far north, and no one to keen him but the black hags that do be flying on the sea?

NORA (*swinging herself round, and throwing out her arms on the clothes*): And isn't it a pitiful thing when there is nothing left of a man who was a great rower and fisher, but a bit of an old shirt and a plain stocking?

CATHLEEN (*after an instant*): Tell me is herself coming, Nora? I hear a little sound on the path.

NORA (*looking out*): She is, Cathleen. She's coming up to the door.

CATHLEEN: Put these things away before she'll come in. Maybe it's easier she'll be after giving her blessing to Bartley, and we won't let on we've heard anything the time he's on the sea.

NORA (*helping* CATHLEEN *to close the bundle*): We'll put them here in the corner.

(*They put them into a hole in the chimney corner.* CATHLEEN *goes back to the spinning-wheel.*)

Will she see it was crying I was?

CATHLEEN: Keep your back to the door the way the light'll not be on you.

(NORA *sits down at the chimney corner, with her back to the door.* MAURYA *comes in very slowly, without looking at the girls, and goes over to her stool at the other side of the fire. The cloth with the bread is still in her hand. The girls look at each other, and* NORA *points to the bundle of bread.*)

(*after spinning for a moment*) You didn't give him his bit of bread?

(MAURYA *begins to keen softly, without turning round.*)

Did you see him riding down?

(MAURYA *goes on keening.*)

(*a little impatiently*) God forgive you; isn't it a better thing to raise your voice and tell what you seen, than to be making lamentation for a thing that's done? Did you see Bartley, I'm saying to you.

MAURYA (*with a weak voice*): My heart's broken from this day.

CATHLEEN (*as before*): Did you see Bartley?

MAURYA: I seen the fearfulest thing.

CATHLEEN (*leaves her wheel and looks out*): God forgive you; he's riding the mare now over the green head, and the gray pony behind him.

MAURYA (*starts, so that her shawl falls back from her head and shows her white tossed hair. With a frightened voice*): The gray pony behind him.

CATHLEEN (*coming to the fire*): What is it ails you, at all?

MAURYA (*speaking very slowly*): I've seen the fearfulest thing any person has seen, since the day Bride Dara seen the dead man with the child in his arms.

CATHLEEN and NORA: Uah. (*They crouch down in front of the old woman at the fire.*)

NORA: Tell us what it is you seen.

MAURYA: I went down to the spring well, and I stood there saying a prayer to myself. Then Bartley came alone, and he riding on the red mare with the gray pony behind him. (*She puts up her hands, as if to hide something from her eyes.*) The Son of God spare us, Nora!

CATHLEEN: What is it you seen?

MAURYA: I seen Michael himself.

CATHLEEN (*speaking softly*): You did not, mother; it wasn't Michael you seen, for his body is after being found in the far north, and he's got a clean burial by the grace of God.

MAURYA (*a little defiantly*): I'm after seeing him this day, and he riding and galloping. Bartley came first on the red mare; and I tried to say "God speed you," but something choked the words in my throat. He went by quickly; and "the blessing of God on you," says he, and I could say nothing. I looked up then, and I crying, at the gray pony, and there was Michael upon it—with fine clothes on him, and new shoes on his feet.

CATHLEEN (*begins to keen*): It's destroyed we are from this day. It's destroyed, surely.

NORA: Didn't the young priest say the Almighty God wouldn't leave her destitute with no son living?

MAURYA (*in a low voice, but clearly*): It's little the like of him knows of the sea. . . . Bartley will be lost now, and let you call in Eamon and make me a good coffin out of the white boards, for I won't live after them. I've had a husband, and a husband's father, and six sons in this house—six fine men, though it was a hard birth I had with every one of them and they coming to the world—and some of them were found and some of them were not found, but they're gone now the lot of them. . . . There were Stephen, and Shawn, were lost in the great wind, and found after in the Bay of Gregory of the Golden Mouth, and carried up the two of them on the one plank, and in by that door. (*She pauses for a moment, the girls start as if they heard something through the door that is half open behind them.*)

NORA (*in a whisper*): Did you hear that, Cathleen? Did you hear a noise in the northeast?

CATHLEEN (*in a whisper*): There's someone after crying out by the seashore.

MAURYA (*continues without hearing anything*): There was Sheamus and his father, and his own father again, were lost in a dark night, and not a stick or sign was seen of them when the sun went up. There was Patch after was drowned out of a curragh that turned over. I was sitting here with Bartley, and he a baby, lying on my two knees, and I seen two women, and three women, and four women coming in, and they crossing themselves, and not saying a word. I looked out then, and there were men coming after them, and they holding a thing in the half of a red sail, and water dripping out of it—it was a dry day, Nora—and leaving a track to the door. (*She pauses again with her hand stretched out toward the door. It opens softly and old women begin to come in, crossing themselves on the threshold, and kneeling down in front of the stage with red petticoats over their heads.*)

(*half in a dream, to* CATHLEEN) Is it Patch, or Michael, or what is it at all?

CATHLEEN: Michael is after being found in the far north, and when he is found there how could he be here in this place?

MAURYA: There does be a power of young men floating round in the sea, and what way would they know if it was Michael they had, or another man like him, for when a man is nine days in the sea, and the wind blowing, it's hard set his own mother would be to say what man was it.

CATHLEEN: It's Michael, God spare him, for they're after sending us a bit of his clothes from the far north.

(*She reaches out and hands* MAURYA *the clothes that belonged to* MICHAEL. MAURYA *stands up slowly and takes them in her hands.* NORA *looks out.*)

NORA: They're carrying a thing among them and there's water dripping out of it and leaving a track by the big stones.

CATHLEEN (*in a whisper to the women who have come in*): Is it Bartley it is?

ONE OF THE WOMEN: It is surely, God rest his soul.

(*Two younger women come in and pull out the table. Then men carry in the body of* BARTLEY, *laid on a plank, with a bit of a sail over it, and lay it on the table.*)

CATHLEEN (*to the women, as they are doing so*): What way was he drowned?

ONE OF THE WOMEN: The gray pony knocked him into the sea, and he was washed out where there is a great surf on the white rocks.

(MAURYA *has gone over and knelt down at the head of the table. The women are keening softly and swaying themselves with a slow movement.* CATHLEEN *and* NORA *kneel at the other end of the table. The men kneel near the door.*)

MAURYA (*raising her head and speaking as if she did not see the people around her*): They're all gone now, and there isn't anything more the sea can do to me. . . . I'll have no call now to be up crying and praying when the wind breaks from the south, and you can hear the surf is in the east, and the surf is in the west, making a great stir with the two noises, and they hitting one on the other. I'll have no call now to be going down and getting Holy Water in the dark nights after Samhain, and I won't care what way the sea is when the other women will be keening. (*to* NORA) Give me the Holy Water, Nora, there's a small sup still on the dresser.

(NORA *gives it to her.*)

(*Drops* MICHAEL'S *clothes across* BARTLEY'S *feet, and sprinkles the Holy Water over him.*) It isn't that I haven't prayed for you, Bartley, to the Almighty God. It isn't that I haven't said prayers in the dark night till you wouldn't know what I'd be saying; but it's a great rest I'll have now, and it's time surely. It's a great rest I'll have now, and great sleeping in the long nights after Samhain, if it's only a bit a wet flour we do have to eat, and maybe a fish that would be stinking. (*She kneels down again, crossing herself, and saying prayers under her breath.*)

CATHLEEN (*to an old man*): Maybe yourself and Eamon would make a coffin when the sun rises. We have fine white boards herself bought, God help her, thinking Michael would be found, and I have a new cake you can eat while you'll be working.

THE OLD MAN (*looking at the boards*): Are there nails with them?

CATHLEEN: There are not, Colum; we didn't think of the nails.

ANOTHER MAN: It's a great wonder she wouldn't think of the nails, and all the coffins she's seen made already.

CATHLEEN: It's getting old she is, and broken.

(MAURYA *stands up again very slowly and spreads out the pieces of* MICHAEL'S *clothes beside the body, sprinkling them with the last of the Holy Water.*)

NORA (*in a whisper to* CATHLEEN): She's quiet now and easy; but the day Michael was drowned you could hear her crying out from this to the spring well. It's fonder she was of Michael, and would any one have thought that?

CATHLEEN (*slowly and clearly*): An old woman will be soon tired with anything she will do, and isn't it nine days herself is after crying and keening, and making great sorrow in the house?

MAURYA (*puts the empty cup mouth downwards on the table, and lays her hands together on* BARTLEY'S *feet.*): They're all together this time, and the end is come. May the Almighty God have mercy on Bartley's soul, and on Michael's soul, and on the souls of Sheamus and Patch, and Stephen and Shawn (*bending her head*); and may He have mercy on my soul, Nora, and on the soul of every one is left living in the world. (*She pauses, and the keen rises a little more loudly from the women, then sinks away.*) (*continuing*) Michael has a clean burial in the far north, by the grace of the Almighty God. Bartley will have a fine coffin out of the white boards, and a deep grave surely. What more can we want than that? No man at all can be living forever, and we must be satisfied. (*She kneels down again and the* CURTAIN *falls slowly.*)

Questions

MONICA / PAGE 2

1. What is the significance of the following lines?

THE MAN: Not a very impressive view, is it?

SIMON (*defensively*): Well, you can see the sky—clouds and things.

THE MAN: You can see the sky from a prison cell sometimes.

SIMON (*pompously*): Are you suggesting that my apartment is like a prison cell?

THE MAN: We all live in some kind of prison, don't we?

2. How are Leonard and Simon different? Does this difference have any effect on the theme of the play?

3. How are Simon and Leonard alike? Does this alikeness have any effect on the theme of the play?

4. Is Leonard talking about roses when he says, "Such a beautiful rose. Some of its petals have fallen off. It's sad, isn't it, how quickly things die"? Does this line have any significance for the theme of the play?

5. Is there a conflict in this play between youth and age?

6. What does Leonard mean when he says, "Do you think they'll ever find the secret of eternal youth, Simon? But then that sort of thought doesn't really worry you, does it? Youth is curiously uncurious about age"?

Questions

COMING THROUGH THE RYE / PAGE 20

1. What is the significance of the first speech by The Voice? Who or what is The Voice?

2. This play focuses on three people: Butch, Carroll, and Steve. One is young, one is adult, and one is old. What significance does this fact have to the theme of the play?

3. What does Carroll mean when he says, referring to the reason for Steve's projected murder, "I'm sorry, Steve. Of course, you'll never know once you're out there"?

4. How many themes do you think this play has? What are they?

5. This play is obviously about many aspects of life and death. Why, then, is it included in About Youth? Could it be included in About Death?

6. Do you think Miss Quickly is right in thinking that Butch's fate is unfair?

THE LONG FALL / PAGE 30

1. Early in the play Larkin says, "Two men have fallen since yesterday. You know how it is: a lot of times these things seem to run in threes. No one likes to work with that hanging over him." Since you know the resolution of the play, what are the implications of this line?

2. There are many conflicts in this play. How many can you identify? What do you consider to be the major conflict?

3. Does the major conflict give you a clue to the theme of the play?

4. Did Charlie fall or jump?

5. How do you explain Morgan's reaction at the end of the play?

6. This is a play which concerns moral choices: Charlie's, Morgan's, Nick's, and Larkin's. What are these choices? Why are they important in the play?

7. Did Charlie need to prove something? If so, what was it? Did he prove it?

8. Is Charlie mature? Is Morgan mature? Who is the most mature person in the play?

THE ROPE / PAGE 46

1. Why is Luke alienated? Is he right or wrong?

2. Why is Sweeny alienated? Is he right or wrong?

3. Why is Annie alienated? Is she right or wrong?

4. This play seems to concern greed. Do you think greed is the real theme of the play?

5. What are the implications of the ending?

6. Bentley continually quotes the scriptures. Are the particular scriptures important? Do the other characters in the play understand them? Do they even listen to them? If they did, would the outcome of the play be different?

7. Did Bentley love his second wife? How do you know?

CRAWLING ARNOLD / PAGE 65

1. Why does Arnold crawl when he enters the house? Does his crawling have something to do with his particular alienation?

2. Why is Millie alienated?

3. Is Arnold alienated from his parents or from society in general? maybe from both?

4. What is the significance of Arnold's line, "As an adult my values encompassed a rigid good, a rigid evil, and a mush everything-in-between. As a child I've rediscovered one value I had completely forgotten existed. . . . Being naughty"?

5. What is Miss Sympathy's function in the play?

6. What do the characters' names mean? Do the names help you to understand what Feiffer is trying to say?

7. Do you find this play funny? Why?

THE BRIDGE / PAGE 82

1. What is the major conflict in this play?

2. Is the conflict natural or forced?

3. Why does Joseph, at the end of the play, stay up on the bridge?

4. Who is more alienated in this play, Joseph or Pablo?

5. What is Pablo alienated from?

6. How is Pablo induced not to jump? Is he "talked out of it," as happens in movies?

HERE WE ARE / PAGE 103

1. What is the major conflict in this play? It is never really stated, although He and She are constantly thinking about it.

2. Can you characterize the boy and the girl? In this play they are under tension. What do you suppose they are like when they are with other boys or other girls?

3. She says, "We won't fight or be nasty or anything. Will we?" He asks the same question later. Can you answer the question? What makes you think so?

4. He says that after they get to the hotel everything will be all right. Do you think it will be? Can you speculate on what their marriage will be like?

5. What do you think Miss Parker is trying to say in this play?

6. This play may have a moral. What do you think it might be?

PYRAMUS AND THISBE / PAGE 111

1. What do you find funny in this play? Why is it funny?

2. Thisbe is played by a man. Do you think this adds to the humor?

3. What is the major conflict in this play? Does the conflict seem like the one in *Romeo and Juliet?* How do the two stories differ?

4. Is there a difference between the quality of the language Pyramus uses and that of Theseus? What is the difference?

5. What does Theseus mean when he says, "As much as we this night have overwatched. / This palpable-gross play that well beguil'ed / The heavy gate of night"?

6. Why do you suppose Moonshine carries a thornbush and leads a dog?

7. Why is Pyramus' last speech comic rather than tragic?

THE GOLDEN AXE / PAGE 118

1. Can you answer Jeb's question in the following lines? "Henry, I ain't sayin' it's wrong for the county to own a piece of ground. But does any man own the air?"

2. What is the significance of the title *The Golden Axe*?

3. What does the following line mean? "Ever' man has got to chop down his own sign sooner or later. And he's got to do it all by himself."

4. Can you describe the courtship in this play? Is the courtship one of the conflicts?

5. Is Jeb right in cutting down the sign? Why? It *is* against the law.

6. Is Jeb "in love" with sunsets?

7. Does this play make fun of so-called national organizations? If so, how?

8. What is the girl on the billboard holding?

SUNDAY COSTS FIVE PESOS / PAGE 138

1. What is the major conflict? Who are involved in it? Should they be involved?

2. How is this courtship different from your idea of American courtship?
3. How is the language in this play different? Do you enjoy the language? Why?
4. Why does Berta insist on being taken away immediately?
5. Do you believe in the fight between the two girls? Why?
6. What customs or practices found in this play seem strange or different to you?
7. What does the title of the play mean?

THE BEER CAN TREE / PAGE 154

1. This play concerns a young man and an old man. Is the play more about age or youth? Why do you think so?
2. Why is Charlie called Snowbound Charlie only in the winter?
3. What is an eyesore?
4. This play is concerned about things other than youth and age. What are they?
5. What does Charlie's past life have to do with his present circumstances?
6. Does Charlie look backward or forward?
7. Can you explain the end of the play? Why does Charlie take off *seven* cans?

SOMETHING UNSPOKEN / PAGE 167

1. What is "unspoken"? Maybe the question need not be answered.
2. Williams is dealing on one level with panic and age in this play. It is obvious, however, that he is dealing with another theme as well. What is it?
3. Can you characterize Cornelia?
4. Grace says that both she and Cornelia are "gray" but that the types of gray are different. What does she mean?
5. What is the significance of the roses?
6. What is the relationship between the two women, other than secretary and employer?

WAITING FOR THE BUS / PAGE 180

1. Why does Edith have such apparent affection for animals? In fact, she refers to them as her children.
2. Andrew keeps notes of the things that have happened to him. What does this signify?

3. Andrew says, "Well, when I subtract the duplication of events, the unimportant incidents, the adventures we started and never finished, the inventions that were failures, the languages that are dead, the characters who are only names, it should come roughly to one small volume." Do you find this sad? Why?

4. What does Andrew mean when he says, "All right, my dear, I'll keep up the game. As long as you can keep up your end, I'll keep up mine"?

5. Does it seem that Edith and Andrew, in their age, have become childish? If so, why do you think this has happened?

6. Do Edith and Andrew have children?

7. Is there a correlation between Andrew and Edith and Adam and Eve?

8. Do Edith and Andrew have a past? Andrew says that it is all an illusion.

THE GOVERNOR'S LADY / PAGE 198

1. Do you agree with Harriet when she says, "Civilization, Gilbert, is the act of tolerating what we loathe"?

2. Although this play is a nightmare about age, it also concerns a number of other things. What are they?

3. Do you think Harriet is right when she speculates that things would have been better if they had had children? Why?

4. Dreams (or nightmares) have significance to the people having them. What is the significance of Harriet's "dream" of Gilbert turning into a gorilla? He was, after all, governor of the colony.

5. Is Harriet, in her nightmare, reliving the guilt of her past?

6. Do the characters in this play look backward or forward? What is the evidence for your answer?

7. In the course of the play, Harriet completely reverses herself in her feelings for Gilbert. Why?

8. The nightmare of this play seemingly occurs between the time Harriet sees the gorilla and the time she kills it. Apparently, because of the nightmare she dies of a heart attack. Yet, the ending is baffling. What do you think it means?

SORRY, WRONG NUMBER / PAGE 223

1. Given all the problems Mrs. Stevenson has with the telephone, what are the implications of the following line? "He's working late tonight, and I was trying to reach him to ask him to come home. I'm an invalid, you know —and it's the maid's night off—and I *hate* to be alone—even though he says

I'm perfectly safe as long as I have the telephone right beside my bed."

2. How is the suspense developed?

3. What, other than the impending murder, adds to the terror?

4. What aspect of death do you think this play illustrates?

5. Do you see any reason for this murder to be committed?

6. What do you suppose Mrs. Stevenson's husband is like?

7. Do the characters other than Mrs. Stevenson seem like people? Why or why not?

HELLO OUT THERE / PAGE 236

1. Why doesn't Mr. Saroyan give the Young Man a name?

2. This is a play with many themes. It could be included in About Youth, About Alienation, About Love, or About Death. Why? Which section do you prefer?

3. There is, in addition to the above themes mentioned in Question 2, another very important theme in this play. What is it?

4. What does Emily mean when she says, "Hello out there"?

5. What does the Young Man mean when he says, "Hello out there"?

6. Does the Young Man really love Emily? How do you know? Does he really expect to escape and meet Emily? How do you know?

7. Did the Young Man commit the crime of which he is accused?

PULLMAN CAR HIAWATHA / PAGE 250

1. What is the function of the Stage Manager? How is this play different from others that you have read?

2. Why does Wilder avoid an emotional treatment of Harriet's death?

3. Why do such characters as Grover's Corners, The Field, and Parkersburg, Ohio, appear in the play at the moment of Harriet's death?

4. Why do the weather, the hours, and the planets have parts in this play?

5. What is the "theological position" of Pullman Car Hiawatha?

6. Harriet speaks after her death. Why?

RIDERS TO THE SEA / PAGE 266

1. Why doesn't Maurya give Bartley her blessing?

2. What does Maurya mean when she says, "In the big world the old people do be leaving things after them for their sons and children, but in this place it is the young men do be leaving things behind for them that do be old"?

Questions

3. What does the title *Riders to the Sea* mean?

4. At the end of the play, Maurya says, "Michael has a clean burial in the far north, by the Grace of the Almighty God. Bartley will have a fine coffin out of the white boards, and a deep grave surely. What more can we want than that? No man at all can be living forever, and we must be satisfied." Can you answer her question: "What more can we want than that"?

5. Refer to Question 4. Do you agree that "... we must be satisfied"?

6. Maurya takes comfort in the rituals of her religion. Why doesn't she blame God for her tragic misfortunes?

2 3 4 5 6 7 8 9 10 DODO 81 80 79 78 77 76 75